T0385158

WHAT YOUR BABY WANTS YOU TO KNOW

WHAT YOUR BABY WANTS YOU TO KNOW

The art and science of bonding with your baby

Marie Derome

For C, O, F, L and H

The information in this book is not intended to be a substitute for medical advice or medical treatment. You are advised to consult a midwife or doctor on any matters relating to your baby's or your own health, and in particular on any matters that may require diagnosis or medical attention. Any use of the information in this book is made on the reader's good judgement and is the reader's sole responsibility.

First published in 2025 by Headline Home
An imprint of Headline Publishing Group Limited

1

Cataloguing in Publication Data is available from the British Library

Hardback ISBN 978 1 0354 2419 1
ebook ISBN 978 1 0354 1448 2

Typeset in 12/16pt Dante MT Std by Jouve (UK), Milton Keynes

Printed and bound in Great Britain by Clays Ltd, Elcograf S.p.A.

MIX
Paper | Supporting
responsible forestry
FSC
www.fsc.org   FSC® C104740

Headline's policy is to use papers that are natural, renewable and recyclable products and made from wood grown in well-managed forests and other controlled sources. The logging and manufacturing processes are expected to conform to the environmental regulations of the country of origin.

Headline Publishing Group Limited
An Hachette UK Company
Carmelite House
50 Victoria Embankment
London EC4Y 0DZ

The authorized representative in the EEA is Hachette Ireland, 8 Castlecourt Centre, Castleknock Road, Castleknock, Dublin 15, D15 YF6A, Ireland

www.headline.co.uk
www.hachette.co.uk

Contents

Three
The Other Side of the Story

Four
What We Do with Our Babies

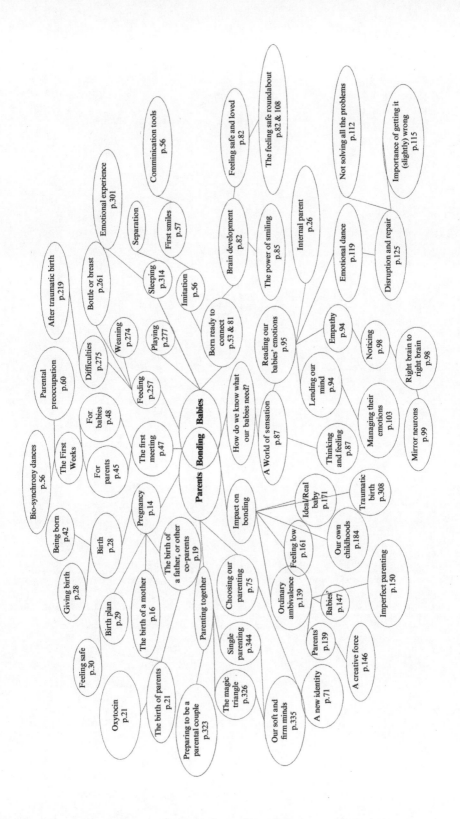

Introduction

t all started when I was pregnant with my first child. As my tummy became bigger so did my worries about my new responsibilities. *What had I done?* What had *we* done?! The fact that I was not alone in this did not diminish the magnitude of the task that lay ahead: how was I, how were we, going to do a good job of being parents, at keeping our baby healthy and happy?

These uneasy feelings lingered on. Once my baby was born – a little boy – I became even more conscious of the strange and somewhat alarming power we parents have over our tiny babies. Of course, my son came with his own big personality, and within hours I could sense his quirky sense of humour, but I also became starkly aware that the way I behaved with him, the way I responded to his smiles or cries, was going to have a huge influence on how he felt about himself and the world around him. On the one hand, this was exciting (and flattering to my ego): to know that the way I loved and cared for him was going somehow to shape him for ever. But on the other hand, it felt totally unnerving: what if I got it wrong? How could I trust myself? I had had no training in being a parent apart from a few antenatal classes, where we were shown how to change nappies and bath babies using unrealistically compliant rubber dolls. In all those years spent at school and university, no one had ever mentioned motherhood, fatherhood or life as a child – not even the basics of what happens when two people begin to interact with their newborn baby. It felt as if society had kept the world of babies and parents, the most intense relationships of our lives, hidden in the dark.

At night, when all was quiet and my baby was at last asleep, fuzzy questions would come into my head. There was so much more I wanted to know – like what was *really* happening between me and my baby, and what all that emotional stuff that was going on between him and me was actually about. I needed to know if I was cooking up the right emotional dishes to nourish my baby's developing sense of self, or if I needed to find a better recipe. So, I turned to books.

As a teenager and young adult, I had particularly valued the way that books had offered me so many different perspectives on the world, different ways of feeling about people and about myself. Surely, I thought, books could help me again, by shining a light on babyhood, motherhood, parenthood, and offering me a surer path for the parenting journey ahead. And they did.

To start with, though, it was tricky to find the *right* books. Most of them were far too prescriptive, telling me firmly and explicitly exactly what I should be doing and how my baby was supposed to develop, amplifying my anxieties and doubts rather than soothing them. Then, one day, I came across some of the books by the paediatrician and psychoanalyst Donald Winnicott, and this opened up a whole new way of looking at my baby. I felt that, at last, I had found someone who not only made me feel freer but also calmer: with his idea of 'good enough' mothering, Winnicott was kindly telling me that I did not have to be perfect, and this felt so reassuring and empowering, especially during those much-disrupted nights. With his focus on the relationship between a baby and their parents, I also felt that Winnicott was saying something even more important: that if I was curious and interested in my baby, then everything else would gently fall into place. It was no longer about rules I was supposed to follow and impose on my baby, so that one day he would turn out the way I thought he should. Rather it was about really getting to know my baby and understanding him.

If being curious felt relatively easy and instant (after all, wasn't my baby the most fascinating thing in the world!?), I soon realised that getting to know someone is a slow process and takes time. I had to stop rushing around, I had to learn to do less and allow my baby to do more. My main job as a curious mother was to take the time to be attentive, to notice the movement of his eyes searching for mine when I came closer to him, the movement of his lips when he smelled the milk I fed him, of his face when the wind closed the door with a bang. I had to notice how his little body moved when he heard his daddy's voice coming into the room, how his legs wriggled as I took his nappy off, how his body became heavier and floppier as he slowly fell asleep.

By observing him and noticing all these thousands of incredible little things that he was doing, I realised that it was okay for him to be hungry sometimes, and tired sometimes. I didn't have to feed him immediately at the very first little cry, or wrap him up and put him in his cot at the very first yawn. I learned to allow him to feel happy and cross, instead of constantly trying to smooth things out for him and eliminate all his frustrations. In other words, I learned to let my baby be himself a lot of the time. And, for an anxious mother, that is not always easy!

But slowly, by watching him attentively, I realised that in order to find the answers I so desperately wanted, it was often simply a case of waiting for him to give them to me. *He* had the answers I sought. I 'only' had to look, to listen and to be open, and then I could understand what he wanted, what he needed, what he liked and what he did not like, what made him happy and made him laugh, and what made him cross and sad. I simply had to accept that, a lot of the time, he was the teacher and I was the student. And, luckily, he was a very willing and fun teacher, teaching me his language: a baby language that I had long forgotten but was keen to relearn.

By learning his language on his terms, I could slowly translate the world for him, putting words and meaning to what was going on around him, but also inside him. I was, in a way, lending him my brain so he could borrow it to make sense of the noises around him, of the weird sensations in his tummy when he was hungry or too full, of the warmth of the sun or the cold wind on his skin, of the dark of the night and the light in the morning, of the poo and pee that made him dirty and wet, of the rage he felt when I took too long to feed him, of the dizziness when his dad threw him in the air, and the confusion of his mummy and daddy disappearing and reappearing, as if coming in and out of existence.

Gradually, in the back and forth between my old brain and my baby boy's brand new one, the world and all its complexity began to fall into place for him, and therefore also for me as a parent. Imagining what my baby could be feeling became my favourite game, and every time my little boy seemed to think I had guessed right, it felt like winning the jackpot and popping open a bottle of champagne, as I was flooded by all these lovely feelings (thank you, hormones!) that gave me a sense of being present and content, and helped me to love him even more than before. Of course, there were also many, many times when I got it wrong, and that felt very different . . . horrible, at times . . . but now I could manage those feelings without falling apart. I had come to realise there was always a way back to feeling safe together, by adjusting my attention a little, re-calibrating the space between us, and re-finding our connection: our happy, easy little dance.

One fundamental thing I slowly began to understand is that it is difficult to see properly if you are too close. Moving back a little helped me see the bigger picture and accept that he and I were very much separate beings, that what I liked he might not like, what made me happy might not necessarily make him happy, what made me feel anxious he might find soothing. By remembering to be a curious parent, I was gently allowing my son to be himself. I was allowing him to have his own needs, which were all very different from mine. He and I were very close, but nevertheless we were two very different people. And that is surely the joy of parenthood: to have the privilege of watching so intensely as our babies grow up and become themselves. We help them when needed, of course: protecting, nourishing and steering sometimes. But we are not making or moulding our babies. Instead, we are giving them what they need to become themselves *by* themselves.

What I found especially amazing when observing my baby – and being led by what I was hearing and seeing, as well as not overthinking what I needed to do – was that it naturally created a space between him and me of just the right distance. And it was in that space that he could start becoming himself; that he could start to explore, under my careful gaze, the contours of his own body and, indeed, of his own mind. And it was also in that space that I could become myself as a mother. There I, too, learned to explore the contours of my own, new, mothering mind. I discovered, as all mothers must, that being a mother is not always as easy or enjoyable as everyone perhaps feels obliged to say it is; but also that it can sometimes be effortless and almost ecstatic in a way that no one else could ever have explained to me either.

After this first little boy, we had another boy and then a girl. And in the middle of all this we also adopted a little girl – but that is another story (though also, of course, part of the same story too). The infinite value of being curious and attentive is certainly not restricted to just our relationships with our babies – biological or otherwise. Being curious and attentive is the thing that makes our relationships with all the people around us (partners, family members, friends, work colleagues etc) more authentic and meaningful and, in the end, more enjoyable.

With four kids, I had my hands full when it came to being curious. But I also realised I wanted to know more about children in general, about relationships, about the human psyche. In particular, I really, really wanted to understand what all that emotional stuff that goes on between my kids and me (and, indeed, between all kids and their parents) was actually about. So I decided to jump right in and start the intense and slow training (over six years) to become a qualified Child and Adolescent Psychotherapist. Coincidentally, one of the key early features of the training is something called 'Baby Observation', where every trainee has to observe a newborn baby and their parent(s) for one hour every week until the baby's second birthday. Keeping our gaze on the baby and noticing every tiny detail of how they interact with their parent, and the world around them, is how, as psychotherapists, we learn to 'see' all the unspoken ways in which babies effectively tell us what is going on with them and how they feel. We learn how to recognise when fear and anxiety have got in the way of curiosity and attentiveness, and how to help parents and children get back on track. It is also through this close study that we get the measure of how powerful and impactful our early interactions with our babies are, and this is why I have included quite a lot of anecdotal baby observations and case studies in this book. They are a brilliant way of conveying the dynamics of parenthood, and I'm sure you will find them as fascinating – and, more importantly, as helpful – as I do.

Training to be a child psychotherapist also opened the door to a world of psychoanalytic theories (and, later, the neuroscientific discoveries that support a lot of those theories), all of which I found fascinating and reassuring. The psychoanalytic world is one that is not afraid of wandering into the dark labyrinth of the mind. It is, in part, about extending our curiosity and attentiveness to embrace the things that frighten us or shame us. As a mother I found this very helpful! Because, at times, it felt difficult to acknowledge, even to myself, that I was not that perfect loving mother I was working so hard to be. Indeed, there were times when being with my baby did not feel enjoyable at all and I found myself missing my old job and life; when, as a mother, I did not feel up to the job, when I felt I had messed up and been (yet again) a rubbish parent; when doubts crippled my mind, and I began to think that maybe walking out of the house, leaving everything behind, seemed the only sensible option, for all of us . . .

So it was liberating to discover that I was not alone and that, actually, it was completely normal and even healthy to have those ambivalent feelings about motherhood. I loved being a mother but I also hated it. I hated it because, at times, it made me feel inadequate, helpless, persecuted, trapped, enraged and guilty. And all these consuming feelings are not easy to navigate when you have to look after a baby and you feel so, so tired.

Yes, it is hard to be a parent. Parenthood is tough. It is possibly the hardest thing that any of us will ever do . . . The pregnancy, the birth, the feeding, the cleaning, the disrupted sleep, the relentless demands on your body and on your mind, the boredom that comes with playing the same game again and again, answering the same questions a million times, the endless negotiations with toddlers, the sense of loss of identity, but also the constant worry about our babies, which continues, of course, long after they have stopped being babies. The list of drawbacks is long.

I have been a child psychotherapist and a mother for many years now and, a few years ago, I began to feel that I wanted to share more widely the incredible things all the babies in my life (at home *and* in my clinic) had taught me. So I started to write this book, a book nourished by both my professional and personal journeys into the world of babies and their parents, written in the same kind and compassionate everyday language that I use with parents who come to see me at my clinic, full of questions and worries. That is why, although it is firmly grounded in psychoanalytic and attachment theories and developmental psychology, and backed up by the latest neuroscientific research, you won't find any off-putting technical jargon.

This book is going to take you on a journey to the beating heart of parenting, and show you all the many different ways we can be with our babies – all those tiny things we do all day (and sometimes all night too), and which we are often barely aware of, but which ultimately form the bedrock of our bond with our babies. It is those many tiny things, when we get them right (and this book is all about helping you with that), that make our babies feel loved and safe, but also free to become who they want to be.

As part of that journey to discover the best way to form a powerful and nurturing bond with your baby, we are also going to explore the *other* side of the story of babies and parents, the side that is too often kept hidden. That's the story of when things are *not* going so well and loving our babies is *not* that easy. And it's a surprisingly common one. I am confident, though, that after reading the sections about how our own childhood experiences, or a traumatic birth, for example, can impact on how we relate to our babies, quite a number of you are going to say to yourselves: of course! Now I understand why I feel the way I do – I am not a freak; it all makes sense. And I know that this realisation will in itself be enough to make you feel a little lighter, and give you hope that things between you and your baby (or your co-parent) can change.

I have written this book to support you to be the parent *you* want to be; it's a book that will free you from guilt, a book that will help you turn down the volume of the sometimes harsh voice in your head that shouts that you are not doing enough, that you are doing it the wrong way, so that you can hear in its place a kind voice, of reason and reassurance. It's also a book full of practical and fun suggestions on how to make the parenting journey enjoyable and authentic. So, at night, when all is quiet and your baby is at last asleep, and fuzzy questions come into your head, I hope that reaching for this book will help you realise that, actually, you are doing a pretty good job at being a parent.

Your baby may not know it, but they will be glad that, while they were sleeping, you read even just a few more pages. And when they wake up again, and are ready for your attention, for your curiosity, you'll be ready to give it with a renewed sense of wonder and excitement.

NB: *This book is for mothers, fathers, biological and adoptive parents, females and males; it is also for co-parents, step-parents and grandparents, and anyone who is or is going to be involved closely in your baby's life and wants to understand more about their emotional world.*

All clinical material and baby observation excerpts used in this book have been anonymised.

One
The Very Beginning

1

The first nine months of life

I t is easy to think that our babies' lives start on the day they are born, and that not much happens until we meet them – until we start to get to know them, and give them a name. But we now know that our babies' lives start way before birth: not just in our tummies but also in our minds. Of course, none of us remembers the period of life that we spend in our mother's womb, as it stays buried deep in our unconscious. But it is a life nonetheless, and one that we cannot ignore if we want to truly understand our babies and create a healthy relationship with them.

So let us try to imagine what life might be like for our babies *before* they are born. Let us try to imagine what it is like to grow from a cell into a human being, to be tucked up inside for nine months before emerging into the world for the first time . . . If we try to understand our babies' experiences in utero, we are more likely to understand them once they are in our arms, still covered in vernix. It will make it easier to empathise with our babies as they grow and help create that deep emotional connection with them that will carry them throughout their lives.

Life in paradise: the baby

For our babies, the time in our tummies is a little bit like a long holiday in a five-star luxury hotel nestled in an extraordinary isolated paradise. Wishes are granted without question, without even calling room service. For our babies' ultimate comfort, our wombs transform themselves into this palatial accommodation where unfailing demand and supply go hand in hand: there is no need for our babies to breathe or to eat or even to poo or pee. All the oxygen and food they need is delivered seamlessly through the umbilical cord, which also serves as a waste extractor, carrying anything that is no longer required out again. And, on top of that, this incredible temple of provision continuously moulds itself around our babies, giving them just the right amount of space to feel both cosy and roomy, so that they can sleep peacefully, or, when they choose, do amazing somersaults and practise their kick boxing.

For nine months, our babies grow in a pampered pleasure dome where – provided the pregnancy is straightforward and the atmosphere at home relatively relaxed – their overwhelming feeling is one of satisfaction: our babies feel totally understood. They have all they need and nothing else to wish for. And that makes them feel very special. And very powerful.

Creating the paradise: the mother

Let us now picture what it is like for the mother to experience pregnancy, how we grow our babies in our tummies, as this is going to help us understand ourselves as mothers. During pregnancy our bodies undergo momentous physiological changes, which have a colossal impact on our state of mind, on how we relate to ourselves, to the people around us and, eventually, to our

14

babies. Some of the physiological changes are evident – such as the slow swelling of our tummies. But some are more hidden; for instance, the changes that occur in our brain – specifically the release of certain key hormones.

Generally, this whole process starts without us even knowing that we are pregnant. We may have wished to have a baby, consciously or unconsciously, but apart from the sexual encounter (or the in vitro fertilising) required for fertilisation to happen, the rest of the pregnancy journey is pretty much beyond our control. Once the victorious sperm has made the arduous trip up to our fallopian tubes to fertilise our egg, and they have fused together and implanted in the wall of our uterus, all we can do is watch our tummies slowly become bigger and bigger. And this loss of control can be simultaneously a relief *and* frightening. Our bodies, however, know how to deal with pregnancy without the interference of our conscious mind. They have become the most sophisticated architects and most trustworthy builders: they construct this perfect palace so effectively that we don't even have to make a snagging list!

At an emotional level, it can feel pretty extraordinary to find that we are able to grow a little human being from scratch, and grant their every wish so that they can come into this world perfectly formed and ready to connect and interact with us – all seemingly without much input from us and, assuming all goes well, without any difficult decisions having to be made. (Of course, it may not have *felt* entirely effortless – especially the giving up of certain foods, the morning sickness and general nausea, the sheer exhaustion . . .)

And, like our babies, we too feel quite special and powerful – omnipotent, the psychoanalyst would say – to have been able to achieve this incredible feat of harmony and engineering. Indeed, we have managed to create for our babies a world almost without gravity, where their needs are met instantly. But, of course, we know that everything is soon going to change. And that can leave us with big, and at times worrying, questions: how am I going to understand what my baby needs? How will I know what to do? How will I love my baby?

These big questions can be both exciting and terrifying, but it is important to remember that, as our pregnancy progresses, a silent yet monumental metamorphosis is slowly taking place in our brains (and also in the brain of our partner or fellow carer). It's a metamorphosis that is going to turn us from mere human beings into *parents*, and will prepare us to tackle the incredibly demanding task of looking after our babies.

The birth of a mother

Alongside the momentous physiological changes we undergo during pregnancy – our tummies becoming rounder and rounder, our breasts growing, our hands and feet swelling, our joints loosening, our skin changing (and, of course, there may well be nausea and exhaustion too) – are those that take place in the brain. And these are no less dramatic.

Thanks to relatively recent advances in neurosciences research,[1] we now know that during the few months before and after our babies are born our brain is at its most plastic and malleable, and that it goes through the quickest and biggest restructuring that it has gone through since we were tiny babies ourselves (even bigger than that during puberty). And it's all happening in order to get us ready to look after our babies. The changes are so striking and distinct that it is even possible for a computer algorithm to assess women's brain scans and relatively easily pick out those who are pregnant or new mothers, as opposed to those who aren't.

We can only conclude that looking after a newborn baby is such a specialised and demanding task that we need a newly adapted brain in order to do it.[2] We need a brain that can stay focused on the task 24/7, no matter what other exciting things are happening next door; a brain that can enjoy the repetitiveness of looking after babies and cope with the stress of life with a newborn; and one that makes sure we still find our babies cute at 3 a.m., when they have kept us awake for hours, if not days . . .

The main hormone (sometimes referred to as a neurotransmitter) at work in this new, incredibly resilient and creative brain is oxytocin. This very ancient hormone evolved around 500 million years ago. It is not exclusive to humans, but the way we have come to use it is key to what makes us human: it is at the heart of our capacity to socialise with others, and to bond closely with the people we love.[3] And it is especially key to ensuring that we love and care for our babies. It has variously been nicknamed the 'love hormone', the 'cuddle hormone' and the 'bonding hormone'. And it is going to be a vital and welcome companion during our parenting journey.

Our new mother's brain

When we get pregnant, a very complex chain reaction of hormonal changes is set in motion, mostly kicked off by a dramatic increase in our production of oxytocin. Oxytocin becomes the chief con- ductor of a big hormonal orchestra (with dopamine, prolactin, cortisol and adrenaline, among many other hormones, all playing a part). It conducts the amazing symphony that is going to be the background music for our relationship with our babies.

Oxytocin is produced in the deepest and most ancient part of our brain – in the hypothalamus, in our limbic system. And it travels to the many different regions of our brain that have to do with caring. There, it supports a process of 'synaptic pruning': getting rid of certain connections between brain cells in order to facilitate and encourage the creation of new ones. In other words, during pregnancy, some parts of our brains shrink – the ones that are no longer useful; while some others expand – those that are essential to keep us on task when it comes to caring for our babies.

Some of the 'grey matter' in our hippocampus, for example – the area that has to do with memory – shrinks. Remembering the title or the plot of the film we watched last night, for example, is not a priority in our life right now, as it won't particularly help us in the job of keeping our babies alive and well (you may have heard people talk about 'foggy mummy brain' syndrome or similar?).

At the same time, many other parts of our brain, especially our ancient mammalian brain, expand in volume, activating our more primitive care-giving neural network. Our amygdala – the part that effectively acts as our danger alarm – starts firing faster, helping us to focus on our babies as we become super vigilant about keeping them safe. To balance this, the part of our brains that produces dopamine expands too. This helps to ensure that we are not entirely overwhelmed by fretting and worrying about our babies. On the contrary, loaded up with this reward hormone, we find our babies' smiles, smells and soft skin the most gratifying things in the world, sending us into a euphoric whirlwind of happy feelings. And even their poo and pee and sick doesn't bother us too much, not as it might have done in our former lives.

The boost in our oxytocin also spreads to more recent (in evolutionary terms) and therefore more cognitive parts of our brains. These are the areas that have to do with our capacity to be curious and empathic, and which are going to help us imagine, understand and respond to what our babies are feeling and what they need from us.

So, you see, those initial questions – how am I going to understand what my baby wants and needs? how will I know what to do? how will I love my baby? – are no longer so very terrifying. All of these changes are preparing you, first as your baby grows inside you, and then for when you meet them in the outside world – every day your brain is getting better equipped to help you find the answers. And get this: it's not just your brain that is changing, it's your co-parent's brain too!

The birth of a father, or other co-parents

For the other parent, be they fathers, other mothers, or co-habiting carers, pregnancy can feel a bit like watching their loved one get on a train for a long journey and waiting for them to come back, nine months later, with a baby. It is easy to feel that, as the other parent, they are not totally part of the adventure, leaving them with some big questions that they may try to bury or avoid: how will I fall in love with our baby? How will I know how to be a dad or co-carer? How will I understand what our baby wants and needs?

Although their body doesn't go through the same obvious external changes as the mother's does during pregnancy (actually, some fathers' breasts do grow a bit!), fathers and co-parents, too, are being biologically primed to be a parent. In the last decade, research on fathers' and co-parents' brains has made huge leaps, showing that, during the few months before and after the birth of their babies, their brain is also highly plastic and goes through a major re-structuring so that they too can be ready to look after their babies.[4] And this research has revealed that the hormone key to this reshaping, once again, is oxytocin. This surprised the researchers, as oxytocin had long been associated only with biological motherhood.

There are key differences, though, as you might expect. In mothers, the reshaping is triggered from deep inside their brains by hormonal changes due to pregnancy. In fathers and co-parents, the changes are triggered externally, through their interaction and shared planning with their partner, and through caring for both mother and child during pregnancy and after the baby's birth. The amount of oxytocin created in the brains of fathers and co-parents essentially depends on how much interest they take, how much support they offer during the pregnancy, and then how actively involved and engaged they are day-to-day (and night-to-night) in their baby's care.

When fathers are involved from early on in the pregnancy, their level of testosterone decreases. This is in part because they are now less motivated to make a baby, and more motivated to ensure the survival of the one they have just made. The ebbing of the testosterone tide makes space for their oxytocin to flow and soar. This then kickstarts a chain of hormonal reactions whereby, like their pregnant partner, their amygdala expands, making them more vigilant and ready to ward off any danger. At the same time, their dopamine level increases, and with it their capacity to take pleasure in being with their babies (starting from even when the baby is still in their partner's tummy). For fathers, and co-parents too, the increase in their oxytocin level impacts on the cognitive parts of their brain, making them more curious about their babies and more empathic with them.

The brains of fathers and co-parents thus go through a metamorphosis all of their own, turning them from mere human companions/observers into *the actual other parent*. With this comes a heightened ability to focus on their babies, to take pleasure in them and imagine their feelings and emotions. So, thanks to oxytocin, they too can feel a little more confident that evolution has got a plan to get them ready to meet and look after their babies, and build a strong and enjoyable relationship with them.

And there's more good news: this incredible metamorphosis goes beyond gender and biological affiliation. It happens to anyone and everyone involved in the active care of a baby. So, whether it be other mothers, other fathers, adoptive parents, grandparents, elder siblings or even professional nannies, the more hands-on they are, the more caring and committed they are, the bigger the surge in oxytocin, ensuring that their brains adapt to the new situation and that they have the required 'tools' to look after the babies that are about to become a new and lasting part of their world.

The birth of parents

Even though mothers and fathers metamorphose into parents in very different ways, they generally do so in synchrony, with the changes in their brains mimicking and complementing each other. A growing body of research has been measuring the level of oxytocin in parents who are in a loving and supportive relationship, both at various points during the pregnancy and in the months and years following the birth of their babies. And the results are extraordinary: both mothers and fathers have rising levels of oxytocin at the same time, and often at almost exactly the same levels. This is called bio-behavioural synchrony: parents' brains enter into a sort of joyous dance together, where the same neural nurturing network gets activated, preparing them both at the same time for the monumental task of caring for their baby. From an evolutionary perspective, these findings are not really so surprising: looking after a newborn baby is such an all-consuming task that, if mothers *and* fathers (or co-parents) work as a team, there will obviously be a greater chance of their baby staying alive and well.[5]

How to boost prenatal bonding and enhance the synchronic dance

Some of us find we are able to get ready emotionally for our babies during pregnancy naturally without many worries or much effort. But, as with any big upcoming event in our lives, the anticipation will be overlaid with various degrees of anxiety about just how easy, or hard, it will be to become a parent and to form a warm and loving bond with our babies. For all their amazing powers, the brain chemicals of pregnancy do not instantly make us perfect, worry-free parents. We are too human for that!

If, for mothers, the oxytocin boost comes from simply getting pregnant, for fathers and co-parents it is all about being emotionally committed and actively involved. So, let's see what both parties can do to 'max out' on oxytocin, in order to ensure we keep dancing with our partner that exhilarating oxytocin dance. Remember: the closer parents are in the joint enterprise of pregnancy, the better synchronised their levels of oxytocin are going to be. Below are some ideas for having more 'together time' that can help boost the whole process.

Co-parenting activities we can do together to boost prenatal bonding

- Go to prenatal and scan appointments together – hearing the train-like thumping heartbeat of unborn babies is always moving for both parents. For fathers/co-parents, it is, after the blue line on the dip stick, the first concrete evidence that, yes, there is a baby in there. The new 4D scans are even better than the old 2D black-and-white ones at helping fathers feel more connected to their unborn babies. They can watch (and rewatch) their babies in action, moving around, sticking their tongues out, sucking their thumbs, or simply yawning.

- Join an antenatal class together – this is a helpful way of starting to create common knowledge and language about your baby's development, the different birth options and scenarios, feeding techniques, sleep rhythms and all-round needs (of parents as well as babies). It is also a great way to meet other parents and start putting together a support network, which will be so important in the coming months and years as you all go through similar experiences. If possible, try to choose an antenatal class that discusses not just the practical but also the emotional aspects of becoming a parent. It is helpful, as parents, to become more aware of your feelings and emotions, and also where they are coming from. Soon you will need to imagine what your baby's emotions and feelings are too, and being in touch with your own is certainly an important part of that.

- Indulge in some 'tummy time' – for both mums and dads, talking to an unborn baby in warm reassuring tones, even just telling them what you are up to, is a great habit to get into. We know that, from twenty-four weeks or maybe even earlier, babies can hear, and soon recognise, their parents' voices. But, even before this, talking to your baby, reading them stories and singing them songs regularly will help release the warm glow and flow of oxytocin and strengthen your bond with them.

- Share the love – there is nothing like witnessing each other's affection for the new baby to get the oxytocin chain reaction going. So, caress your tummy and ask your partner to do it too. Touch is a very powerful trigger for oxytocin, and babies will often react to your tummy being rubbed with little kicks and wriggles. These are signs that the warm feelings that you are getting are being reciprocated and enjoyed by them too.

- Play with your baby – when your baby kicks or pushes with their elbows or feet against the inside of your tummy, you can respond by pushing gently on their protruding limbs to start a little kicking game. This is the beginning of all the cuddling and tickling and toe squeezing games you are going to play after they are born. But it is also the all-important beginning of turn-taking. As we are going to discover very soon, the taking of turns with our babies – the exchange of touching, squeezing, looking, listening and speaking – is going to be absolutely fundamental to our bonding with them. And the touch part of that can start when they are still in our tummies.

A few ideas for co-parents showing support

- Communicate your support – being attentive to the impact of the pregnancy on your partner's emotions and physical well-being is a great way for fathers/co-parents to be more invested in becoming a parent. Asking how she is feeling and what help she would like tells her she is not alone in this, and therefore a little more relaxed.

- Become an equipment expert, so you can share the frustration! – one (potentially) 'easy' way for fathers and co-parents to feel actively involved is to invest time and energy in becoming the expert in car seats, prams and baby monitors etc. You could also use (or work on) your DIY skills to prepare the baby's room and set up (without too much swearing) the various bits of flat-pack furniture that is soon going to appear in the house . . .

- Reinvest in household chores – unless you are already a 50/50 couple, this is a good time to explore how to share all the tasks involved in the running of the home more equally. Shopping and cooking together, or taking turns to do so, for instance, will enhance that bio-behavioural synchrony, so can be a useful preparation for looking after your baby together (See also Chapter 17 – Babies and the family).

- Another useful approach for both parents during pregnancy is to create a mental and emotional space to 'be with' your baby, well before they are actually born. There are two ways to do this – visualisation and noticing. You may enjoy both of them, and ring the changes, or you may find just one of them feels right for you.

Visualisation: from sports performance to coping with stress, we know that visualisation exercises can be very powerful. And visualising our babies in our tummies – imagining how they might feel, what they might be doing – can be a very powerful and positive exercise.

Noticing: noticing is subtly different to visualising. It's a form of mindfulness and it means tuning into and accepting things as they are, without judgement. So, try to notice how we feel about being pregnant and having a baby growing inside our tummies. What are those food cravings like, and how new and strange is that feeling of someone inside us, moving and kicking? It's okay to be disturbed or even frightened by these thoughts and feelings. Indeed, noticing that we are feeling a bit apprehensive may well make us less so. Noticing when we are happy or even exultant in our pregnancy is fine too. However, if the thoughts become too scary, it is important to stop and seek professional help. (Similarly, if scary thoughts are coming to you outside of such mindfulness exercises – if they feel like they are intrusive and outside our control – then you should talk to your GP or seek other professional help.)

Pressing pause

But before it's possible to do any of the above exercises successfully, it might be a good idea simply to press PAUSE. Some of us deal with the uncertainty and sheer newness of being pregnant by arranging a constant and endless series of distractions for ourselves. Working, cooking, calling friends, watching TV, checking Instagram, renovating a house . . . By staying almost unfeasibly busy and engaged with other matters, we can absolve ourselves from thinking about our babies, and how being pregnant is making us feel.

There's no exact prescription for where or how you pause, but if you recognise what I've just described, I think you already know what's required. Sit down or lie down somewhere private and comfortable. Turn off all devices. Give yourself at least half an hour. Don't necessarily leap to a visualisation or noticing exercise; simply remind yourself that you are pregnant, that your body and your life are changing, and see where the thought takes you. If you find you are jumping up within minutes to answer an email or start cooking supper, that's okay. Just make sure you give pausing another go tomorrow. And if you are really finding it hard to put yourself in a quiet, reflective place, then you could do worse than reading another chapter or two of this book. Indeed, a lot of parents find reading and learning about the development of babies really calming and reassuring. So, let's keep reading . . .

2
Giving birth

Of course, everyone is incredibly excited about that very first meeting. But before we can lock eyes with our babies, we need to undergo a journey: the momentous journey of giving birth. This journey, the most natural of all, is as ancient as humankind, and despite myriad of extraordinary medical advances, it will still, more often than not, be pretty much as our ancestors experienced it millions of years ago in the dark corners of their caves. The experience of giving birth is, no matter what, always both exhilarating *and* perilous. It takes us to the limits of our minds and our bodies, to the frontiers of life and death. We should all – mothers, fathers, partners and babies – emerge from it unscathed, all being well. But, at the same time, it is an experience that will change us for ever, in ways that are hard to describe, but which are important to try to understand.

Trusting our bodies

For our babies, being born is a one-way journey they have never undertaken before and will never undertake again. It is an experience they will never consciously remember. But it is also a journey whose excitement and drama, frustration and danger, at a deeper level, will never be forgotten. And we will come to explore the consequences of that for our relationship with our baby in due course, especially when, as is sadly not infrequently the case, the journey is traumatic (see Chapter 13 – Healing from a traumatic birth.)

We may choose to have several babies, and thereby get a little bit used to the experience of giving birth. But however many babies we have, each journey is unique and unpredictable. No matter how much preparation we do, no matter how many birth plans we write, we can't guarantee for ourselves the 'perfect birth'. Such a thing (despite all we read on Instagram or celebrity blogs) does not exist. As we will see in this chapter, giving birth rarely turns out exactly as we dream it might – we may plan, as is only natural, but we shouldn't wish too hard, or try to control it too much.

Birth plans

It is often more useful to think of a birth plan as a wish list, and be prepared to manage our disappointment if we don't get all of the things we hoped for. Or perhaps be happily surprised, should we get something nice that we had not thought of beforehand. Even more helpful is to, instead, think our birth plan as a springboard that allows us to explore in detail all the different ways of birthing, rather than something to stick to, or insist upon.

While exploring our birthing options, it is important not to catastrophise. Remember that, at the end of the day, our bodies will generally do what they need to do and, just as during pregnancy when we left the growing of our babies to our bodies, our bodies know how to give birth. They have been designed carefully through millions of years of evolution to let our babies travel safely from their little five-star palaces into the world. So, trusting our bodies, and creating a safe and calm environment where they can do their job with as little interference as possible (and hopefully produce as much oxytocin as possible), is essential. That should be at the heart of our birth plan (and central to any decisions taken by those assisting us). However, there are quite a few things that we can do to help our bodies be at the peak of their capabilities.

As with anyone preparing for an extreme physical challenge, we first need to look after ourselves: giving birth is no mean feat. Having a healthy diet filled with fresh veg and fruits (and ideally pulses and nuts and seeds too), as well as taking regular exercise – all these things help keep our body in top condition. If possible, take some time off work before your due date too. Giving birth is exhausting, and being rested before going into labour gives your body an extra chance to relax into the process and do its job properly. Ultimately, though, the thing that will give your body the best chance of being at its most efficient and effective when giving birth is feeling safe. Let's look at how that works.

Feeling safe

Our bodies and minds are intrinsically linked and cannot be separated. So, how we feel impacts hugely on what type of hormones our brain releases and, therefore, on how our bodies function. And it is when we are feeling calm and safe that our brain can best do what's so useful when we give birth: deliver us the right blend of hormones, which are designed to help us during this extraordinary time.

Our brains are like attentive mixologists in the trendiest of bars, in that they intuitively know what cocktail of hormones our bodies need, depending on our mood. So if, when in labour, we arrive at the 'labour bar' feeling safe and calm, our brain mixologist will serve us a deliciously sweet and soothing glass of oxytocin-based cocktail. Oxytocin, which was discovered at the beginning of the twentieth century and given a name derived from the Greek, meaning 'quick birth', is designed to kickstart our labour and accompany each of our contractions. By lowering our blood pressure and suppressing the production of the stress hormone cortisol, this oxytocin cocktail helps us feel less anxious, making labour more bearable, i.e. less physically painful and less frightening.[1]

If, on the other hand, we arrive at the 'labour bar' stressed, anxious and on high alert, the attentive brain mixologist will discern a different need and serve us a cocktail full of the sharp notes of adrenaline and cortisol, to help get us ready to run away from danger, or even fight it. Unfortunately, this also means that our contractions will slow down, and sometimes stop all together. This is a not uncommon experience: our contractions start calmly at home, often in the night, and once they get into a gentle but effective rhythm, we decide that it is time to go to hospital. We excitedly pack our bag, get into the car, but then the traffic is slow and we struggle to find a parking space, and of course we haven't downloaded the right app for the parking ticket and the contactless payment doesn't work ... After walking through endless hospital corridors, we finally arrive at the birthing unit; we don't recognise any of the midwives, but one of them examines us anyway, and tells us ... that our contractions have stopped, so we are sent back home again.

Giving birth is a moment in our lives when our connection not only with our human ancestors but with all mammals is at its most evident. Animals instinctively know that giving birth when on high alert is not conducive to a safe birth. The pregnant doe, as the daylight fades, starts roaming the woods for the quietest and safest place, somewhere dark, hidden; the ewe finds the darkest corner of the lambing shed, away from the other sheep. There is an intrinsic knowledge shared by pregnant mammals that finding a safe place to give birth, away from interference and distraction, is a priority. It makes birth easier and calmer, and it makes bonding afterwards easier too.

Labour is a time for us to slip gently back into our mammalian brain – where our hypothalamus dependably produces oxytocin, reducing the effects of stress, inducing feelings of pleasure and euphoria, and ultimately supporting us to bond, love and care for our babies. It is a time when we need to try to leave behind all the distractions associated with our neo-cortex, i.e. our thinking and problem-solving brain. We need to stop making to-do lists, checking emails or the latest Instagram posts from our favourite celebrities, or even reading the section on giving birth in this book.

And, like our mammal friends, we also need to avoid as far as possible stimulating our 'reptilian brain', that primitive part of our brain that is mostly preoccupied with survival. When we are scared and feeling unsafe, it is this part of the brain that takes over, directing all our blood and oxygen to the organs essential for survival – to our legs so we can run away, to our arms to enable us to defend ourselves and fight off attackers.

In short, when we are feeling unsafe and scared, we stop producing oxytocin – the hormone essential for maintaining our contractions – and our bodies simply stop giving birth. When the body is under stress, oxytocin becomes the 'shy hormone'; it goes and hides until it is safe to come out again. This is obviously helpful for the doe who has been sniffed out by a predator and needs to stop her contractions so she can run away fast. But, for us, in our highly controlled and structured Western world – or anywhere else in the world, for that matter – we should never be in that frightened state when in labour.

We shouldn't be, but quite often we are . . . Unfortunately, the modern medical system does not always give mothers the respect and care they deserve – this is a subject we will return to a bit later in the book (particularly in Chapter 13), and it is an important one. As a society we can (and need to) agree to help mothers feel safe when they give birth. They need to be seen as a whole human being, with a mind, a body, and a hopeful plan; they are not just machines delivering babies. The humanity of a birthing mother needs to be fully recognised, enhanced even, and never diminished or disrespected.

Choosing a safe place

As we can see, giving birth is an experience of two extremes: we are at our most powerful and yet also at our most vulnerable. When giving birth, our bodies perform this most incredible act. And yet, at that very moment, they cannot do anything else. Not even the basic tasks of protecting and defending themselves. Indeed, giving birth is so all-encompassing that our bodies and minds need all the energy they can muster to stay focused. So, like our cavewomen ancestors, we need to find or create an environment that we trust will protect us.

However, because we are humans and have a very complex mind, this feeling of safety, and how best we are going to achieve it, is a very subjective one. In most cases it's going to depend on an intricate combination of our culture, our personality, and our past experiences.

For some mothers, feeling safe means being at home, in a familiar room and close to the people and things that make them feel secure every day. Others find more security and calmness in a medical environment, with the reassuring sounds of beeping machines and the knowledge that trained professionals are there to respond to anything untoward. Even the knowledge that the option of surgery is close by, with the possibility of opening up our tummy to end the pain and release the baby, is a genuine comfort for some. For many of us these days, a blended combination of the natural and the medical feels right – a home birth with a midwife who can offer pain relief, and the knowledge that the hospital is just a short car ride away; or a hospital with a birthing centre that has softly furnished rooms and birthing pools.

But nobody can tell us what feels safe for us. We have to find it out for ourselves. And, unfortunately, unlike our animal friends, we have lost some of our instinctive and intuitive feelings in this respect. Our man-made environment is so complicated, and so full of choices that are not of our making or design, that we can feel lost, even a little alarmed. And as we know, that can take us straight back into the wrong part of our brains, where we are apt to sip the wrong hormone cocktail in the labour bar.

So it is very important, while pregnant, to spend time exploring which choices make us feel safe and which make us feel scared. Luckily, we have quite a few months in which to do this. And we have partners, friends and professionals who can (or should be able to) help us with the task.

Exploring what feels safe

Basically, we need to get curious about ourselves: we need to dig deep into our conscious and unconscious mind. And, as ever, oxytocin can help us out here. The increase in oxytocin production in our brain during pregnancy actually encourages us to be more explorative with our emotions. It even increases our desire for new social interactions: we want to know ourselves better and we also want to learn from others. Pregnancy is often a time when we form new or stronger bonds – with our parents, siblings and friends – around the experience of motherhood and fatherhood. We search the internet, we listen to podcasts, we read books, we join antenatal groups. We want to know about other people's experiences.

When it comes to understanding your relationship with feeling safe or not, you might want to revisit some past experiences where you felt safe, and also some where you did not. It might at times feel difficult to do this. Talk to your midwife and doctor, to your partner and friends. Talking to a therapist might be a good idea too, especially if you have gone through some previous traumatic events in your life, or if your own childhood was difficult.* Designing a birth plan or birth wishes with support from partners and midwives can be key to helping you clarify what you need to feel relaxed and calm.

Inevitably, when trying to work out what feels safe for you, you may meet people with strong opinions on the matter, and who think they know what is best for you better than you do yourself. It might be the fanatical home-birth mother (or midwife) whose view is that hospitals are dangerous, hostile places. Or, conversely, a pro-hospital birther who wants to persuade you that home birth is a reckless and self-centred proposition. The more insistent they are, the more you can be sure they are not hearing you, or seeing who you really are.

It is not always easy to keep a steady head when it comes to deciding where feels right to give birth, so it is important to take your time and allow your mind to explore, to ask lots of questions. This really

* I have included a list of associations that you might find useful at the end of this book (see p.369).

is worth the effort. There's a whole raft of research showing that the safer we feel, the 'easier' the birth, because the safer we feel the more oxytocin (remember that word derives from the Greek for 'quick birth') our brain will produce (up to four times the normal amount), with all its incredible pain relief and relaxing qualities. Even if labour is long and at times painful, even when there has been synthetic pain relief and other interventions, it is very clear from the research that mothers who report feeling safe throughout rate their birth as 'easier' and 'more positive'.[2]

In Chapter 13 – Healing from a traumatic birth, however, we will look at the other side of the birth story and how being scared while giving birth often leads to feeling traumatised. We will also explore how both scenarios – feeling safe and feeling scared – impact on how we bond with our babies.

Common features of feeling safe

Even though this feeling of safety is highly subjective, research tells us that there are some common features that can help us stay calmly in our mammalian brain, where oxytocin production is optimal. For instance, keeping the light in the room very low and keeping noise levels down (which often means asking those present to talk calmly and softly). Removing or muting devices and machines, including phones and clocks, is also a good idea, as such devices are highly likely to re-activate our neo-cortex/thinking brain.

Some of us will be reassured by the background noise of the machine that monitors our babies' heart rate. But others may become anxious and frightened as we try to analyse the meaning of the different beeps. If this is the case, perhaps ask the midwives to turn the sound off (they can still see what's going on on the screen).

One thing almost all mothers-to-be agree upon is that having some-one they love and trust alongside them during their labour is a fantastically helpful factor in feeling safe. Like our ancestors, we feel hugely reassured if we know that someone else is ready to fight away the predatory beasts lurking at the entrance of the cave (or deal with an over-anxious phone call from a soon-to-be grandparent or maybe the critical tone of an increasingly impatient midwife).

And this is a very good reason for having an officially designated birthing partner, who has (latterly at least) been close to us and helped us plan our birth. This can be the father or other mother of our babies, or it can be our own mothers or sisters or best friends. Or a professional doula or midwife. When we hear information from someone we love and trust, we tend to trust that information too, and our level of oxytocin rises. As we know, this helps us relax and feel good, but perhaps more surprisingly, studies have shown that the information is also stored away more effectively and recalled more easily.

Agreeing a few things ahead of time can be helpful. A birthing part-ner may help us to negotiate with midwives and doctors if we feel that we need more time and privacy before they step up their med-ical intervention. They may translate medical jargon for us into gentle reassurance at a time when we have switched off our thinking brain. They may take care of our other children if they are nearby and explain what is happening. And they may make or bring that all-important cup of tea . . .

Most of all, the reassuring voice of someone we love and trust, the gentle patting of their hands on our back, or just their silent presence, helps our brain to release more and more oxytocin, allowing our bodies to relax and concentrate on giving birth.

Birthing options

Most of us, in the Western world at least, have a certain degree of choice in the way we give birth. Some mothers choose the 'natural' way to give birth, trying to stay away from medical interference as much as possible: for them, home is where they feel safe and they generally give birth in the peace and quiet of a favourite room or in the warm waters of a birthing pool. With the support of their partner and a midwife who, ideally, they have got to know well in the last few months, they are actively involved in the birth process, and retain as much control as possible over how their babies are going to be born. Their midwife will also have kept the nearby hospital up to date with the progress of the pregnancy, so that it is ready to welcome them if there is a need for a medical intervention.

But the majority of mothers choose to go to hospital or a medical birthing centre. Relying on the expertise of midwives and doctors, they are happy to relinquish some of their control and hand over some of the decisions. At this very anxious time, they want to be told, or at least reminded, what to do.

Those women who have given birth before are very likely to be informed by their previous experience next time around. The precipitous birth mothers, whose babies tend to shoot out of their bodies with little warning, may choose to stay at home, particularly if there is a risk their baby is going to be born on the way to hospital in the taxi or the car park. Others may have had complications during a previous pregnancy or have some medical condition that makes them feel that a hospital birth is the only safe and sensible option.

But whatever option we have chosen, it is important we feel that it was indeed our choice: an informed, considered and un-coerced decision based on unhurried research, conversations with trusted partners and previous experience, if we have it, leading to a plan that makes *us* feel safe.

The birth journey

We can think of pregnancy as being like a long river journey. For nine months we have been gently bobbing on the surface of the river, enjoying the ride. But as we reach the final stretch, we know that all this is about to change and that we will need to jump into a canoe, one we feel is safest to negotiate the rocky bends in the river and dangerous rapids ahead.

We also know that, at the end of the river, we will find the sea; that after the narrow confines of the riverbanks, we will emerge into this infinite environment, where everything seems different and new. For us mothers and fathers and co-parents, we will have become the guardian of new lives, a responsibility like no other. For our babies, they will have left their five-star palaces and entered the earthly world of (physical and emotional) gravity, hunger and noise.

Every mother has their own unique river journey and their own idea how they are going to negotiate the last stretch. But if we cannot choose our rivers or know in advance how the last stretch will flow and unfold, we can, however, choose our canoes (metaphorically speaking). And as we have been exploring, we need to choose the one that we feel is safest and suits best our way of paddling. After months of research and soul searching, and many conversations, some of us go for the high-end model with all the latest tech, while others prefer the old-fashioned one, with just a wooden paddle. Ultimately what is important is that we feel confident with our canoe, that we can trust it to bear us safely down the river. Once the journey has started, there is no stopping it.

For the lucky few, we travel the last stretch of the river quickly, negotiating relatively easily the rapids, avoiding getting stuck in the bends
or thrown overboard by the big rocks. But, generally, for most of us,
the last stretch of the journey is long, winding and, at times, frighten-
ingly turbulent. If so, we hope that along the way there will be calm
pools where we can rest, admire the vegetation, imagine how our
babies are managing their part of the journey (they too have their
own version of our river trip), get some nourishing supplies and
encouragements from our partners, and some reassurance from the
medical staff, before the current pushes us forcefully to the next stage
of our labour.

There may be times when we feel that the canoe is getting dangerously close to a big rock, half hidden in the water, or a scarily turbulent
whirlpool. So, we paddle harder and harder and yet it doesn't seem to
make a difference. But then along comes a friendly current, which
draws us away from the danger, sets us back in the flow of the main
river, and we feel calm again. We catch our breath while floating in
another lovely pool, where we can imagine our baby again and enjoy
hearing the loving and reassuring voice of our partners. Then, like
the muscles of our tummies, the river narrows again, pushing our
canoe into what now seems like impossibly small ravines heaving
with powerful currents. This time it feels like nothing we do is
making a difference, the paddle has become useless as the space is too
narrow and we have to let go and trust that the river knows the way
to the sea. And it generally does.

But for some of us, though, riding the last stretch of the river was
never an option. Or perhaps it had to be interrupted mid-course. The
medical staff is shouting from the bank that it's too dangerous, too
many bends, too many rapids, our paddle is too small, our canoe has
a hole in it. But they also tell us that they are going to rescue us and

make us safe. They have done it many times before. Here comes the helicopter to winch us up to safety, lift us up above the dangerous rapids and the sinking canoe. It's going to take us straight to the sea, to meet our baby even sooner than we thought . . .

Our babies' journey

Of course, our babies experience this momentous journey too, but very differently from us. For them it is more like being little contortionists who have decided that it is time to get out of a very cramped cave. And the only way out is down a very narrow tunnel and an even more narrow exit. Again and again, helped and encouraged along the way by pushes and squeezes from our pulsing, contracting uterus, they have to turn and twist their little bodies – that are now starting to feel not so little – in very precise ways, discovering at the same time the power of their tiny growing muscles as they wriggle and writhe. As they leave our uterus and enter our birth canal, their incredibly malleable head gets compressed: the still-forming skull bones ride over each other, overlapping to allow the whole round head to morph into an elongated bean-shape that can now slowly slip down through the narrow birth canal. And after more twisting of their bodies, and as if scraping the tip of their noses on our spines, they can finally exit our bodies, hopefully head first.

We can never remember consciously what it was like for us when we were born, nor can we ever understand exactly what our babies are feeling, and indeed thinking, when they make this extraordinary journey. But we can use our imagination, perhaps aided by deep stirrings in our unconscious, to know that it must be exhilarating and frightening at the same time, involving perhaps the most intense sensations, some pleasurable and some painful, that we – and they – will ever feel. By imagining, even visualising, what is happening for our baby on this journey, we can encourage, accompany and reassure them with our mind's eye, even as our bodies are showing them the way to go.

Although our babies' journeys are so very different from ours, the two remain intimately connected. This is not just because we help each other negotiate the bends and narrow passages, feeling each other's bodies and responding mutually to each wriggle and pulse. It's also because our baby is sharing that special cocktail of hormones – albeit in suitable baby-sized doses carefully measured out by our genius mixologist – as it passes through the placenta from our bloodstream into theirs. This oxytocin cocktail not only eases our physical pain, it also eases the pain the baby feels on being born. It will have an amnesic effect on our memories too: it will soon help us both forget a little just how painful and scary the birth was, and to hold on to the more euphoric part of the experience. Often, for us mothers, it is not until we have another baby that we fully and consciously remember how painful giving birth is.

And one thing we can be certain of, even if we can never measure it or ask for a report, is that when our babies finally emerge into that ocean of air and gravity, hunger and noise, they experience an intensity of change and newness that will never be repeated or matched during the whole of the rest of their lives. Even if it is not laid down in conscious memory, it is certainly acknowledged and recorded in every cell of this new person's body. It's like a personal 'big bang', laying the foundations for everything that follows. Their universe has just begun and the momentous event that launched it into being will be with them for ever.

After the birth journey

We, as mothers, certainly feel a version of the momentousness that our baby experiences on being born. And fathers or co-parents do too. We may well feel totally elated by the river journey, especially when the last stretch has gone as we had hoped it would. And so we come out feeling stronger and more confident. But it is also not rare to feel disappointed when things have not gone the way we had imagined they would. And that is very hard to bear. The trauma from a difficult birth is, unfortunately, too little acknowledged by professionals, who perpetuate an age-old societal expectation that if mother and baby have both come out of that turbulent journey alive, then everyone should be grateful and not dwell too long on the emotional and psychological impact of the birth.

The truth is that, no matter how 'easy' the birth is, giving birth and being born are and will always be physically and emotionally traumatic events, experiences that stay with us and our babies, often at an unconscious level, for the rest of our lives and theirs. Some of us instinctively know that talking about the birth of our babies can be helpful, and we will find the time to do this in a calm and helpful way with friends or family members. But sometimes the experience has been so overwhelmingly confusing and traumatic that it is difficult to put it into words, let alone to share it with anyone. We will be exploring the aftermath of traumatic birth in more detail later in the book (see Chapter 13 – Healing from a traumatic birth). Suffice to say here that, while there are various things we can do to help us 'process' our experience, in some cases finding a therapeutic space is essential. In talking to a trained therapist, we can tell our story, our very own scary story, without being judged or interrupted. We can express our disappointment that we did not 'manage' the perfect birth we had been sold in the books we read or on social media; express our very real fear that we thought we were dying; admit to our guilt that we have 'let down' our babies, and confide our anger that we were not listened to by those around us. And, hopefully, at the end of the therapeutic process, we will finally be able to enjoy the relief that we and our babies are indeed alive, despite all that we went through.

3
At last, we meet . . .

Meeting our babies

We have finally made it to the open sea of motherhood. We are in shock, exhausted, and it is hard to keep a steady head, as the cocktail of hormones that has helped us give birth and is now going to help us bond with our babies has reached its peak of intensity. Our brains are swimming in a pool of oxytocin, prolactin (there to stimulate our milk production) and even adrenaline, which gave us that last boost of energy to push our babies into the world.

Our babies have now swapped the sanctuary of our tummies for the safe haven of our arms. They are naked, still covered by protective vernix, and we feel their skin against ours (a simple form of contact, but one which, yes, releases yet more oxytocin). Time, which was speeding past us only a few minutes ago, seems to have slowed right down. At last we can look at our babies: the baby we have imagined and fantasied about for months is now replaced by a real one. Their big, wide-open eyes invite us to dive deep into our feelings.

Meeting our babies for the first time, like giving birth, is an experience that is loaded with pre-conceived ideas. There is an expectation that, as mothers (and fathers and co-parents, to a lesser extent), we should love our babies straight away, that it is in our biological make up to fall in love with them instantly, and that, if we don't, it must be because there is something wrong with us. So many books, films and now Instagram accounts continue to perpetuate this myth.

In the hours after giving birth, as we stare at our babies' little faces and meet their eyes, so many feelings rush through us. Some wonderful feelings, full of love and gratitude, but also some rather more ambivalent feelings, laced with confusion and contradictions.

As we scan their little bodies for the first time, some of us feel a sense of knowing our babies already, enjoying the sort of intimacy that comes from having already spent nine months together. But, for a lot of us, our babies can feel almost alarmingly present and real: who is this intimidating stranger?! Perhaps we find it difficult to recognise them; or had imagined our babies to be very different from what they actually look like. Maybe we find them quite ugly. Perhaps we are disappointed that they are a girl or a boy. Or we are worrying already that they might be like us, with all our imperfections, or that they might be like their dad, with all his annoying habits. We might also feel confused and upset about the way our babies were born and can now only see them through the lenses of the traumatic birth we have just experienced. And we are wondering how we will ever be able to love someone who has taken us through so much fear and pain. We might even find those big eyes are already judging and critical of our ability to be a mother. This is especially likely if the birth has been difficult.

The fact is that most of us enter parenthood somewhere in the middle of the two extremes. Despite what we see on social media and in glossy magazines, very few of us enter parenthood from the love extreme, with our feelings for this new red, wrinkly and totally helpless being all-consuming and self-evident. And some of us might even enter parenthood from the other extreme, where looking at this noisy wriggling creature is almost unbearable. Such a feeling is often triggered by some past trauma that is interfering with the bonding process. If this is your experience, then it is very important to seek professional support, where you can talk about, explore, and make sense of these feelings in a safe space. (We will look at all these more conflicted aspects of parenthood in more detail in Part Three. I have also put some links at the end of book for some helpful organisations to contact if you think you may be suffering from post-natal depression.)

Meeting our new selves

Meeting our babies is not just meeting our babies. It is also meeting ourselves, or at least a new version of ourselves, as a parent. Through growing, giving birth to and caring for our babies, we not only get to know them, but we also get to know ourselves better, and in a different way.

And when we get to know our babies, we soon discover that, as with any other relationship, our feelings about the other person are never constant and straightforward. Just as when we became lovingly involved with our partners, we discovered that the same person can evoke in us not only feelings of love but also of annoyance and sometimes even of fierce hatred. It may be the same with our babies. Being a parent is to enter a whole new relationship, perhaps the most significant in our lives, one that will, at times, test us to the extreme. This hopefully infrequent but less happy aspect of parenting can be hard to acknowledge and reconcile, especially in a society that still expects mothers to love (with a capital L) their baby 24/7. The knock-on effect is that we may also struggle with our perception and understanding of who we are. Just as we will find we do not have exclusively loving and positive feelings for our baby, we may not always love the new parent we have become either.

When we enter the world of parenthood, we become a tightrope artist, the balancing poles of our emotions wobbling precariously between the two extremes of love and hate, or at least between love and frustration/confusion. We will return often to this theme of parental ambivalence throughout this book (and especially in Chapter 9 – When loving our babies is hard).

But it's not unusual to find that one minute we may feel that we already know our babies, that nine months of pregnancy has given us an intimate knowledge of them and an unconditional love, and the next we feel that our babies are total strangers, and we become dizzy thinking of how long it will take to get to know them. The good news is that it is through this getting to know them, through taking care of them, and interacting with them, exploring their needs, and noticing our own feelings, that we will slowly and steadily fall truly in love with them. And we will love them for who they are, more than for who we thought or hoped they were going to be.

When our babies first meet us

While we may not be entirely sure how we feel about our babies when we first meet them, one thing is certain: they are pretty clear as to how they feel about us. For them, we are no intimidating stranger but rather a long-lost friend that they can't wait to catch up with. During the last nine months, they have acquired an extraordinarily deep knowledge of us. They know the intricacies of our heartbeat: its fast pace when we were running late for the bus, its quieter rhythm when we were relaxing after a long day. They have heard all the most intimate functions of our body. The sound of our blood rushing through our arteries, our stomach digesting our food, even our bottom farting; of our voice as we sang, talked, shouted, argued or laughed with our partner. They even learned our smell while they were in our tummies! In many ways, they know us inside out. And as soon as they are born, they have a powerful instinct to start exploring our outside, so they can achieve intense intimacy with that too.

Just after birth, our babies are generally very calm – and yet, paradoxically, also in an incredible state of alertness. Instantly they recognise our voice and their other parent's voice. They know who we are, they have heard us before, and research confirms they will consistently turn their heads in the direction of their parents' voices, or the voice they know, rather than of that of a stranger.[1]

Our voices, once muffled by the placenta and our tummies, are now clear and unmistakably ours. And for our babies it is very reassuring to know that, while everything has changed for them, we are still here for them, close by and available. The sounds of our bodies are also soothing: several studies have shown that, when nestled in our arms, their little heads against our chests, our babies recognise our heartbeat, the distinctive, reassuring rhythm that for nine months has been a constant companion to them. And so, as they settle in our enveloping arms, that soothing pulse helps them regulate their own heartbeat as well as their body temperature and even their mood.[2]

When we first meet our babies, we generally start exploring them with our eyes, scanning their faces and bodies. However, our babies start with their noses. For them, just after birth, the nose is the most important organ: through the taste of our amniotic fluid, they have learned our smell in utero. And they will soon know the smell of our breast milk just as intimately. Immediately after birth, they are like puppies or piglets, sniffing us out and searching for our nipples. No one can fool them in this mission. Researchers have tried – by putting milk-infused breast pads on either side of a newborn baby's head, one with their mother's milk, the other from an imposter-mum. Days-old babies unmistakably and consistently turn their head towards the pad with their mother's milk on it, ignoring the other one. Likewise, if a just-born baby is left alone on their mother's tummy, they will behave like almost every other infant mammal, slowly wriggling towards her breasts, following the scent of their favourite food, looking for and generally finding the nipple all on their own.

And we respond to their wriggling and searching: the skin-to-skin contact just after we have given birth, as well as the pressure of our baby's little elbows and knees on our tummies and eventually on our breasts, creates yet another surge of oxytocin in our brain. This also helps our uterus to contract one more time to deliver the placenta and, eventually, stop the bleeding, and also causes a surge of the pro-lactin hormone that triggers the production of milk.

However, if a newborn's first interaction with the world is through their sense of smell, sight comes a close second. One thing that utterly fascinates our babies, arguably even more than our breasts, is our face, which, over the next few months and years, will become the most important part of our bodies for them. It is from the multifarious muscles of our faces, and the thousands of expressions that we make with them, that they will learn not only about us but also about themselves and the world around them (We'll explore this more in the next part of this book).

As soon as they are born, babies very much want to know what we look like. Guided by our voice, when they are close enough (newborn babies do not see clearly beyond 20 centimetres, because their eyes have not had a chance to get much practice in the darkness of our tummies), they start to learn the contours of our face, its lines, its shapes, its characteristic crinkles, pouts, frowns and smiles.[3]

Within hours of being born, they are able to distinguish us from a stranger. Researchers have shown hours-old babies pictures of their mother and pictures of strangers and, unmistakably, they spend more time looking at their mother.[4] When we hold our moments-old baby in our arms, when they lift their head towards our face and slowly open their big eyes, they are actively looking at us, scanning our features, and storing them in their memory bank. It is as if they are discovering us for the first time, but yet also recognising us as their long-lost friend.

Not only do they like looking at our faces, they also love it when we look back at them. Research has shown that very young babies can tell when someone is looking at them or away from them. And they much prefer it when we look at them directly![5] Feeling that we have our eyes on them makes them feel more protected, safer and, of course, loved.

4

Born ready

For nine long months we have nurtured our babies in our tummies – in that time they have grown from a single cell into a human being. And yet they are born totally helpless, lacking the most basic skills to survive on their own. You could even say that all human babies are born months, if not years, premature. It will take them four months, for example, before they can hold their neck up on their own or roll over on their tummy, six months before they can sit up, nine months before they can stand and around a year or more before they can walk and start saying a few words. It will take another eighteen months before they acquire the most basic survival skills, such as running from danger and feeding themselves. And, one might argue, another two decades or more before they can make their own bed and clean up their own dishes – if we are lucky!

This helplessness at birth is the trade-off for having babies with highly developed brains, which need to be protected in big heads. In order for babies to be relatively independent straight after birth, they would have to have be born with a brain the size of a two-year-old's (i.e. roughly 80 per cent of its adult size). However, because we humans walk upright on our two feet, our pelvis has stayed relatively narrow, and clearly there is no way that we could give birth to a baby with a head this size.

At the moment when they are born, a baby's highly sophisticated brain actually has more neurones than it will ever have – approximately 100 billion of them, ready to form a super-sophisticated network of connections. And yet, unbelievable though it may now seem, babies were for centuries regarded as not just helpless but without intention or direction. The general assumption was – and sometimes still is – that they are passive little beings with no emotional life, whose body movements are the result of uncontrolled, spontaneous reflexes. Compared to adults, they were deemed 'boring', and barely worthy of research. It was even assumed that they did not feel pain – a belief that, until the mid-80s, was still widely held among members of the medical profession and so meant that babies were often not given any pain relief, even during invasive surgical procedures.[1]

Not a boring blob of clay

Needless to say, parents have long intuitively known that their babies are not boring – let alone little blobs of clay waiting to be shaped! – that they can certainly feel pain, and that they very much have 'a mind of their own'. But it is only with the advances of science and new technology, such as Magnetic Resonance Imaging (MRI scans) and 4D CT scans, that it has become possible to prove babies' incredible emotional vitality and capacity to connect. For a few decades now, researchers have been busy scanning mother's tummies, and wiring up parents' and babies' heads to see what part of their brain is active when they interact. And they have also been filming and micro-editing babies' most minute interactions with their parents and the world around them. What we now know is that our babies have the ability not only to react to social interaction with us but also to initiate and maintain many of these interactions. They have a very impressive range of communication skills, and are well equipped and motivated to participate in a two-way relationship. They are, as the saying goes, born ready!

And, indeed, they are born ready because, even while they were still in our tummies, they were already practising this two-way relationship. In a recent study, thirty-weeks-pregnant mothers were asked to talk freely to their foetus while watching a live 4D scan of their unborn babies' reaction. The researchers found that the foetus responded much more actively (more sucking, hand movement and mouth opening) when their mothers talked to them in an interactive way, as if they were having a 'conversation' with them – for instance, telling their unborn babies what they saw them doing on the screen and wondering what it meant and how they felt – than when they chatted to them in a non-interactive way, with the 4D scan screen turned off. The same was observed when the mothers were touching their tummies. The foetus reacted more when the touch was interactive, as if the mums were sort of playing a game with their foetus, than when they were stroking their tummies without looking at the scan screen.[2]

Therefore, way before they are born, our babies can distinguish between when we are talking to them thoughtfully and meaningfully, noticing and commenting on what they are doing, as opposed to when, for example, we are chatting to a friend on the phone. Long before they are born, they have a sense of what a loving and caring connection feels like, and have already started to know how good it feels to be in the forefront of someone's mind. So, it's no wonder that, as soon as they are born, our 'helpless' babies want to carry on that relationship with us – and indeed take it to the next level.

. . . But no words yet

Although our babies are born ready to relate, they lack one of the most useful tools with which to communicate with us: words. To remedy this, they have had to master the art of non-verbal communication using their whole body. And master it they have – with their arms, legs, hands and feet, and with their face, with its dozens of muscles, their mouth, nose, eyes and eyebrows. They use all of these and more, in a deliberate and reliable way, to tell us how they feel, what they like, what they don't like, what they want more of or less of . . . As soon as they are born, our babies invite us, with their big beautiful eyes, to dance the most incredible and precise dance that we will ever dance. Without words, they will manage to engage us in some of the most intimate and transforming conversations we will ever have.

The imitation game

The conversation starts right at the beginning: our babies are in our arms, they look at us intently and what do they do? They start to imitate us! Studies have shown that if we stick our tongue out, there's an excellent chance that our hours-old baby will stick out theirs too.[3] If we make an O shape with our mouth, they too will make a little O shape with their mouth. Some other studies have even shown newborn babies being able to lift one, two or three fingers up, copying the adult in front of them.[4] It might look like at first sight as if our babies are just learning 'new tricks', but in fact their imitations are very much intended: they are a way to start a communicative and cooperative relationship with us.[5] Because what do we do when they start imitating us? We instinctively start to imitate them back! And then they imitate us again, and we imitate them in return . . . And there we are: we have entered this everlasting dance of back and forth with our babies, through which they will learn about us, about themselves and the world around them.

How do we know that our newborn babies are not just little parrots copying us for the sake of it? That they are using physical and vocal imitation as a way of getting to know us and to communicate with us; and that the 'imitation game' pays dividends in bonding and understanding? We know this because of multiple studies, which have shown that changing our facial expression also changes the way we feel (for example, when you are cross, try smiling and staying cross . . . it is almost impossible!). So, by trying to copy some of our facial expressions, babies get a sense of how we feel, who we are and what is going on around them. In turn, by inciting us to imitate them, they enable us to get a sense of how they feel.

Imitation is our babies' first step towards 'feeling for' another human being, dipping their toes (and fingers, and noses) into the welcoming waters of empathy and socialisation.[6] It is the first of the many steps in the dance that our babies will invite us to perform with them – during which we both start collecting vital information to be deposited in the bank of our shared experience, a bank that we will draw on to build our understanding of each other.[7]

The invisible dance

Even more incredibly, there is also an invisible, visceral dance, corresponding to the physical one, which we and our babies engage in with our nervous and hormonal systems and with our brain synapses. In the same way that both ours and our partners' oxytocin rose in tandem during pregnancy, now our babies' hormonal and nervous systems as well as their brain are going to start dancing synchronically with ours. We saw earlier how, with our first skin-to-skin contact after birth, their heartbeat and body temperature adjusted to ours; well, their oxytocin level also follows ours, as does their brain (the same part of both of our brains is activated when we are together).

Of course, to dance all these dances we need to be close to our babies, to spend time with them. And, for that, our babies have evolved quite a few irresistible tools that make us want to spend a lot of time with them.

They even know how to smile . . .

One of their most powerful tools is their smile. They have been practising it since the twenty-third week of pregnancy, and, soon after they are born, they are keen to show us just how good they are. Frame by frame micro-editing of videos of days-old babies shows that they not only smile with their mouth but also with their eyes, making their cheeks move upward a little.[8] Most scientists now agree that these smiles are not just 'reflex' smiles, attributed in some old-school parenting books to a successful fart, but have clear social meaning and purpose. So next time someone tells you that your baby's smiles are only the result of 'wind', you can ignore them or politely tell them the science says otherwise.

And this really matters, because our response to our babies' smiles depends on the meanings we attribute to them. If we think they are all about farts, we might ignore or even dismiss them, but if we understand that their smiles are intentional and meaningful we will respond to them in kind, entering again that dance of back-and-forth communication.

There is a very good reason why our babies smile at us from day one. MRI scans have shown that, when we see our babies smiling, our brains fill with dopamine, the reward hormone.[9] A smile from our babies makes us feel happy, even as euphoric as if we had just won the lottery or found the most extraordinary treasure! So, no wonder we spend so much time looking at our newborn babies. One research paper observed that when a mother first holds her baby, she spends an extraordinary 80 per cent of her time looking at her baby – with 40 per cent of that time concentrating on her baby's face and 34 per cent actually smiling at her newborn.[10]

Arms and legs . . .

Because our babies have no words yet, they have to use not just their face but their whole body to engage us and communicate with us, to let us know how they are feeling and what they need. And for this they especially like to use their arms and legs. Until quite recently it was thought that babies had little control over their bodies. The latest research says differently, suggesting that over 75 per cent of their arm and leg movements are very much intentional.[11] And that this actually starts when they are in our tummies, with those kicks and elbow nudges. Studies show that they are even able to put their thumbs in their mouths with great accuracy. Carefully observe your newborn baby and you will find that it is possible to tell if they are happy or sad just by looking at the movements of their arms and legs. Happy babies share their joy by vigorously moving their arms and legs; when they are sad, their arms and legs will be less active.

In addition to this, our babies' movements are often quite precisely coordinated. Micro-editing of videos of babies shows very clearly that they use their arms and legs in harmony with their facial expressions and early vocalisations. Later on, we will notice how this harmonious coordination includes us, how their body movements become very quickly coordinated with ours, and vice versa, making the special dance even more special and fluid. It takes two to tango, and very often it is our baby that takes the lead.

No words but a voice . . .

Although our babies do not have words yet, they certainly have a voice. And they are ready to use it right from the beginning, and with an incredible sense of timing. There is a fascinating study of fathers interacting with their two-to-four-day-old babies that strongly sug-gests our newborns know from birth how to be in a conversation with someone.[12] The researchers filmed the fathers holding their tiny babies in their arms, looking at them and vocalising with them. When they then micro-edited their recordings, the fathers and babies were shown to be responding to each other within one to three seconds, which is the ideal temporal window for 'turn-taking' and recognised to be the basis for all meaningful conversations. It also became evident that the newborn babies in the studies were engaging in these conversations to establish a connection, rather than to seek immediate protection or care. So, way before they have learned how to speak words, babies nevertheless know how to listen and 'talk' to us. From the very begin-ning, with both their bodies and their voices, they start a conversation with us, their parents. It's a two-way performance, of simultaneous conversation and dance, and it will last a lifetime.

Survival necessity . . .

Forming an emotional bond with us is an existential necessity for our babies, which they undertake with huge vitality and enthusiasm from the moment they are born. When still in our tummies they have had some experience of how good and safe it feels to be in the forefront our minds, and instinctively, once born, they know how to draw us close to them, so we not only don't forget them but also understand what they need from us. Using every inch of their little body, they invite us to look at them with immense curiosity, hoping to mesmerise us with their faces and their thousands of different expressions.

Parental 'preoccupation'

And, indeed, in a matter of days, or hours even, we will very likely become mesmerised. Like incredibly strong little magnets, our babies pull us close to them: making us want to hold them all the time, to look at them, study their face for hours, squeeze their little hands, caress their little feet, check their ears, count their toes . . . And soon we no longer quite recognise our former selves. We used to be gregarious and curious about things happening around us, but now our field of vision has shrunk and we have become fixated on our babies, almost hypnotised by them. What on earth has happened to us?

What's happened to us is simple: we have become a parent! And with this crazy, obsessional parental love comes a degree of fear. One of the most monumental steps into parenthood is coming face to face with the utter vulnerability of our babies, including the frightening reality that they could die. From now on, we have someone in the world we care about more than we care for ourselves. And we will worry, with more or less intensity, about our baby's safety and health for the rest of our lives. Of course, we have known for a long time how fragile life is (maybe since the moment we were ourselves born). But most of the time, in order to live a more or less relaxed life, we have managed to put this thought to the back of our minds. When our babies are born, the fragility of life comes back to the fore in a very primal way.

The next monumental step of parenthood is the realisation of our baby's absolute dependence on us. Within minutes of them being in our arms, we start to appreciate, even if unconsciously, the massive extent of the task ahead: our babies need our near constant input and attention just to stay alive. And, especially for the first few weeks, caring for them will be the most demanding job that we have and will ever have done. Some of you may be familiar with the story in the Asterix comics about his friend Obelix, who fell into the druids' magic potion when he was a baby, which gave him everlasting strength. What happens to us as parents is something similar. It is as if, in order to make sure we can do our job properly, we fall into the magic potion of parenthood, a potion that has the power to transform us into incredibly focused and strong people, ready to engage with the monumental task ahead: keeping alive our helpless babies and allowing them to grow into happy human beings!

The paediatrician and psychoanalyst Donald Winnicott describes the first few weeks of parenthood as a sort of illness, but an illness that is essential to create the initial bond between us and our babies. Even though our babies are ready from the word go to interact with us, and have a panoply of lovely tools to catch our attention, we also need to be in a certain state of mind to be able to see and hear all these cues they are sending us. Indeed, most of their signals are so minute and quick that generally only the parents of a new baby can intuitively notice them (no wonder the researchers studying infant behaviour need their frame-by-frame editing facilities!). It is in order to make us more receptive to our baby's tiny signals that our brain undergoes such a huge transformation during pregnancy and birth (and, again, this is true for both parents). The amygdala, an almond-shaped set of neurones deep within our brain, and key for processing memory and emotion, has a growth spurt during this period and becomes even more sensitive to the incredible cocktails made by our personal brain mixologist. It expands to take on even more oxytocin, prolactin and dopamine, so we develop the deepest possible empathy for our babies, which in turn allows us not only to intuitively notice and read the minute changes in their expression but also to reap the maximum reward from these interactions, so that we not only respond sensitively to their incredible neediness but feel good while we are doing it!

Winnicott calls this state Primary Maternal Preoccupation.[13] It's when our caring part takes over all the other parts of our personalities. We become so engrossed by our babies that not much else captures our attention – indeed, we can barely look after our own needs. This is perhaps the origin of the 'slummy mummy' trope. Attention to personal grooming may be one of the casualties, along with anything else on our pre-baby to-do list. If we behaved like this outside early parenting, doctors might indeed conclude that we were suffering from some sort of mental illness. And this illness is not restricted to mothers: fathers and co-parents too, if they are hands on and spend enough time with their babies, can also develop it and become totally preoccupied with their newborn.

From our tummies to our minds . . .

The first three months of a baby's life has sometimes been described as the 'fourth trimester', as it's when babies are at their most vulnerable, so one could argue that it would have been a better idea to keep them in our tummies for a little bit longer! But, as we covered earlier, as humans we are not physically adapted to give birth to babies larger than their current full-term size. To compensate for this arguably premature birth, something extraordinary seems to happen within us: it is as if, as they leave the sanctuary of our tummies, we welcome our babies into the safe haven of our minds. They reside at almost all times in our thoughts, plans and feelings. Our heads replace our bodies as the places where we look after them, where we keep them safe. Thanks to our new hyper-vigilance, we notice their every movement: their mouths opening a little, their arms slightly reaching in the air, their legs kicking, their eyebrows frowning, their noses wrinkling, their fingers curling. And with our newly super-abundant empathy, we are able to interpret and respond sensitively to their micro-messages and countless needs. Our mind becomes our new tummy, with its safe protecting walls, and its incredible capacity to imagine what it is like for our babies . . .

A golden time . . . but also a shock

Before we leave this golden time of the first few weeks after birth, marvelling at our baby's remarkable readiness to engage, their beautiful abilities to harmonise with us in their dance, we need to consider another perspective. Being born, and giving birth, is also really hard. And perhaps the hardest part is the transition from one reality to another.

Up until the birth, we mothers and babies have both been living for nine months in a state of omnipotence, feeling special and powerful. We have been together in a supreme symbiosis of mutual understanding, where our baby's wishes did not even need to be whispered, and yet were effortlessly, magically granted by our internal five-star luxury hotel. As long as there have been no complications, pregnancy for both of us has been easy-peasy, certainly in the light of what is coming up next . . .

Imagine what a shock it must be, then, for our babies to find out that, after they are born, the pampering is over: suddenly they are besieged by needs that they feel they have to satisfy all by themselves. It's like they are standing naked on the street outside the luxury hotel, barred from going back in, and they don't know where they are going to sleep or where the next meal is coming from.

They have become the chief agents of their own survival: they have to use their lungs to breathe, they have to learn how to suck, using their mouth and tongue, they have to use their muscles to contract their bowels and bladder to get rid of their poo and pee. Their body is no longer protected by the reassuring, cushiony placenta. Maybe just a few hours ago it felt cramped and stifling inside: the urge to move beyond it was unstoppable. But now they have been flung from the mattress, as it were, and the duvet and the pillow have been ripped away. The walls of the cosy room they knew so well have dissolved into nothingness. The space around them now feels like a limitless void – and that is quite alarming, to say the least.

Their skin, which had been kept at the same perfect temperature for months, now feels the cold. Soon they will experience hunger and thirst for the very first time, and will have to wait for, or shout for, their food (and even when they learn to call room service, they won't always get a reply). They are quickly going to realise that their needs are no longer understood instantly. And now that they have become physically separate from us for the first time, they may experience perhaps the most intense and distressing of all human emotions: loneliness.

For babies (and let's not forget that we were all once babies, so this is a universal experience), being born is the ultimate realisation that life is not going to be perfect. It turns out that we are not so magically powerful as we thought, just a few hours ago. In the process of being born, babies discover that they are vulnerable little beings who need us to stay alive. And to survive they will have to create relationships, they will have to make themselves understood, they will have to accept compromises and learn that the perfect mother, who only a few minutes ago could understand them as if by magic, is simply not quite so good at understanding their needs anymore, and even worse at fulfilling them instantly. Yes, our babies have all the tools to navigate this new state of being, far more so than we have tended to give them credit for before. But that doesn't mean it's going to be easy . . .

This dawning realisation may be equally shocking for us mothers. Suddenly we cannot offer the infallible luxury treatment to our babies anymore, and we can no longer grant our babies all their wishes . . . motherhood has just moved from instinctive to inadequate. It is as if gravity has filled the gap between us and our babies, as if we and our babies have, through the process of birth, become human again, instead of omnipotent super-humans. From now on, we will both have to play by the rules of the human condition, not to mention the laws of physics and biology.

It will take us time to accept this new reality, and even more time not to feel too guilty about it! Indeed, this sudden fall from grace may explain some of the mythology of the 'perfect mother' – women's inevitable and desperate attempts to be the same perfect mother after the birth that they once thought they were, when they were all that their babies ever needed, ever wanted, ever hoped for.

That said, the experience of that exceptional state of omnipotence during pregnancy is a vitally important one: even though it has now come to an end, it provides an essential foundation for both babies and mothers to prepare them for their new roles in the 'real world'.

For babies, it means that they won't be shy to demand what they need to survive. And when they get fed, and cuddled, and gently rocked, it will indeed feel like some sort of return to the 'good old days', when everything was done for them. And that will feel amazing and help them to be strong and brave and ready to face the world. For mothers emerging blinking from this state of omnipotence, back into some version of everyday reality where a baby is a whole new person to be looked after (and maybe not the only one!), the shock is buffered by the interim state of 'Primary Maternal Preoccupation', which we touched on earlier. This is essential, as it means that we will devote ourselves, and surrender entirely, to the incredibly demanding task of caring for our babies. And when we succeed, as we will, it is one of the best feelings we can know, better even than when it was all effortless and easy because our babies were inside us.

One thing we will need to accept and come to terms with, though, is that most of the decisions and responsibilities in this new reality will rest with us. But at the same time (and this is all too easy to forget) we are going to be getting a huge amount of help from this small and helpless-looking person. Because, actually, it turns out our babies are much better at telling us what they need than it might at first seem.

We may no longer be bonded flesh to flesh as we once were, but both mother and baby have the most powerful instincts, and all the right tools, to make a new kind of bond, and the most important one of all: the emotional bond that will open the doors to new ways to communicate with each other, and allow us to enter into those conversations and dances that will make our babies feel complete and hopeful human beings. And it may very well complete us too.

Two

Bonding with Our Babies

5
Alone with our babies ... Who am I?

Bored already?

Up until now, life as a new parent has been incredibly exhilarating: the pregnancy, our bodies changing, our mood changing, giving birth, meeting our babies, falling slowly (or instantly) in love with them, the feeding, the sleep or lack thereof, the dressing and undressing of our babies, the nappy changing, the visits from grandparents, relatives, friends (all with their –mostly – friendly advice), our new status as a mother or father, as a pair of parents . . . learning how to set up a car seat, putting a pushchair together . . . It has been exciting and exhausting, there's been little time to think . . .

But now what? The excitement of all these 'firsts' is beginning to wear off. Things, at times, are starting to feel quite repetitive, and even a bit tedious. And some of us might be worried that it is the start of the 'boring' phase of our life with our baby. That babies are boring during the pre-talking phase, when they are seemingly just feeding, eating and sleeping, is still a very prevalent belief in Western society – a belief that's perhaps not widely spoken about but still quietly assumed, that babies are not only boring but also kind of stupid, and that, until they can talk in full sentences, there is very little need to engage properly with them at an emotional or intellectual level. And, yes, bits of life with babies *can* be boring, let's not kid ourselves; the logistics of looking after a baby can feel quite dull – a lot more washing to be done, more shopping, nappies to change, bottles to sterilise, pushchairs to fold and unfold, car seats to carry – but hopefully no more than is the case with most worthwhile things in life, where there is always a boring side.

Letting go of the old life . . .

It is often hard for us parents, especially first-time parents, to accept that we cannot live the same life we had when we were childfree. And yet a lot of us try to pretend we can. We think that surely a baby doesn't have to change everything. Yes, we'll have to take some time off work, but there's no need not to carry on socialising, going on holiday, the gym, that yoga class, or book club, the cinema, parties etc. And then, of course, life catches up with us, and we realise that a baby actually changes quite a lot and we can't carry on at the same speed. We have to slow down. And that can feel very scary. The idea of being all day with a baby, who has no crazy schedule to meet, and not much of a social life just yet, can feel fearfully monotonous. What do babies do all day? Sleep, eat, refuse to sleep, poo, pee, fart, burp, sleep, eat, refuse to sleep, poo, pee, fart, burp, ad eternum.

So it is tempting to fill our weeks with activities: Monday – Mini Mozart baby group, just in case there is a Mozart hidden in our babies; Tuesday – Pukka Mama, where we are all hoping to learn some magic massage stroke that will put our babies to sleep on demand (but, failing that, we know that a nice massage is good for bonding); Wednesday – Messy Monkey, where our babies can explore their Jackson Pollack sides, splashing water and paint all over the place, and we don't even have to tidy up; Thursday – Buggy Fit, as it is never too early to start rebuilding our strength and reconnecting with our core and glutes; Friday – Baby Yoga and Breath, where we can catch our breath and relax a little while visualising . . . our old child-free life . . .

Slowing down is not always easy. Modern culture has conditioned us to be ambitious individual achievers from a very young age. So, allowing ourself to surrender to the diktat of a newborn baby, whose diary is filled mostly with poos and burps and a few naps, is not easy. That is partly why so many of us are, at some point or another, tempted to run away from our babies, or run towards as many activity groups or other distractions as we can possibly find: Mini-Mozart music class, Baby Yoga, Buggy Fit . . . These can be great, of course, but are we really doing them for our babies? Or to fill the scary gap that is left in our lives? Going back to work quickly after our babies are born can feel like another safe escape route, especially as it allows us not to face head on our new identity as a parent. But maybe that activity gap, and that parent identity, don't have to be quite so scary after all. Perhaps we can acknowledge our fear, and still embrace the new version of ourselves.

A new identity – the biggest job there is

One of the barriers to taking on our new role is that being a full-time parent is not generally given very good press. Telling someone you meet that 'all' you do all day (and night) is look after your baby is never a great opening line, is it? Rarely (if ever) do people respond: 'Oh, how amazing – tell me more about this incredibly fascinating work . . .'

Our post-Second World War Western society, with its paternalistic (and often outright sexist) bias, has generally been keen to promote the idea that bringing up a baby is an easy-peasy hobby requiring no specific skills and therefore merits little social recognition or financial support. It is scarcely a job, and if it is, it is a menial one that frankly could be done by anybody, but is especially suited to women.

This failure to value childcare is in large part because it has often been regarded as essentially a physical job. 'All' you need to do is to keep them clean, dressed, away from danger and give them the right food so they can grow big and strong. And indeed we do, understandably, spend a lot of time and energy thinking about their physical needs. We think about what they eat, how much and when. We worry that they are eating too often or not often enough, we worry about the quality of our milk, whether our breasts are producing enough, whether the spicy meal we ate last night affects the taste of our milk, or whether we bought the best powdered milk, should we get a different make, should we use a bottle with a wide teat or a narrow one, should we feed them when they seem hungry or when we think it is time to eat. We worry about how we pick them up, are we holding them in the right position, tighter, looser, are we holding the head right . . . It's all too easy to slip into that mode where we obsess over our baby's physical needs, as perhaps society expects us to do.

But what about our baby's mind? What about their personality? Although there are stacks and stacks of books that promise to help us with looking after their bodies, when it comes to thinking about our baby's developing brain, and their inner life, information is sparse. And yet in the same way that our babies need the right food to grow a healthy body, they also need the right emotional food to grow a well-functioning brain and a healthy mind. Mind and body are vitally connected and integrated: nourish one and you nourish the other, and it is the two in combination that helps our small, wriggling babies become healthy, happy, kind and caring people.

So, yes, providing the brain food for our babies – emotional sustenance, love – is a big job, pretty much the biggest there is. Much of it generally comes intuitively, because our brain is hard-wired for us to care for our babies, but that doesn't necessarily mean we do it without effort. We are going to need to step up to it. Luckily, when we do, we are going to find it is one of the most fulfilling and meaningful things we can do with our lives. Indeed, this job, the job of nurturing our babies emotionally, is what this book is all about. And we are going to be talking much more about it in the pages to come.

Babies may look pretty helpless, and in many ways they are, but, from the moment they are born, they want and need us to engage with them as socially and emotionally intelligent beings. Our babies are born ready, ready to be shown how to be a human being, ready to be clever, ready to be funny, ready to interact with us and build that essential emotional bond that will sustain them throughout their lives. And we have a huge role to play in this more invisible task of looking after our babies' emotions and helping them to make sense of them, as well as to learn to regulate them.

At one level this might sound scary, and certainly more complicated than just having to look after their bodily needs. And perhaps it is. There will be times when it doesn't go according to plan, and the fear and even the boredom kick in again (we are going to learn some strategies for coping with that too). But it is also a lot more interesting. Building a rich emotional bond with our babies is what makes our job as parents much more exciting and enjoyable. And I will show you how.

Putting on our 'New-Life-Baby-Lenses'

Our babies are here and they need us completely – there is no magic escape. And if we slow right down, stop looking back longingly at our old life (I know it is not easy – it is so tempting now to look back with rose-tinted glasses) and allow ourselves to embrace our new one, with our babies at the centre, we will see that, actually, babies are neither boring nor stupid, and, as it turns out, our very own baby is the most fascinating of all. We may find it a pity that other people can't see it – of course, that is their prerogative! – but we don't let this worry us, because we know it is really our job to see it, and that this is why our relationship with them is going to be so special.

All big events alter the way we perceive things; often, without us even noticing, they change the lenses through which we look at our lives. Bringing a new human being into the world is one of these life-altering events. So now we need to look at things a bit differently. We need to put on our New-Life-Baby-Lenses and put away the Pre-Baby Old-Life ones . . .

Our New-Life-Baby-Lenses are sometimes a bit like a microscope and sometimes a bit like a pair of binoculars; through them we are going to see staggering things that will fill us with a gratifying sense of wonder, excitement and purpose. Indeed, if we allow ourselves to slow down and get into the rhythm of our baby, if we allow ourselves to be curious, then we will do the best thing ever: we will get to know our baby, and our baby will get to know us, and we will dis-cover a little being that is certainly more fascinating and captivating than any boxset we have ever watched.

This is because not only are we the actors in this new relationship drama but also, and most importantly, we are the scriptwriters too. Yes, it is our job to write the script and decide the story line. And this can feel both exciting and daunting at the same time, as we suddenly realise what a huge responsibility it is to be in charge of the plot: we can take the story with our baby in whatever direction we want.

Quite a thought, isn't it? Life with our baby may well be a little less dull now . . .

Deciding what sort of parents we want to be

In the first weeks after giving birth, it is easy to feel that we have no control at all when it comes to our babies. Indeed, it is sometimes easier to feel that they are controlling us. They seem to dictate our every move, from when we sleep to when we eat and when we shower, and sometimes it feels like we even need their permission to go and have a pee . . . But this is something of an illusion, if we think about it. Of course, these tiny beings, who have hardly any independent movement and no words to shout at us yet, can't really make us do anything. The reverse is the case. They need us to get almost anything done. They need us to be fed, to be cleaned, and to be put somewhere warm and calm, away from bright lights and frightening noises.

This utter dependency on us is, as we might imagine, a very scary thing for our babies, and most of the time they'd rather not know about it or feel it. They are vulnerable and, as a result, they are often quite amazingly adept at flipping the power dynamic and making us feel totally and utterly powerless in the face of their continuous demands. But, actually, it is important to remind ourselves of the enormous power and control we have over them. We are the all-powerful adults, and they are the powerless, defenceless babies. And how we decide we are going to use our power – or, in other words, how we are going to parent them – is going to impact the rest of their lives, and our lives too.

Most of us have a sense of how we would like our babies' lives to unfold: as we hold their tiny bodies in our arms, lose ourselves in their big beautiful eyes, we imagine a curious toddler, an inquisitive child who loves learning and is invited to all their friends' birthday parties, a quizzical, adventurous teenager who discovers the world (in a safe way), a confident young adult who stands up for their friends and opinions, and an adult comfortable with their choices at work and in their intimate life, and (cherry on the cake) who loves to ring us with their latest exciting news.

In other words, we hope that our babies will grow into healthy, independent, confident, kind, compassionate and generous human beings who have been able to fulfil their potential and become whoever they wanted to be . . . No mean task.

If this is how we see the story unfolding, more or less, then there is a very exciting script to write and this book will certainly help you with the job. The opening scene of episode one should perhaps be a long close-up of our faces, looking into the distance, pondering what sort of parents we want to be and what sort of relationship we want to have with our babies. Do we want to be a compassionate parent who is curious about their child and interested in what they have to say? (Yes!) Or an authoritarian one who thinks they know the truth/ all the answers and are ready to impose it no matter what? (Er, no?) Do we want a relationship with our children based on love and trust? (Yes, obviously.) Or on fear and suspicion? (Hardly!) Do we want our children to feel happy and safe? Or scared and stressed? (The former, of course.) Do we want our children to become relaxed and generous or anxious and self-centred? (Are you kidding me?)

I have made these questions deliberately crude because I want to underscore just how huge an influence we have on our babies' futures. We are all the product of relationships and there are none more influential than the first relationships in our lives. Our parents shaped us and, in turn, we are going to shape our babies. Indeed, as

parents we shape our baby's brains, we shape their minds and personalities, we shape their physiological systems and even their immune
systems.[1] This is why it is vital to ask ourselves these fundamental
questions now, because how we respond to our baby's needs right
from the beginning is going to influence who they become.

If only we had magic glasses

If we had some magic glasses (even more amazing than the new-
parent lenses we have just had fitted) that could enable us to see all
that is happening between us and our babies, we would observe a
rich and constant traffic going back and forth between us of emotion
and information. We would see how everything we do, from the
clear physical interventions of feeding and changing their nappies to
the interactive flicker of eye contact and the smallest squeeze, tickle
or caress, affects our babies both physiologically and emotionally.
Stroking their cheek will increase their oxytocin levels and their love
for us, picking them up when they cry will slow their heart rate, a
smile will affect the growth of their brain. The same smile will make
them feel loved, a soothing voice will make them feel safe, a shouting
voice will make them feel scared.

In turn, we too are affected deeply by our babies: their cries will
make our heart rate rise, a scream will increase our cortisol level, and
a smile from them will send our dopamine level rocketing. From
now on, we have entered that never-ending dance as our emotional
and physiological lives are inextricably linked with our babies' and
vice versa. And as we shall see, this is most especially true in the first
two years of their lives, when their dependence on us is at its highest,
and the new neural connections in their developing brains are accumulating at their most rapid rate.

6

Building our babies' brains

It is all about connections

Our babies are social animals who are desperate to form a relationship with their parents in order to survive. And their brains, which start to develop within weeks of conception and continue to evolve until early adulthood, are perfectly designed for this mission. To maximise the chances of survival, our babies' brains are designed to adapt to the environment they are born into, and also to adapt to whatever approach their parents take in looking after them. This means they can adapt to very challenging environments – including, if required, neglectful or abusive environments/parents. The primary motivation in all new human beings is survival. But, of course, we want our babies to do more than just survive! We want them to thrive, and develop into healthy, happy children, who are resilient and self-assured enough to grow into confident adults. To do that we need to nurture their infant brains. And we should not be surprised (or indeed stressed or ashamed) to realise that we might need some help and direction as we accompany them on this vitally transformative early journey.

Our babies' brains

Although babies are born with all the neurons they will ever need (around 100 billion), their brains at birth are hugely underdeveloped in the sense that they lack the vital synaptic connections between these neurons – they have got the kit, as it were, but it needs assembling. It is these synaptic connections that make the brain a useful organ that will gradually enable our babies to engage in complicated physical activities and allow them, eventually, to think for themselves. Without them our babies would never learn to talk, walk, eat on their own, play, write, read, dream, ride a bike, make friends, fall in love. And by far the most important stimulus – or food, if you like – for encouraging and nourishing these synaptic connections is social and emotional interaction, i.e. interaction with another human being.

For any baby, their parents – the people they meet within seconds of their being born, the people who have brought them into the world – are the most obvious, and best, candidates. At this stage, our babies have no need of anyone else: we are their favourite people in the world, and we should never forget that. Of course they will love to meet their grandparents, aunties, uncles . . . But at this stage there is no rush to socialise our babies too widely. We're here! This is exactly what parents are for! And for the next year at least we are going to be their favourite playmates: our facial expressions, the different tones of our voice, the million ways our body moves . . . all these will be the most fascinating things that our babies will ever watch. They *never* get bored of watching us. On the contrary, they can't get enough of us, because it is through us, through the way we move in the world and react to things around us, that they come to understand what's going on around them (i.e. whether they are safe or not) and get a sense of who they are.

Baby's neural network

So, let's look a little more closely at our baby's brain, so we can understand how it all works. Imagine for a moment billions of Lego pieces rattling around in a brand new box. Our job is to help them put the pieces together to create a stable and functional structure. And don't worry: we are not on our own in this incredibly important work; we have the best of all possible assistants – our babies themselves. They are born extremely curious, ready to explore and eager to learn.

Every stimulus from the outside world adds to our baby's neural network – the light coming through the window, the noise of the vacuum cleaner, the soft breeze on their skin – laying down memories and defining the expectations of future encounters. But even richer and more vital in establishing these meaningful connections and fast-tracking development are their hundreds and thousands of interactions with us, their parent. Our hand gently caressing their cheek, the taste of the milk, the tone of our voice, our smiling face (especially our smiling face, as we will see later), all send signals through our baby's nervous system to their brain, stimulating neurons to fire up and connect. Over time and with the repetition of all this firing up and connecting, the microcircuitry of the brain becomes more and more robust and starts forming a dense neural web, linking the different regions of the brain together. This creates a stable structure where information flows smoothly and quickly from one part of the brain to the other. And, although stable, this structure also has the ability to be malleable and adaptable – sometimes referred to as 'plastic' – shifting and adjusting to new experiences and information throughout our lives.

An efficient web of connections is essential for a baby to develop a well-integrated and yet plastic brain. By the age of three they will already have around 1,000 trillion connections – and these are the foundations of their future brain health. But then, over the next two decades, a tough selection process occurs, called 'pruning', whereby only the connections that are used regularly are going to stay, while the others, the ones that are not used enough, gradually disappear. By the time they are adults, just half of a toddler's 1,000 trillion connections will remain.

As I've mentioned, in order to maximise survival, our babies' brains are incredibly good at adapting to whatever parenting style they happen to get. And it is very much the quality and nature of their relationship with us – how consistently and compassionately we respond to their needs, the richness, frequency and dependability of our interactions – that will shape our babies' brains and will determine whether they have a strong or weak foundation for their future learning, behaviour, health and general ability to cope with life and enjoy it.

The idea that our babies' brains are shaped by its environment – much of which we provide, of course, via the everyday experiences we share with them – is a stark reminder of the importance of nurture over nature. And this can go both ways: our power over our little babies can feel both exciting (when we think we have got it right) and overwhelming (when we think we have got it wrong). So, before you read the next section, please remember two things: firstly, even though the peak of the brain's plasticity – its ability to adapt to its environment – is during the first three years of life, our brain carries on changing and adapting to its environment throughout our lives. However, its plasticity decreases with age, and so it is easier to change things when we are two than when we are fifty-two. That doesn't mean it is not possible to change our ways, our outlook or our behaviours when we are adults – it is just that bit harder. And that is especially true if the things – feelings, behaviours, ideas about ourselves – that we want to change are the ones that were established when we were very little. This is why there is so much emphasis in my work as a child psychotherapist on children's early years, because life is dramatically easier if parents get things more or less 'right' the first time around. No pressure, folks!

The second thing to remember is that the structure of the brain is built over time and through repetition. What is going to have an impact are the experiences that happen again and again, several times a day, day after day and over a long period of time. So, if on the odd occasion we realise we have not responded to our babies' needs as sensitively as we retrospectively feel we should have, we don't need to worry, as we have almost certainly not scarred them for life. There is, thank goodness, some margin for error in parenting. And actually, by being less than perfect once in a while, and not entirely consistent in our responses, we will have helped them grow a little more resilient. We will talk more about this later.

Feeling safe and loved

Another way of looking at our new baby's brain is to imagine it to be like a giant and dense virgin forest with billions of short, narrow and as-yet unconnected paths leading to nowhere in particular. Our baby's brain cannot keep track of, or maintain, all these short, narrow, directionless paths – they would simply get lost or stuck or very confused. With time, though, the paths that are used repeatedly will slowly start to become bigger and more established and they will turn into lanes, then roads and ultimately highways. Meanwhile, the others, the ones that are rarely used or not used at all, will vanish, as the forest plants grow over them. What we want is for our children to have an extensive network of healthy lanes, roads and highways that connect seamlessly to each other and with all the different regions and hemispheres of their brain. We don't want any dead ends, traffic jams or road rage issues. We want nice, smooth (emission free!!) highways that transport information, and indeed emotions, from A to B in a steady flow.

Ideally what we want at the centre of this network is a massive roundabout called 'Feeling Safe'. This is one of the most important feelings that we should try to instil in our babies, as it is only when they feel emotionally safe that their nervous system can relax, allowing for a healthy development of every other aspect of their personalities.

But 'feeling safe' doesn't need to be an endless, uninterrupted loop from which there is no exit or re-entry. Indeed, flowing from the Feeling Safe Roundabout will be many different lanes and roads and even other highways that will allow our babies to explore the world in an exciting way. For instance, there will be the highway called Feeling Loved, which is not without its risks of disappointment and rejection – although, as long as these offshoot roads ultimately lead back to the Feeling Safe Roundabout (which requires being dependably loved by their parents), then babies can learn to navigate the riskier byways of Feeling Loved in order to form trusting relationships with friends, teachers, lovers, partners . . .

Another road coming off the Feeling Safe Roundabout will be one called Feeling Relaxed, which will lead to our babies feeling able to play and learn and be creative. And there will be other lanes and byways, such as Feeling Curious, which will lead them to be interested in others as well as the world around them, as well as Feeling Kind and Feeling Confident . . . All of these will help our babies to be able to trust, learn, explore, take risks, fail and, most importantly, bounce back from setbacks, because they know they can always return to the Feeling Safe Roundabout.

Of course, there will be darker, more difficult lanes too: the likes of Feeling Scared, Feeling Angry and Frustrated, of Feeling Sad and Feeling Lonely. But if the Feeling Safe Roundabout is well established at the centre of the network, and our babies have learned reliable ways of finding their way back to it, then it should be easier for them not to get lost for too long in these scarier lanes before they return to their safe place.

Let's get building

How do we create this incredible network in our babies' brains? By being with them! By looking after them, communicating with them, forming a relationship with them. The way we react to our babies' cries, the way we greet their smiles, the way we hold them when we feed them, dress them, undress them, change their nappy, clean their bottoms, massage their tummies, the way we chat to them, tell them little stories, sing them songs, smile at them, rock them, cuddle them, strap them in their pushchair, take them out to the park, put them to sleep . . . All this is what our babies are made of. It is through these very mundane yet enormously nurturing everyday tasks that we communicate with them and let them know how we feel about them, how much we love them, how important they are to us and how we are going to make sure they are okay.

When, for example, we hold them tight against our chest when they cry, when we soothe them to sleep, lay them carefully on the changing mat, talk to them softly while undressing them, smile at them, we can reasonably imagine the most jaw-dropping fireworks in their brain, as their neurons fire up and connect, consolidating and nurturing the all-important Feeling Safe Roundabout with its hundreds of related emotional lanes, roads and highways. If we can keep this in mind when feeding our babies, when changing yet again another dirty nappy, picking them up when they cry, calming them in the middle of the night, bathing them, playing with them, then looking after our babies becomes so much more thrilling and meaningful, because we know that all of it is contributing to the growth of their brain health.

The power of smiling

Of all the interactions, the one that perhaps best epitomises the power of what passes between us and our babies, and how it impacts their brain and body, is smiling. If we had those magical glasses through which we could see the flow of energy and information moving back and forth from us to our babies, when we smile we would see the nervous and hormonal systems in their body and the neural pathways in their brain light up like bright flashing neon lights at the fun fair.

Lily (eight weeks)

Henry is sitting on the sofa with Lily lying on his knees. He is bending over, looking at her. Although he is not saying anything, it is possible to see all the love he has for his daughter written on his face. Lily, too, is looking at him. She has a serious look on her face. They stay like that for a moment. Slowly, Henry starts smiling, a gentle soft smile. Lily frowns a little more. Henry frowns a little too. After a second or two he smiles again. Lily then joins in, and as if in slow motion – her eyes open wide, her mouth stretches to the sides, her nose crinkles, and her whole face lights up with a smile. Henry's smile widens, as if matching Lily's.

It is very simple interactions like this moment of togetherness above that will help Lily's brain to grow 'big and strong'. Every time we look tenderly at our babies, every time we smile at them, they can see the pleasure on our faces and they get the message that they are valued, that we enjoy being with them, that we love them. Their heart rate rises a little and feel-good hormones, like endorphins, dopamine and oxytocin, flood their brain, encouraging their brain to grow, with more firing up and wiring up of neurons. Each smile adds a layer to the Feeling Loved path, turning it, over time, into a smoother and straighter road that always leads back to the Feeling Safe Roundabout. And the great thing about smiling at our babies is that it makes us parents feel good too. Like our babies, we get flooded with endorphins and dopamine; and the more we smile, the more we want to smile. It is a virtuous circle!

7

How do we know what our babies need?

A world of sensation

However much we are aware of this positive, feel-good cycle, however much we recognise the importance of the quality of our interactions, it can feel like a daunting task to try to be constantly understanding and responding to our babies' needs. They have no words yet to tell us what they like and dislike. How do we know if we are we getting things right?

Let's try for a moment to imagine what it is like to be a newborn baby, so we can enter their world and understand a little more what they might need from us.

Thinking and feeling

Newborn babies do not *think* the world around them, they *feel* it. And this is because the two hemispheres of their brains that have to do with thinking and feeling grow at a very different speed. Their (left) Thinking brain – with its love of logic and order, problems solving and making sense of things – is very slow to develop and won't be properly active until they are around three and a half. Whereas their (right) Feeling brain – all about emotional and social connections – grows super-fast in their first two years, allowing them to concentrate all their efforts on creating that vital relationship with us.

Linking sensations with emotions

Because newborns cannot think logically yet, cannot make even simple causal connections, they have no choice but to link the sensations they are experiencing with the emotions they are feeling. These sensations travel through their nervous system to their super-active right/Feeling hemisphere, giving rise to primitive and basic emotions: happiness, excitement, love, trust, sadness, anger, fear, surprise or disgust. This means that our babies live in a world of continuous sensations, which for them lack obvious explanations. *We* may know that our babies' feelings and reactions are caused by sound, light, shadow, taste, smell, touch on their skin, perhaps a tightness of their muscles, but *they* don't really know where these sensations are coming from or why they are happening. Indeed, their underdeveloped left/Thinking, order-loving hemisphere won't know for quite a few years where these emotions come from or what to do with them. They won't know how to distinguish, name and classify them, or how to react appropriately to them. As you can imagine, this must make their world almost constantly surprising, and at times really quite alarming.

We could perhaps describe our babies at this point as highly emotionally active but almost totally emotionally illiterate. And our task is to help them with this, to help them become fluent at reading their emotions and managing them, and for that we will have to sort of lend them our own fully functioning brains. But more of that in a short while. For now, let's try to stay in the moment, like our babies do, and imagine what the world feels like for them. Staying in the moment is what some of us try to do when we meditate, after all, to get our thinking brain to shush for a while.

Staying in the moment

Sit with your eyes shut and try to just listen to the world around you. Notice how many sounds you can hear and how the different sounds affect you. You can do the same with each of your senses – shut your eyes and notice all the different materials that are touching your body, notice the different tastes in your mouth, even the light that comes through your shut eyes, etc. Of course, you only have to think for a second and you can recognise and picture the sources of these sensations. But, now, put yourself in baby mode . . . try to zone out those 'identifications' and focus on the sensations, as if they are arising unbidden from sources unknown. With a little practice, you can actually do this . . . and you may start to find these sensations a bit unnerving, frightening even. Just as, for much of the time, they are for our babies.

It can, at times, be overwhelming to be in a world of unexplained sensations, especially when they are not very pleasant. For our babies, the tightness of their muscles in their tummies (when they are hungry), the loud bang of the door slamming shut in a draught (as they lay calmly on their playmat), the light that, in a split second, is replaced by pure darkness (as they are put to bed), the out-of-the-blue warm water on their skin (as they are dipped into the bath), then the cold air and the harshness of the towel (as they are dried), the violent contraction of all their muscles (as they sneeze) . . . it's a lot.

Luckily, and vitally for their wellbeing, there are also lots of much nicer sensations too: the taste of milk on their lips, a soothing voice, and gentle, cuddling arms . . . and even more luckily, and equally vitally, many of these are coming from us, the parent. But at the very beginning all these sensations, whether pleasant or unpleasant, are very hard to interpret or understand for our babies, because they have no idea where they come from or what their purpose is. They have no idea that it is because they are hungry that they have this very unpleasant feeling in their tummy, or that they got spooked because the wind blew the door shut. For them these painful sensations must feel like random attacks on their mind and body, and that is perhaps why our babies can respond so dramatically and seem sometimes almost inconsolable in their distress.

Noah (two days)

Noah is fast asleep. Suddenly he wakes up and, within seconds, he is screaming at the top of his lungs. Becky, his mother, shocked by the strength of his screaming, picks him up straight away. She sits him on her knees, holding him with her hand on his front, and taps gently on his back. After a few taps Noah produces a huge burp.

Noah was fast asleep when he started to feel a strange and painful sensation, which woke him up. He had no idea that it was just a bit of wind trapped in his tummy. For him it was a sudden ambush of discomfort.

But he is also learning that the cuddle that he got afterwards, and which makes him feel better, does come from somewhere. And he can take this on board because the cuddle seems to be coming in a pretty reliable and consistent way. He is also certainly noticing that, as well as being a nice feeling, it comes with a nice smell that is now familiar, and with a gentle calming voice that always sounds the same.

Babies make connections between what goes on inside their body or around them and what they feel through repeated experiences over time. At first they have no notion that the milk gently filling up their tummy is making them feel calm and full, or that the sudden loud noise is making them feel scared, or that their crankiness and grumpiness is because they are tired or windy. They have not made the link yet but when these common physical experiences repeatedly coincide with the same emotions, they can slowly start to make the connection between them. They start to associate certain sensations and experiences with feeling relaxed, peaceful, joyful and playful; and others with feeling restless, agitated, distressed, sad, angry and lonely. They are slowly entering the world of emotional literacy.

Peter (eleven days)

Peter has been in his Moses basket for a little while when he starts crying. In no time the crying turns into full-blown screaming. His mother picks him up gently, firmly placing her hand behind his neck. She holds him against her shoulder and walks a little around the room. The screaming goes down a notch and sounds more like crying now. After more walking, his mother sits on the sofa and starts unbuttoning her shirt. As Peter's head is getting near her breast, his crying goes down a further notch. His mum now presses his face into her breast and the crying instantly stops; Peter is now feeding avidly and noisily . . .

Peter is still very little: he could not bear for too long the aching/painful sensation of hunger in his tummy and he was soon overwhelmed by some sort of fearful feeling, a sense of loneliness or insecurity perhaps. Not only has he not yet made the link that it is because he is hungry that he is feeling these horrible cramps, but he also doesn't yet know for sure that he has a mummy who can replace these painful sensations with calming ones that come from the delicious taste of warm milk. It will take many, many feeding sessions, but gradually Peter will learn to associate that crampy-tummy sensation with hunger, and hunger with mummy picking him up and talking in a calm voice, mummy's breast with warm milk and a full tummy, and feeling calm again. Gradually the sensation will become 'associatively meaningful', as we sometimes say in the therapy room. What this means for Peter is that he connects this sequence of events in his developing mind, and no longer finds it inexplicable, surprising or scary. And this will be hugely reassuring for Peter. We could also say he is starting to become more emotionally literate.

If Peter's mummy manages to be relatively consistent in the way she responds to his screaming and crying, he will soon associate her with a nice warm safe feeling: he will trust that his mummy is not going to let him scream for ever and that she is going to try to find out as quickly as she can why he is crying and act on it. And soon, armed with this ever increasing trust in his mother's ability to look after him, Peter will be able to let her know that he is hungry in a less dramatic way. As he gains a better understanding of his sensations, he will develop an array of more subtle (and less noisy!) techniques to communicate his hunger. He will learn the 'gurgle shout' that means 'Oi, Mum!' Physical gestures, like putting his hand in his mouth, may also become effective. And screaming the house down will become a last resort.

Peter (two months)

Peter has been lying on his playmat for about ten minutes. He has been making lovely sounds, as if talking to the mobile that is hanging over him. He has now gone quiet, and he is looking around the room and putting his hands in his mouth, sucking noisily on them with an insistent gurgle. His mum, who has been catching up on some emails, notices the change in the noises and she looks down at Peter. Their eyes meet and she says: 'Oh, you have had a lovely play but I think you are getting hungry.' She puts her hand on her right breast, then the left one, and says: 'I think the left one is ready for you.' As she is bending towards Peter, he moves his legs and arms rapidly and excitedly. Once in his mother's arms, he calms down a little, but as his mother is struggling to unclip her bra he starts making louder noises. Mum says that, yes, she knows he is hungry and how difficult it is to wait when his little tummy is feeling so empty. Peter watches his mum intently and when, finally, the bra is unclipped, settles quickly into feeding . . .

Peter is a little older now and he has started to learn and recognise the signs (his mummy's voice, her tone, her smell, the way she picks him up) suggesting that his mummy has not forgotten him, that she is thinking of him and is going to make sure he is okay. What a relief it must be for Peter to be able to make a link between his mummy's noticing him, picking him up, and his feeling calmer, safer.

This also is very good news for us parents, because it means that Peter is now able to wait a little longer when he is hungry and not react quite so fearfully to the first aching sensation in his tummy. It's a two-way street. He understands that his mummy has got much better at spotting his signs of hunger, and he is confident she will be giving him some nice warm milk soon. And his mummy knows she doesn't have to panic and rush over to him (which might even escalate his anxiety). She knows now he can cope with a little waiting.

Gradually Peter's world is starting to make more sense: when he was very little, it was easy for him to get lost, at the first painful sensation, in the big dark forest of his brain, with its tiny dead-end paths. But, a few months on, the paths of trust, love and feeling understood – always leading to the Feeling Safe Roundabout – have become stronger, wider and straighter. This helps Peter not to fall apart at the onset of the first unpleasant twinge in his body.

Lacking the tools (a grown-up, thinking brain) to make sense of sensations, both pleasant and unpleasant, our babies are compelled to share their emotions with us, as it is only through our feedback, through the way we react to them, that they will learn to associate them with recurring events and attribute meanings to them.

Lending our mind to our babies

To help our babies make sense of the world, we use the incredible tool that is our own mind: through our fantastic capacity for empathy, we are able to imagine what life is like for our babies and what they might be feeling. When we watch them smile, when we hear them cry, when we see their body stiffen and arch as we gently lower them into a warm bath, when we watch their startled faces when the door bangs, when we see them shivering in the cold wind, our capacity for empathy kicks in.

Like our babies, we too use mostly the right/Feeling hemisphere of our brain when we care for them. Since we have become parents – with its impact on our hormonal system – there has been a surge in activity in our right/Feeling hemisphere. Too much thinking is not that useful when you are dealing with a little person who cannot speak.

Noticing and feeling your way along are much better. Our capacity for empathy is enhanced and sustained by our newly elevated level of oxytocin, which makes us more sensitive to our babies' emotions and better at reading their subtle body language. We become acutely aware of the most minute changes in their facial expressions – their eyebrows going up or down, their lips wobbling or smiling, their little nose curling up – and of the movement of their body, as they wave their arms about or kick their legs, or their breathing speeds up or slows down.

Our extra-strong parental empathy is almost a superpower that enables us not merely to recognise our baby's needs, but almost to feel them by proxy, as if we were lending them our brain and mind. Indeed, we can pretty much suspend our own feelings and needs and, in their place, feel our baby's joy, their pain, their excitement, their fear, their loneliness. On top of that, we can intuit what they need from us to help them cope with and manage these feelings. As we spend more and more time with our babies, we get better and better at noticing their likes and dislikes and at giving them more of that emotional food that makes them excited, engaged and happy, and we also know their many signs of upset and distress, and, crucially, how to make them feel better.

Anifa (five weeks)

Rael is holding his daughter, Anifa, in the crook of his arm. He is talking to Anifa's mum about a complicated plan for the evening. When Anifa's mum leaves the room, Rael starts looking for something in his bag. He hasn't noticed that Anifa is staring at him, eyes wide open. Now she makes a noise that catches her dad's attention and finally he notices his daughter's intent stare. He stops rummaging, and carries her over to the sofa, where he sits down with her facing him on his knees. He stares back. As soon as Anifa senses that she has her daddy's attention, her expression changes: she narrows her eyes, her mouth opens a little as if trying to say 'O . . .' in turn. Rael's eyes widen and he follows the subtle up and down movements of Anifa's head, the opening and shutting of her mouth. Anifa's eyes are now wide open again. When Rael is sure that Anifa is not about to cry, he relaxes. His smile widens and he starts imitating her facial expressions: his eyebrows go up and down, following hers, his mouth forms an O shape just as she does, and he copies her 'O, O, O, O, O' sounds. This back and forth between Anifa and her daddy goes on for a couple of minutes.

To start with, Rael was distracted, but now he is able to allow his mind to notice Anifa's desire for connection. He has a long to-do list, and is dying for a cup of tea, but for a moment he suspends his own needs and wishes and lets Anifa take the lead. He watches her attentively, allowing his mind to imagine what she is feeling and what she wants (and needs) from him: a daddy who is trying to get to know his daughter by engaging in a simple baby 'conversation' based on dad and baby imitating each other. Anifa is craving moments of connection and togetherness like this; she's hungry for the right emotional food for her brain to grow and expand, and for her mind to develop a sense of self.

Anifa is still looking intently at her daddy, but she is no longer smiling and her face is now quite serious. She is moving only her arms, reaching out towards her dad's mouth. As Rael continues making the O shape and sound with his mouth and moving his eyebrows up and down, Anifa frowns. She turns her head, stops looking at her daddy and focuses her gaze on her hands. When Anifa starts rubbing her face, Rael stops his interactions, and makes a downwards shape with his mouth as if a little disappointed. Anifa looks at her hands again, and then, after more face rubbing, looks at her daddy. Rael seems delighted and goes back straight away to where they had left it: he widens his eyes and makes more O sounds, adding in a little rocking. Anifa's eyes are now wide open, as if a little startled. Her body stiffens, and she yawns and gives a little cry. As the cry doesn't last, Rael rocks her little more, trying to get her attention back. Anifa looks at him again, but after another yawn, she shuts her eyes and starts crying. Still looking at his daughter, Rael's face now becomes softer, calmer. He brings Anifa closer to his body. There is no more eye-to-eye contact. Instead, he gets up and walks around the room, rocking her very gently and giving her soft little kisses on the top of her head. In less than a minute she is asleep.

Anifa has been enjoying this intense moment of connection with her daddy, but now she is tired. She is only a few weeks old and cannot yet manage long periods of turn-taking interaction. The only way she can tell her daddy is to move her gaze away from him by turning her head to the side. But her daddy doesn't get it straight away. So she rubs her face. Yet again he doesn't get it. So she cries a little. It takes a bit of time for Rael to forget his own enjoyment in the exchange (his own brain is getting lots of dopamine from it) and to return to a place where he can again put himself in Anifa's place and sense that she is 'full' of the little imitation game they have been playing: he has given her enough of the delicious emotional food she wanted. What she needs now is to have some quiet time to digest this food and let her brain process all the intense firings up of Feeling Loved and Safe that have been triggered by this moment of closeness. Sleep is a good time to get that done.

Noticing and learning how to read our babies

As we spend more time with our babies, we get better at reading their body language and noticing all the minute and super-fast responses (often almost invisible, yet somehow perceptible – more later about this), as well as at empathising with what they are feeling. The relationship we have with our babies during their first two years of life has often been called a right brain to right brain relationship, in which our special ability to read our babies' mind fosters their ability to read our mind, which in turn allows them eventually to read other people's minds – giving them the gift of empathy, which will make them feel truly human. It is also through this complex process that they will learn to read their own mind and develop this all-important sense of who they are.

Marie Derome

Intuition-mirror neurons (Mentalisation)

Trying to imagine what our babies are going through is partly an instinctive and intuitive activity, but it is also a skill that we develop over time. Scattered around in different places in our brain we all have what are called 'mirror neurons': these are the neurons that fire up in our brain when we do something, but also when we watch someone else doing something, almost as if we were doing the action ourselves. Some scientists think that these neurons play a major part in the complex network in our brain that deals with our capacity to empathise with others – in this case our babies – as they allow us to mentally put ourselves in their place, see the world through their eyes, and thus get a sense of what they might be feeling. And this is a two-way street: watching us will fire up our babies 'mirror neurons' too, so that, in time, they too will be able to empathise and see the world through other people's eyes.[1]

However, for some of us, our neural network that deals with empathy might be less developed than we might want. This might be because we are on the autistic spectrum (it seems that autistic people's mirror neurons do not work so efficiently). Or it might be because we experienced some significant period of neglect or trauma as a baby. Or simply because our own parents were not very curious about us when we were babies and did not spend much time imagining what we were going through or responding to our emotional needs. Whatever the cause, this might have affected some regions of our brain and left them relatively under-developed.

So, for some of us, it will take a bit more effort and a little longer to find our way towards being able to imagine what it is like for our babies and to empathise with them. To start with, it might feel more like a cognitive and forced activity than an instinctive one,

99

and we might, therefore, feel a little self-conscious. But that's okay, because the more we do it, the more we spend time observing and interacting with our babies and trying to imagine what they are feeling, the better we get at it. And our babies will always be grateful for the effort we are making, even if we get it a bit wrong sometimes. They'd rather we tried than didn't bother! And they are usually kind enough to reward our efforts by making their pleasure clear. We know that, in turn, this will make us feel good, which, in turn, reinforces our confidence, so that a little less effort may be required next time.

The simple wondering game

Look at your baby and ask them: I wonder what you might be feeling now, I wonder what you want, I wonder what is upsetting you, I wonder what you are looking at, I wonder why you are smiling, I wonder what you are trying to tell me . . . and then, still observing your baby as closely as possible, notice the subtle movement of their body and the changes on their faces. Let the answers (as it is likely that there will more than one) slowly emerge in your mind . . .

The idea of 'faking it till you make it' can often sound a bit cynical, and perhaps less than ideal when you are interacting with your baby. But, really, there is no shame in it. And every parent, even the expert empathiser, knows the feeling of 'making an effort' with their child even if they don't always 100 per cent feel like it. Luckily, we also know the feeling of being surprised by just how much fun even these slightly forced interactions turn out to be.

How to help our babies manage their emotions

In the same way our babies need us to empathise with them and imagine what they are going through so they can begin to root their sensations and emotions in the world, and process their meanings, they also need us to help them manage these emotions. Since their left/Thinking brain, with its love for order, is so immature, they have no way to interpret and manage their emotions on their own. Having no (Thinking) brakes yet, our babies, when left alone with their emotions, can quickly get overwhelmed by them, and that can feel quite scary and upsetting for them.

It's worth bearing in mind that this apparent problem is really an asset. Our baby's brain is well designed for survival. Having a highly functioning left brain, with its structured thinking and pragmatic decision making, is actually not very useful when you are still so totally physically helpless and cannot do anything for yourself – not even run away! By contrast, having an overactive right brain, with its superpowered ability to connect emotionally to the persons you are totally dependent on, and who will do everything for you, is extremely useful.

That is why our babies are so good, with their big beautiful eyes, at drawing us in, and inviting us to 'read' them. And why, with their insatiable appetite for observing us – they can't get enough of our faces – they get more and more fluent at reading us in turn. Thus, the way we react to our babies' display of emotions is very important to them. It is from our reactions, which they scrutinise constantly and so carefully, that they will take their cue to as to how they should react. Are they in genuine danger and so should scream even louder, or are they free from danger and therefore able to relax and feel safe? Over time, and with repetition and consistency in our responses, they learn from us what the world around them is like and how they themselves should feel about it.

Helping our babies manage their emotions is no small job. With no words yet, and not much control either, they have a very primitive and at times a very dramatic way of expressing their emotions. Because they haven't got the filter of a thinking brain yet, their emotional display is often large scale and tsunami-like: their emotions explode as if out of nowhere, like a huge storm that vanishes as suddenly as it has erupted, with very little transition in between. Screaming at the top of their lungs can be followed by gigantic smiles within seconds, and vice versa. They will often use their whole body (arms, legs, face, eyes, voice . . .), because this is the only tool they have to express and communicate their emotions to us. But this means that, at times, they can appear out of control (or dysregulated, as a therapist would say). And it will be like that until the two hemispheres of their brain, the Thinking and the Feeling brains, can talk to each other better and work together. And that is not going to start until they're well into their third year.

So what is it we need to do to help our babies manage their emotions? When our babies smile, it is generally easy to respond: we give them a smile back. But when they cry and scream, we have to do something more complicated, less instinctive, as we know it won't be helpful to cry or scream back at them. Remember: the aim is to make them feel safe as much as we can. And when they act their emotions out with their 'whole body' expressions and unfettered vocalisations, to us parents, who have largely replaced this physical vocabulary with actual words and subtle hand signals, this can feel quite surprising. At times, babies can appear out of control, as if they are being assaulted by terrifying, primitive, meaningless sensations and emotions. But we should try not to become alarmed, or defensive even. All they need from us, all they are begging us to do, is that we take these over-sized, terrifying and primitive sensations and emotions away from them. Picking them up to give them a cuddle, accompanied by sooth-ing words, is usually a good start.

Processing and managing their feelings for them: our mind-kitchen

But there's a little bit more to it than that. When we soothe and com-fort our babies, we are not just removing their fear and pain, we are helping them to process and manage these feelings. This is possible, and necessary, because usually we are not taking the horrible feel-ings completely away. We are merely diluting them with nice ones. It's almost as if we are taking some of the pain into ourselves, and swapping it for some of our calm (it helps a lot to remain calm!) and our love. With our words of comfort ('There, there . . . Mummy's here . . . Daddy's coming . . . was that a bit frightening . . .?') we are even giving them back these scary feelings, but in their proper pro-portion, cut down to a size and shape they can now manage, so that they can feel safe and calm again. In this way we are managing their emotions for them, until such a time as they can manage them for themselves.

This sounds like an amazing piece of work, and it is. But we have the tools for the job. We have our mind, and our imagination, which together become a sort of 'mind-kitchen'. Here, in our mind-kitchen, we can turn their undigestible primitive sensations and emotions (like metaphorical raw carrots, unwashed leeks and knobbly potatoes) and transform them into something that is much more palatable and comforting (a smooth, warm and tasty soup) that they can now eat and digest easily and feel nourished by.

Noah (three weeks)

Baby Noah is laying on his back, gazing around the room. His dad is busy on his computer. Suddenly Noah starts crying. His cry instantly turns into a scream – he screws up his face, his arms are flapping and his legs are going up and down rapidly. His dad quickly picks him up, but Noah's body stiffens and he arches his back in such a way that it makes it awkward for his dad to hold him . . . He manages to put him on his shoulder, walking around the room, saying oh, oh, oh as he bounces him up and down gently . . . Noah is still arching his back; his screaming stops for a few seconds but then it starts again . . . His eyes are now full of tears.

We don't know why Noah has suddenly got upset, but we can see that he finds it impossible to deal with the sensations and emotions that are assaulting him: pain somewhere in his body, loneliness, feeling too cold or too hot? Whatever the sensations and emotions, they are too big, raw and confusing for him to be able to deal with them and digest them on his own. For Noah, it is a bit like having to eat a soup made of as yet unwashed and uncut vegetables – the aforementioned carrots, leeks and potatoes, which are totally indigestible. All Noah wants is to get rid of all these upsetting sensations and he does that by forcefully throwing them at his father through his relentless screaming and tensing of his body. Luckily for Noah, his father, whose brain is still under the spell of parenthood, can for a moment suspend his own thoughts and needs, and is able to receive his son's distress and use it to try to imagine what is going on for Noah, and what might be making him so upset.

Noah's dad looks puzzled. He lays Noah on the sofa and sits beside him. He starts to talk to him and softly massage his tummy. The screaming doesn't stop but Noah's dad carries on gently massaging his baby, saying: 'What is the matter, oh, oh . . .' Noah is intently looking at his dad's face, as if trying to say: 'Please, make it stop . . .' Noah's dad starts talking to his son: 'I am sorry you are having such tough time . . . it looks very painful . . . What is it? Is it in your tummy? Do you have little farts in there?' Noah is now crying rather than screaming. This goes on for a while until Noah's dad decides to wrap him up in his baby blanket. Gently he puts the blanket around him with only his little hands coming out at the top. Noah's crying is now more like a constant whimpering. 'Oh, you like that, my darling . . .' Noah's dad takes a big breath and says: 'It is so hard to see you so upset . . . if only you could tell me . . .' Noah is now trying to put his hands in his mouth, as if wanting to suck them. But this seems to aggravate things, and after each attempt at sucking on his hands, Noah starts crying again. His dad helps him keep the hands near his mouth, but again the crying carries on. 'Perhaps you are hungry, my little one?' Noah's dad takes him in his arms and, bouncing him up and down, walks to the kitchen, where he makes a bottle for him. While the bottle is warming, Noah's dad turns him around, as if wanting to show him what is going on. 'You see, I am making a bottle. Maybe that will help you feel better? We just need to wait a little . . . I know it is hard to wait . . .'

Noah's dad is not throwing these inedible raw emotions back at Noah by shouting at him, or ignoring them by leaving the room, nor is he joining in the panic and getting out of control himself by screaming and crying. On the contrary, he stays calm and open to the experience his son is having, receiving his son's raw sensations and emotions and allowing them to osmose into his own mind. He imagines what feelings Noah is having and, like a good cook, he checks them, sorts them out, metaphorically washes them, cuts them up and finally cooks them into a comforting emotional soup that Noah can digest. And this comforting soup is made of his calm voice, his gentle caresses and massage, the rhythmic rocking, his concerned face, soft words . . .

Even though Noah is still screaming, he is also starting to sip this comforting 'soup', where the lumpy veg has been mixed with, and seasoned by, all of these new sensations generated by his father's careful, assured movements, and calm reassuring talking. This is how Noah knows that his daddy has understood him and is dealing with all the panicky sensations inside him. Noah has already started to associate his daddy's smell and face, his calm and soothing voice, his gentle rocking, his confident hold on his body, with feeling safe. Those are cues that, since birth, have sent signals to his brain that things are okay, that he is loved by his parents. Each repetition of this sort of experience adds one more layer to the path to the Feeling Safe Roundabout.

It also allows Noah to slowly build his left brain, until one day he will be able to think about his sensations and emotions on his own instead of acting them out and throwing them at his daddy to deal with. He will be able to be his own emotional cook, and when he feels pleasant and unpleasant emotions, he will be able to make sense of them on his own, linking them to whatever has caused them. His Feeling brain and his Thinking brain will be able to work together to make his emotions meaningful and manageable. His emotions will make sense to him – he will have an understanding of their roots and causes, and that will give Noah a great sense of comfort, which will sustain him throughout his life.

For our babies, being out of control can be a terrifying experience, a bit like falling without anyone to catch them. So when we help them manage their overwhelming emotions, we are saying to them: 'Don't worry, you are not going to fall. I am here to catch you.' By feeling emotionally held by us, our babies slowly learn to think about how they feel and why, rather than simply acting their scary feelings out, and this eventually will make them feel much safer.

Helping our babies to get back to the Feeling Safe Roundabout

When our babies cry and scream, we can think of them as having left the Feeling Safe Roundabout and beginning to get lost in the darker and scarier lanes of solitude, fear and sadness. It is inevitable that our babies will venture into those lanes. They are part of life and we would not know what a happy lane was if we never ventured into the scary and sad lanes. But what is important for our babies is that they learn to find their way back as quickly as possible into the lighter, brighter lanes, where they feel they are not alone, and that their upset matters to us. They are a long way from having their driving licence, and so we need to be their chauffeurs. It's our job to drive them safely back through difficult roads to the comfort of the Feeling Safe Roundabout.

Kristy (six weeks)

While her baby girl, Kristy, is napping, Paula quickly tidies up the kitchen, making quite a lot of noise as she cleans the pots and pans in the sink. The kitchen is all neat now and all is silent. Tired, Paula sits down with a cup of tea. She is about to take a sip when Kristy starts crying. With a deep sigh, she gets up and walks towards the Moses basket where Kristy has been having her nap. Kristy's crying is loud. As it takes a little a moment for Paula to reach Kristy, Kirsty's crying intensifies. Paula starts talking to Kristy: 'I can hear you, sweetheart. I am on my way, here I am.' Before she picks up Kristy, Paula looks at her for a second and their eyes meet. The crying subsides a little. Paula picks up Kristy and holds her tight against her chest, giving her little kisses on the top of her head. She wonders aloud what the matter could be? 'You woke up and you could not see me and that made you all sad? I was here, having a cup of tea . . . Shall we have a big cuddle now?' Kristy has stopped crying. Paula is now sitting down on the sofa, holding Kristy on her knees facing her. They look at each other. Paula talks softly to her daughter. They stay like that for while.

On waking up and experiencing the silence instead of the noises of her mummy pottering in the kitchen, little Kristy had started to go down the lane of 'I feel abandoned, alone and scared'. Paula, by talking reassuringly, smiling tenderly and holding her warmly, very quickly 'rescued' her daughter and brought her back into the lane of 'I feel loved, calm and safe'. At a physiological level, Kristy's heart rate had gone up and the stress hormone cortisol was flooding her brain. On hearing her mother's voice, looking at her face and her tender smile, and finally by being in her mummy's arms and smelling her delicious smell and feeling her warm kisses, her heart rate lowered, and the stress hormone, cortisol, in her body was replaced by the happier hormone of oxytocin. If this is repeated as often as possible when Kristy gets upset, Kristy's brain will slowly but steadily get wired around a greater sense of safety and, one day, she will even know the way back to the Feeling Safe Roundabout on her own. And that will be very useful, as we will see later, for when she starts being more independent.

When it is not easy to manage our babies' emotions

There will be times, of course, when we will find it hard to process our baby's emotions. It is not always easy to get inside our babies' minds and imagine what's going on for them. Sometimes, their distress takes us too much by surprise, or we are too tired or our to-do list has become too long and stressful. And when they start crying or screaming, we can become quite overwhelmed and embark with them into the darker lanes of our own brains. Suddenly it feels as if there are far too many raw ingredients for us to sort out quickly, our mind-kitchen is a bit of a mess, we haven't had time to tidy it up from last time, and the first soup we throw together turns out to be a bit lumpy and hard for our baby to digest . . .

Annabel (two months)

Annabel has woken up suddenly, and starts crying almost immediately. Theo, her mum, goes straight to pick her up. As Annabel's crying continues, she decides to feed her. As Theo is unclipping her bra, Annabel's cry intensifies and, when Theo offers her breast, Annabel turns her head away sharply. Theo tries gently to turn Annabel's head towards the breast, but again Annabel turns her head away, stiffening her body. Theo looks desperate, her eyes begin welling up and she starts walking up and down the room, rocking Annabel . . . but Annabel's distress just seems to escalate . . . Theo becomes very alarmed, tears are now rolling out of her eyes, and her own body is more and more rigid, and her rocking of Annabel seems to follow the intensity of the crying . . .

Annabel woke up with sensations and emotions that are too much for her, and all she wants is to get rid of them and give them to her mum to deal with. It is as if Annabel is throwing her very raw emotions (fear, sadness, anger perhaps?) at Theo, but they are coming so fast that Theo is struggling to identify them and know what to do with them. There is no more space left within Theo for thinking and processing Annabel's upset feelings, and soon Annabel's distress becomes Theo's distress too. It is as if she has taken her baby's distress inside herself so thoroughly that she is now flooded by her baby's panic.

Theo goes to the kitchen, drinks a glass of water and opens the window a little. Her breathing seems to slow down. She is now holding her baby tightly against her chest, whispering in her baby's ear some soothing words. Theo sits on the sofa, doing slow forwards and backwards movements. Annabel is no longer screaming. She is rubbing her face on her mother's chest. Gently,

Theo moves her away from her chest so they can look at each other's faces: 'Gosh, that was a big upset . . . What was it? What was so scary? You're better now? . . . Do you think you would like to eat a little?' Theo offers her breast to Annabel, who this time takes it straight away. She is now feeding noisily, her little hand caressing her mother's chest.

After being flooded by her baby's distress, Theo is able to regain some sense of herself and starts to process her baby's difficult feelings. Theo's emotional soup was a bit lumpy, but in the end Annabel decided her intentions were good, and she was happy to take it.

It can be quite difficult at times to get it right when we try to imagine what's going on for our babies, but the good news for us parents is that a lot of the time it is not just about getting it right or wrong, it is mostly about *trying*. Just trying to imagine what they are going through and helping them manage their difficult emotions is often enough to make our babies feel better. When our babies feel that we are trying to understand them, they feel thought about, they feel valued, they feel loved. This means they are not so alone with their emotions, which in time will give them confidence and help them to become more resourceful and resilient.

8

The power of being thought about

Facing all the feelings rather than solving all the problems

What matters most to our babies is to feel that we are interested in them, curious about their wants and needs. Indeed, with their incredible learning brains, they become adept pretty quickly at sensing our good intentions and can appreciate that we are acting with them in the forefront of our minds. This is true even when we don't quite succeed in solving their problems straight away or in understanding fully what the problem is that they are trying to tell us about.

Ultimately it is this feeling of being worthy of interest that will allow them to develop a mind of their own and be curious about themselves. What could be better than knowing you are being thought about, feeling that someone is curious about you, and truly trying to understand what is going on for you, and not just when you are happy and smiling but also when you are scared, confused and screaming.

Joe (five months)

Joe fell asleep in the car and his mother brought the seat with him still in it into the house. He has now been sleeping for a little while in his car seat. Every now and then he extends his legs and then brings them back towards his tummy. As he does this, a little smile appears on his face. He is now extending his arms over his head. His eyelids are flickering, and he is making cranky little noises. Joe seems to be slowly waking up. After more stretching of his legs and arms, he opens his eyes and blinks a few times. He looks neither sad nor happy. After staring into space for a short moment, he starts looking around the room as if searching for something. He makes more loud noises, this time as if calling for someone. Every time he makes a noise, his legs and arms become a little more active. Then he stays still for a bit as if waiting for something to happen. After making more noises and doing more twisting in his car seat, he starts crying. Soon the crying turns into screaming.

His mum, Gabriella, has heard him and enters the room quickly, but although she is saying to Joe: 'I am here, I am coming . . .', because of the seat's position, Joe cannot see her. Suddenly she appears, as if out of nowhere, in front of him. She kneels down and sits cross-legged in front of Joe, putting her hand gently on his legs. Joe is a little startled to begin with, but he is now looking intently at Gabriella's face and Gabriella is looking intently at Joe's. She takes hold of his hands and moves them very gently up and down, saying: 'I am here, my little one, I am here . . . I know you were all on your own . . .' Joe starts looking at his mum. Joe's crying has now stopped and, as

Gabriella initiates a gentle smile, Joe's face radiates with his own smile in return. Jo and Gabriella stay like that for a while, their eyes locked on each other, delighting in each other's presence and pleasure. Gabriella then says: 'Shall we go and play on your mat now? Do you think you are ready?' Jo kicks his legs and moves his arms forwards, as if saying: 'Yes, let's go. I am ready.'

Gabriella may well have felt annoyed with herself initially for not preventing Joe's distress. It is so hard for us not to feel guilty when our diverted attention leads to our baby screaming and becoming upset. And part of Gabriella must have wanted to make the screaming stop straight away, perhaps by taking Joe out of his seat and distracting him. This might have been quite effective in stopping the crying, but it would also have sent a message to Joe that his upset was something that could not be faced by either of them, and needed to be quashed and silenced above all else.

Instead, Gabriella allowed Joe to express his distress in her presence, and gave him time to re-connect with her before they moved to another activity. Before taking him out of his car seat, she came to his level, looked at him and, talking to him, she put words to his distress. This allowed Joe to feel that his upset mattered to his mother, that there was nothing to be ashamed of, that she could face it and deal with. It also gave him an opportunity to reconnect with her and her with him: recognising his mother's face and her smile filled him with joy and reassured him that he was not alone. And it was with this knowledge that they could both be excited about their next activity and their next adventure.

Solving all our babies' problems straight away would be like denying them the opportunity to explore the necessary adventure of conflicting and scary emotions. Ultimately it would stifle their need to develop an emotional life of their own. But demonstrating we can share in those emotions is equally important. Our babies want us to accompany them in all their emotions, and that includes acknowledging and sharing their most difficult feelings, not simply doing all we can to prevent or curtail them.

By not distracting our babies when they are upset, or even when they hurt themselves, but instead acknowledging (and putting into words) their upset or their pain, we gently help them regulate their emotions, and allow them to get a sense of themselves in the fullest way possible. Ultimately this deepens our bond of love, as after this period of shared emotion, our babies are fully ready to feel not merely relief but real joy and pleasure.

Allowing time to re-connect with our babies when we might feel that we have let them down is also a chance for us parents to slowly come to terms with our own parenting imperfections, and realise that being less than perfect is actually one of our best tools for preparing them for the real world, and for an imperfect but exciting life.

The power of getting it (slightly) wrong

When our babies are tiny, their level of tolerance for us not understanding them fully and so getting it wrong is pretty low. And that is because, as we have covered, they have not yet experienced sufficient repetition of caring and loving interactions with us to build the necessary structure in their brain to create dependable pathways back to the Feeling Safe Roundabout. But as they grow older, they don't actually need us to get it right immediately every time. Odd as it sounds, sometimes they actually quite like it when we get it just a little bit wrong. To satisfy their urge to learn, and to stimulate them to grow emotionally and cognitively, they need interactions that surprise them, puzzle them, and get them excited. If we always respond constantly and perfectly to our babies' needs, we actually start to distort their sense of the reality of our imperfect world. Even babies can sense that this is not how life is. Always being on the Feeling Safe Roundabout becomes boring for them, stifling even, and prevents them from developing psychologically. Small doses of surprise and unpredictability are actually quite useful ingredients when it comes to helping them develop a mind of their own.

Iris (twenty days)

Iris is nestled comfortably in her mother's arms. She is looking intently at her mother's face. Tia, her mother, looks at Iris with a serious expression on her face too. Iris relaxes a little and moves her head slightly up and down. Tia follows her and does the same, gently moving her head up and down. Tia starts smiling, but Iris grimaces and turns her head away. At this, Tia stops smiling straight away. Iris looks at her mother again with a serious look. Her eyes are wide open, and she now seems to be scanning the room as if looking for something. She brings her left hand to her mouth and starts sucking on it. Quickly she gets frustrated and starts crying. Tia, who has already made her a bottle, offers it to her. Iris stops crying immediately and starts feeding straight away.

Iris is still very little and wants her mummy to respond to her with quite exact precision. She finds any mismatched interactions between her and her mummy quite difficult to bear. Remember, she hasn't long been out of the perfect five-star tummy-palace and is not yet used to the slowness of the new room service (see Chapter 1 – The first nine months of life). So she doesn't want a smiling mummy when she is feeling so serious and maybe a little anxious. She wants and needs her mummy's face to reflect exactly how she herself is feeling inside. And when she is hungry, she wants her bottle now . . .

Iris (twenty weeks)

Iris is safely strapped into her highchair, which Tia has placed alongside the kitchen work top. Tia is busy making lunch. Iris is relaxed and looking around. When she manages to see her mother, she follows her with her gaze and moves her legs up and down excitedly. Every now and then Tia stops what she is doing for a few seconds and looks at Iris. Each time, Iris smiles broadly at her mother, making gurgling noises. Tia imitates her baby's cooing and adds: 'I know you want to chat, but I have to cook first, then we will chat; is that okay?' Iris seems okay with the plan. She carries on following her mother with her eyes. When Tia bends down to get something from the cupboard, Iris keeps looking in the direction where her mother was, as if waiting for her to reappear. And, as she does reappear, Iris starts kicking her legs more energetically, making slightly louder gurgling noises. Tia comes closer to her baby and, smiling, she puts her hands in front of Iris's little feet and lets them kick her hands. 'What strong legs,' she says.

Tia then hears the phone ringing and disappears briefly into the next room to get it. Iris keeps looking in the direction her mother has disappeared. She seems a little disappointed that the kicking game has had to stop. She is now looking around the room again, making more gentle gurgling noises. Her mother comes back into the room, talking to a friend on the phone. Iris turns her head in the direction of her mother, frowning a little. She stays like that for a while, but her mother doesn't notice her. For a few seconds she goes back to inspecting the room, wriggling her legs and moving her arms, but then she makes a loud shrieking noise, as if calling her mum. Tia, who has hung up, hears Iris's call and looks at her. She brings the highchair Iris is sitting in a little closer to her, but as she does that, she also brings her face centimetres away from Iris's face. Iris opens her eyes wide and turns her face away. Tia moves back, saying: 'Oh, sorry, that was a bit too close.' Iris looks at her mum again, her body still a little rigid. Tia waits. After a moment, Iris relaxes and they both look at each other with intensity. Tia smiles at Iris and Iris smiles back, gurgling with great enthusiasm – a much deeper sound than when she gurgles to herself.

When Iris has finished her gurgling, Tia imitates it but adds a little variation with an 'e' sound. All Iris's attention is now focused on her mother's mouth and, with a great effort, she tries to copy the new gurgling sound, her eyes shining with excitement. Tia's face is also tense with anticipation. Iris, as if digging really deep within herself, manages to make a gurgling sound quite similar to her mum's. Tia's face lights up with pride. Iris and Tia carry on their conversation for a few more minutes each trying to imitate the other.

Iris is older now, so she doesn't need a mummy who can pre-empt her every need and wish, like she did when she was just a few days old. There is now some margin for error, and, indeed, this gives mother and baby some room to play with. In Iris's first few months since birth she has come to terms with the fact that getting everything you need as soon as you need it eventually becomes too predictable to be interesting and exciting. And it is certainly not going to help her become the independent adult she needs, one day, to become. On the contrary, she has embraced wholeheartedly the urge to learn that she was born with and which will transform her, gradually, from a helpless baby into a competent young woman.

So she is now enjoying a mum who seems to have a life of her own, who is there, disappears, reappears, gets it right, gets it wrong and then gets it right again. Tia and Iris have created for themselves a routine where mismatch can be repaired, where disconnection is followed by re-connection, and where sometimes these not always perfect interactions can even feel like a fun game. These imperfect interactions mean that Iris and Tia get an opportunity to learn about each other, so that Iris can discover new ways of being with her mother, and therefore with herself and the world around her.

Dancing with our babies

Dancing – literally dancing – with babies is a lovely thing to do. Moving and swaying with them snuggled in our arms is a great way of being in the moment with them. What I'm talking about here, though, is a more metaphorical sort of dance – the precise, instinctive and intuitive body language that we engage in with our babies from the moment they are born, a vital form of communication that is hugely complex and yet barely perceptible to the naked eye.

It is only thanks to the advance of micro-editing in recent decades that researchers have been able to demonstrate that most of what happens between us and our newborn babies takes place in microseconds, without our being aware of it.[1] We tend to react to our babies' movements and expressions within a sixth of a second, for example. Our babies are a little slower, but still super-fast as they react to our movements in about a third of a second. This mutual reaction is so quick that research videos have to be slowed right down to make it detectable: a one-second interaction, for example, has to be broken down into ten or twelve images before you can really see what is going on.

What all this fascinating research shows is that every single interaction with our babies – whether it be changing their nappy, giving them a bath, playing with them, putting them in their car seat, feeding them, consoling them – is a dance made up of symmetry and synchrony. We follow each other in harmony, going towards and moving away from each other at the same moment, each of our respective movements subtly synchronised. We and our babies react almost simultaneously to the most minute changes in each other's facial expression and gestures: an eyebrow going imperceptibly up, a mouth slightly opening, eyes subtly narrowing or opening, the first signs of a hand moving forward, a leg moving away . . .

Liam (five months)

Liam is lying on his mother's knees. They are looking at each other. Liam's eyebrow moves up a little, his mum's follow suit. She asks: 'Hey, what's up?' Liam moves his gaze to her mouth while at the same time making a triangle shape with his. His mum's gaze moves to his mouth, her mouth making a similar triangle shape. Liam's whole body now tenses up, his eyebrows moving up again. His mother tenses her body too, holding her breath. Liam starts gurgling and making beautiful and expressive round noises. He looks very seriously at his mum. His mum's face is tense too, and she is still holding her breath. Liam stops. His mother then copies his gurgling.

Liam and his mum are truly dancing together, but if we could slow down this observation to a twelfth of a second, we would notice that the timing with our babies is both beautifully linked and *near* perfect but (also measurably) *not* perfect. Indeed, the ideal synchrony between us and our babies is one where we follow each other neither too closely nor too distantly. Our babies do not want an instant response from us, but nor do they want to wait too long. What they want is just enough space between us and them to feel that they have had a chance to enter our mind and that our reactions to them follow their, rather than our own, agenda. They want to feel it is about them and not about us.

So it is in moments of near perfect synchrony not-too-close, not-too-distant interactions, that our babies experience being understood with all its incredible impact on their growing sense of safety and trust. And it is in the micro-moments of perfect/imperfect synchrony that they grow emotionally and cognitively.

Ideally, they need some variations in the speed and accuracy of these reactions, so that some are near perfect and others more obviously imperfect, ideally interspersed with each other. Indeed, having everything near perfect all the time would be stifling, but having imperfect all the time would be traumatising. What is important is the sequencing of near perfect and imperfect.

Let's look at some moments of synchrony and what happens when they are broken and then mended.

Anish (four and a half months)

Anish is lying on his back on his play mat with a pillow propping him up. His mum, Mia, is sitting on the floor, facing him. They are chatting. Anish is looking intently at Mia's face and slowly opens his mouth. Mia opens her mouth too. Anish tenses his body, opening his eyes wider (Mia does too) and starts making Aou sounds. After a second or two, Mia joins him, trying to make the same sounds. Anish's face lights up with a huge smile. Mia smiles too – a broad smile. Anish starts again making more Aou sounds . . . Mia follows him . . . The whole time he has been kicking in and out with his little legs. Mia puts her hand on his tummy and rubs it gently. Anish kicks his legs even more rapidly . . .

Anish and Mia are dancing that subtle dance and are beautifully, almost perfectly synchronised with each other: one initiates, the other follows – not too closely, not too far apart – in their dance partner's footsteps, taking it in turn to stop and start. Anish is enjoying seeing reflected on his mother's face his own emotions and mood. Her face has become a mirror where he can see his reflection and read about himself, and he finds being understood by his mother utterly enjoyable and pleasurable.

> The phone pings . . . Mia stops looking at Anish to search for the phone and checks the message. Anish is still looking at Mia's face but he is no longer smiling . . . His eyes are open very wide and he has become quite still. Mia, whose face is slightly looking down to the phone, is now busy replying to the message. Anish now looks around the room. While the texting carries on, he carries on looking around and fixes for quite a long time on the bright light from the desk lamp. Gradually he starts kicking his legs again, looks at his mum, and smiles an hesitant smile. Mia is still looking at her phone, texting. Anish starts making the Aou sounds again while looking intently at his mum. Mia is still engrossed in her phone. Anish becomes more and more agitated, kicking his legs, moving his arms, whimpering more and more loudly . . . Mia is still on her phone, and Anish is now trying to roll over, while starting to cry . . .

The togetherness moment with its synchronised dance between Anish and Mia is broken. The turn taking that had given Anish so much pleasure has stopped, as Mia is no longer responding to

Anish's calls to start the dance again. Anish is no longer seeing his reflection in his mother's face as her face is no longer matching what he is feeling inside. He finds himself alone with his own emotions and he doesn't like that. He needs Mia's face and her voice and her arms and hands to let him know what is going inside him and that he matters to her. He calls her again and again but she doesn't notice him. He calls her again. He is not used to a mum who doesn't notice him. Suddenly he is feeling very much alone and that is scary and upsetting.

Mia looks at Anish, who is making bigger and bigger upset noises, and she smiles. But Anish turns his face away, kicking his legs vigorously. Mia puts the phone away and tries to hold his hand, but he takes it back, making an upset face by pushing his bottom lip forward, and starts crying again. He gives his mum furtive little glances but avoids her eyes. Mia speaks very softly and says: 'I can see you are cross with me . . . That's okay . . . I am sorry for stopping our chat, it was such a good chat.' Anish slowly starts looking at his mum again, then quickly turns his head away again. He brings his hand to his face, and rubs his eyes. Mia puts her hand on his tummy, rubbing it gently. Anish and Mia's eyes meet and this time Anish hold his mummy's gaze. Mia rubs his tummy a little more and Anish start to relax a little: a faint smile appears on his face. Mia imitates the faint smile. Anish slowly makes a bigger smile, which again Mia imitates. He starts kicking his legs and moving his hands towards his mother's face. She moves her face close to him so he can touch her. He gets hold of her hair and pulls her even closer to him.

Mia is back with Anish – she has finished what she had to do and is ready to re-enter the dance again. But Anish is not sure anymore that he can still trust his mum. It has been very upsetting and stressful for him to feel ignored by his mother, and it takes him a little while to feel that his mummy has got him in mind again. Mia is aware of his upset and she gently accepts his cross feelings and his avoidant gaze. She doesn't take them as a rejection of her but as the expression of very legitimate feelings. With her soft voice, her gentle eyes and strong hand on his tummy, she is letting him know that she can deal with those emotions and that he can take his time, there is no rush, she will walk with him the darker lanes and wait for him to be ready to walk back with her to the Feeling Safe Roundabout.

Many of our dances with our babies are disrupted by the ordinary events of everyday life, like a phone ringing, a delivery to sign for, a sibling needing urgent attention, a dinner about to burn, something we have just remembered and which is bothering us . . . There is nothing we can do about it except to try to be aware that we have left the dance – and try not to leave our babies standing on the dance floor on their own for too long. Re-entering the dance is a chance to mend what has been broken, and the more undisrupted dances we have previously had with our babies, the safer they feel, and the easier they will trust us again to be a good dancing companion.

It is useful for our baby to learn that, even when the dance is disrupted – which, of course, makes them feel lonely and confused – there is a very good chance that it won't be for too long. Provided the dance can resume, with those reassuring not-too-close, not-too-far interactions, then the slightly scary break can be an adventure along one of the less travelled byways. It serves to deepen our babies' emotional experiences and broaden their cognitive horizons before we bring them back to the Feeling Safe Roundabout. Our babies are learning through our near-perfect synchrony, through the sometimes inevitable interruption of our shared dances, that life is not perfect, and they are starting to trust, thanks to our loving care, that they can cope with that.

Internal parent: the forever companion

So, when we care for our babies, when we dance with them, when we step into their shoes to see and feel the world through their eyes, when we help them make sense of on their emotions, when we comfort them with calming words or sing them soothing songs, when we play exciting games, when we hold them gently in our arms and also in our minds, when we wonder aloud what the matter could be (even without promising immediately that we can solve it), then we slowly build inside our babies, in their minds but also in their thinking brains and even in their bodily cells, an inner version of our parenting selves. And it is this 'inner parent', with its kind, caring and reassuring voice and dependable, always returning presence, that will keep them company for the rest of their lives.

Kristy (twenty months)

Kristy has been going to nursery a few mornings a week since she was eighteen months. She can walk and run quite confidently and really enjoys the freedom to explore that it gives her.

Kristy is running around the playground with her friends. Suddenly she trips over one of the toy cars and falls. For a few seconds she seems frozen and there is a long silence. As she picks herself

---

up, she looks at her hands and knees. Her bottom lip is wobbling. Again she looks at her hands and then her knees . . . she rubs them . . . she mumbles something inaudible. Her breathing is still tense but slowly it comes back to a more normal rhythm. She looks around and sees one of the teachers. She goes to him and shows him her hands and knees. They have a chat and, as he is about to give them a rub, she runs off to join her friends, who are now playing in the sand pit.

Kristy, like all little children, has fallen many times in the past. Her parents generally managed to stay relatively calm and went through a 'routine inspection': hands, knees, forehead . . . checking for any injuries. But, most importantly, before telling her reassuring words, they always acknowledged how painful the fall might have been and allowed as much time as she needed to recover and feel better.

Kristy is now nearly two and, when she is away from her parents, she manages not to fall apart as soon as she hurts herself. Neither she nor we can hear it, but somewhere deep in her mind there is a voice that takes her through her parents' routine inspection, saying something like 'Oh darling, that was a big fall, it must hurt . . .', empathising with what she has just gone through but also reassuring her that she is okay.

This caring and loving inner voice is made up of all the fun and harmonious 'dances' we have had with our children. It is also strengthened by the gaps between these dances, the more scary journeys away from, and back to, the Feeling Safe Roundabout. Ultimately this inner parenting voice becomes a lifelong companion, with whom our babies turned children, turned adolescents or adults, can have regular, reassuring conversations, and which helps them not only to learn and explore, but also to cope with that feeling of loneliness that comes the moment they leave our physical bodies and enter the world.

Therefore, years later, when they are off to nursery, 'big' school, university or at their first job interview, our inner parent goes with them like the satchel on their back. And when they fall asleep alone at night, or when they play with their friends, when they graze their knee in the playground, when they celebrate their successes and confront the challenges of life, they will always have as company this nourishing internalised voice of our two-way parenting.

The ongoing dance

Our babies are born with an existential longing to connect with us, and it is with their whole being that they engage in the subtle but vital dance of forming a relationship with us. This first dance we dance with them during the first two years of their lives will evolve and change but will form the basis of all of our future interactions and communications – we will continue our dance with them for ever, albeit to different music, with different tunes and rhythms. As they grow older, as they become teenagers and then adults, they will also dance many more dances with other people, some to tunes they have learned with us and others to brand new tunes they have discovered for themselves. Some of these will reinforce the paths to their Feeling Safe Roundabout that we have helped them lay down, and others will divert from those paths and even lay new ones.

The great adventure of their lives will be to find their own dance to take them through the world. And one of the greatest pleasures of ours will be to watch them do it.

Three

The Other Side of the Story

9
When loving our babies is hard

S o far I have mostly been telling the bright side of the story of how we bond with our babies, how we build, right from the beginning, a long and loving relationship with them. But as with every story, there is another side to it: a more shadowy side, a side that is less told, that is not always easy to talk about or even to think about. This is the side of the story that relates to when things do *not* go so well, when loving our babies is not that easy, when caring for them is difficult, when we sometimes want to run away when they cry rather than pick them up and comfort them.

All parents go in and out of the bright side and so spend time on the shadowy side of the story, after which we are no doubt relieved to find ourselves basking again in the sunny light with our beloved babies. This toing and froing from the sun to the shadows and back again is part of ordinary parenthood. But for some of us, once we find ourselves in the shadows, we can struggle to find our way back to the light again. We are caught in the darkness, feeling fearful and anxious, maybe also angry. That can be not only confusing but also scary, and it can undermine our confidence in our parenting.

Before we look into why some of us get stuck there, let's just take some time to describe the more ordinary shadowy side of parenting and think about some of the reasons not only why we all go into the darker realms at times, but also why it is in fact necessary and useful to spend time there. We will find that simply by describing and acknowledging the confusing, uneasy and, at times, frankly frightening feelings that seem sometimes to encircle and trap us, we are already in a much better place to see the paths that can lead us out of them, and back into the light.

How do I know I love my baby? And other feelings . . .

How do I know I love my baby? I am a terrible parent . . . I want to run away . . . Maybe my baby doesn't love me . . . I feel sad . . . sometimes I love my baby, sometimes I don't . . . I want to cry all the time . . . I feel so lonely and bored . . . I can't bear thinking about the birth . . . it was so scary . . . Sometimes I am feeling so angry with my baby . . . I feel totally empty and numb . . . I feel my baby is judging me . . . I hate being a dad/mum.

These are all thoughts and feelings that we can often grapple with at one point or another in our first year(s) with our babies. Our society thrives on the cliché of instant love for our babies, of mothers, fathers and co-parents knowing straight away what to do, of the whole parenting thing being purely instinctive and intuitive, of love at first sight and first sniff . . . But by the time we actually have a baby in our arms, and in our homes, we've already learned it isn't like quite that.

The fact is that none of us are born knowing how to be parents (neither mothers nor fathers). We all *become* parents, not only through a natural physiological process (see Part One) but also and mostly through intense practice and hard work (see Part Two). As we have seen earlier in this book, in the course of the pregnancy, birth and the first few months and years of caring for our babies, a complex hormonal process takes place in order to provide us with different cocktails of hormones that should facilitate the subtle process of bonding with our babies.

But this physiological process is not fool proof, and it can certainly be disrupted very easily by stressful external factors, such as emotional or financial stresses, a traumatic birth, domestic difficulties, previous mental health issues or past trauma . . . And so the hormones associated with stress are never too far away and can throw a spanner into the subtle bonding process and make us at times want to run away from our distressed babies rather than cuddle them.

However it is also important to note that even the 'good hormones' do not have all the answers for us, and that bonding with our babies requires hard work and sheer perseverance. There is nothing instant about knowing what to do and how to be with our babies. It takes time and dedication and *lots* of trial-and-error.

As we have seen in the previous chapters of this book, bonding – creating that special relationship with our babies – is a complicated emotional process and one that is rarely talked about or described. Most of the antenatal classes concentrate on the physical aspects of pregnancy, birth and looking after a baby. Rarely are emotions, feelings, anxieties – whether of the babies or the parents – discussed calmy and at length. As parents, we may be told to expect an 'emotional rollercoaster' and to brace ourselves for intense feelings. But we probably won't get much useful guidance about where those feelings are coming from, and how best to make sure they don't overwhelm us and interfere with our relationship with our babies.

There's generally very little discussion about the impact of being pregnant, giving birth and caring for a baby on the deep emotional state of the parents, and on our innermost feelings. Rarely are parents asked how they *really* feel about being pregnant, how they *really* feel about their baby, especially when they haven't had a proper night's sleep in weeks. Again there is an assumption that pregnant people are all happy and all the same and that, once mothers and babies have 'survived' the birth, we should all be grateful and get on with the rest of the journey, which is far too often painted as all rosy and smooth, without too much fuss.

Whatever we are *really* feeling, we are probably also telling ourselves: how could I possibly complain when both mother and baby are alive? And the world around us is not very ready to help us think differently, or to allow us to be more honest with ourselves. There seems to be a consensus that parents should feel a certain way about their babies and that, if we deviate from that consensus, then surely there must be something wrong with us. Society's hidden but extremely powerful message is: how could we possibly feel sad/lonely/disappointed/scared/regretful/angry or even just confused when we have a healthy baby? And especially if we *wanted* that baby. Society wants us loving and happy, our family wants us loving and happy, our friends want us loving and happy, and these days social media wants us loving and happy too, and posting about our blissful baby days as often as possible. And even our babies may seem to join this conspiracy and want us loving and happy . . . But what if we are just not feeling very loving and happy? And it's a near certainty that's exactly what's happening for most parents a significant amount of the time.

Parenting: a journey of self-discovery

What we often overlook, when we think about the journey to becoming a parent, is how much it is also a journey of self-discovery. When we get pregnant, when we give birth, when we care for our babies, we not only discover who *they* are, we also discover who *we* are. As we have seen, the cornerstone to bonding with our babies is our ability to be curious about their experiences, our capacity to put ourselves in their place and our willingness to accept their emotions and feelings. And it is the same for us as we become parents: we, too, need to be curious about our experience of being a parent and accepting of our new and often surprising emotions and feelings. It's important that we are ready for times when this curiosity can lead us to discover a side of us that we might find unsettling. What if we are not who we thought we were? What if we find we sometimes have negative feelings about our babies we never imagined we would have? We will need to acknowledge those feelings. Because, ultimately, the more aware we are of how we feel – good and bad, happy and sad, exhilarated and terrified, loving and angry – the better it will be for our relationship with our babies. And, indeed, for our relationship with ourselves.

Life will never be the same: gains and losses

Let's not deceive ourselves: having a baby is a massive thing that has a huge impact not only on our bodies and on our minds but also on the way we feel about ourselves and the way society now sees us. Once our babies are born, we will never be the same again. Some of us might feel that is a good thing and can see more easily all the positive changes that being a parent has brought to our lives; but some of us might struggle with that permanent shift and be much more aware of the losses that having a baby brings to our lives.

In a study about the impact of motherhood on women, the 'loss of sense of self' came at the top of a list of unexpected difficult feelings that new mothers had to grapple with during the first few years of their babies' lives.[1] Having a baby undoubtedly turns our lives upside down, and it's often easier to frame our crazy new world in terms of losses rather than gains. Yes, we gain a baby! But we lose our independence and sense of lightness (we are now and for ever responsible for this baby). We lose our freedom of movement and spontaneity (anchored to this tiny being, we can't just go out when we feel like it or when our friends call us to join them at the pub; we can't even watch TV, sleep, or eat when we want!). It may even feel that we lose our freedom of thought (we are so tired and numbed by the repetitiveness of the baby-caring tasks that we may feel our brain has turned into mush). We might also lose our financial autonomy (the parent who stays at home looking after the baby often becomes financially dependent on the other parent). And perhaps we feel we are losing that special romantic relationship with our partner (our partner is no longer primarily our lover and best friend, but perhaps more like a business partner or work colleague with whom we have to divide chores and negotiate responsibilities (see Chapter 17 – Babies and the family). It's likely we will lose some of our confidence too (we probably knew how to be good at our jobs, but looking after a baby can feel like a very challenging task we have not been trained for). Okay, so that is a very long list of losses, which won't apply to every parent all the time. But there's a lot of loss to tune into and reflect on when our tired brains choose to go down that path.

For some parents, the sense of rapidly accumulating losses may come in an overwhelming and unexpected rush, right at the beginning of our parenting experience, almost immediately after the birth. For others this may come later, in bits and pieces, but just as unexpectedly.

The sense of loss can be quite acute and, for a lot of us, it will take months or even years to work through and adapt to the huge challenges of caring for a baby and for us to recover our emotional and social equilibrium.

It can feel very hard to speak about – let alone complain about – all these losses. This will, in part, be due to our fear, conscious or unconscious, of being judged by our society, which remains adamant that parenthood is uncomplicatedly blissful. As this is unhelpful, so let's spend a bit of time thinking honestly about what we miss from our old lives. But, at the same time, let's also remind ourselves about the things that we feel we have gained since our babies have been born. It might even be a good time to sit down and write ourselves a thoughtful and honest letter. Here is a simple template with a few bullet points to get you started, but adapt as you see fit.

Dearest me,

Here are the things I miss from my old life:

1

2

3

4

5

6

7

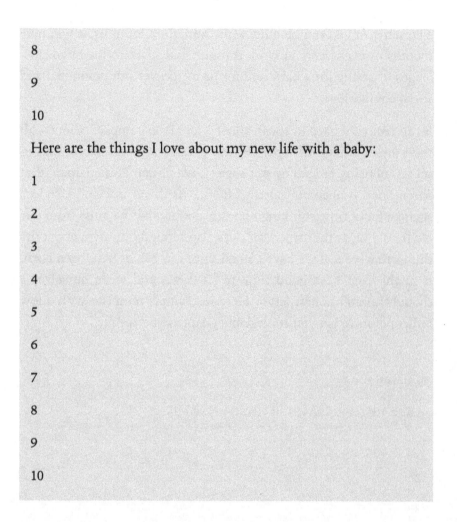

8

9

10

Here are the things I love about my new life with a baby:

1

2

3

4

5

6

7

8

9

10

The list might well feel lopsided, leaning heavily towards what we love about our new life or towards what we feel we have lost since having a baby. We might be surprised, even shocked, that there is so little in one of the lists. And it may be that our predominant emotional state is biasing us in favour of one list or the other. That can change over time, and it's good to acknowledge those changes.

Having our two lists – the things we miss and the things we have gained – roughly equal in length and so roughly balanced would demonstrate that we are in touch with both the gains and the losses, that, for us, being a parent is neither over-idealised nor dramatically demonised. And that's pretty healthy. But we also need to acknowledge that the lists might look quite different depending on the day – and whether we got any sleep the night before, how sore our nipples are, and whether we just had to say no to our friend's birthday party because we are feeling too shattered. And they might be very different lists indeed if we just got a smile from our baby, had a great session of baby yoga and massage, or had a super supportive visit from granny and grandpa . . .

So let's try to stay curious about how we feel about being a new parent and keep coming back to the lists, to add things and cross out others, as our feelings change and evolve.

Next I want to explore an important aspect of this newfound honesty about our feelings regarding our babies, because being aware of how we feel, ultimately, will help us to be aware and more accepting of how our babies are feeling too. And as we have been discovering so far, that is always going to help us create a more authentic and nurturing relationship with them.

Ambivalence: the ultimate taboo

There is one particular feeling that we are highly likely to be unprepared for, as it really doesn't get much recognition from society, the medical profession, or even from the gurus of pregnancy and parenting. In fact, it is still generally seen as a negative, ugly feeling, even a taboo, which makes it very difficult for parents to admit to. I am talking about . . . and brace yourselves here for a very strong word . . . hate.

Just seeing this word, right here on the page, right here in this book about how to bond with our babies and give them all the love they need, probably feels shocking in itself. Some of us might think: 'Are you suggesting that what I feel for my baby is not just pure love? I can't possibly agree with that!' Whereas some others might think, with some relief: 'Oh! You mean I am not the only one who sometimes dislikes my baby?'

Before we get too horrified by the suggestion that we could hate our babies, let's try to deflate this word, which has become too big for its own good, to its normal size. Put in simple terms, hate is merely the opposite of love. And when it comes to our babies, it generally means, for most of us, fleeting feelings of irritation, annoyance, displeasure, exasperation, crossness, momentary feelings of disappointment, indignation, dislike, anger, and even rage perhaps . . .

Babies, and *our* babies especially, because of their utter vulnerability and complete dependence, are masters at evoking in us the widest and wildest range of feelings, from total exhilaration to the deepest despair, and anything and everything in between. No matter how much we have tried (and often mostly succeeded) during our 'grown-up' years to keep our feelings and emotions neatly under control, to restrict their range and moderate their power, now that we are parents, it is as if the lid has been lifted on Pandora's box and all our feelings are loose once again.

At one end of the spectrum, our babies are experts at eliciting incredibly strong feelings of love such as we have never experienced before. With their big eyes and tiny button noses, their wide beguiling smiles, sweet smell and silk-soft skin, they draw on our deepest wells of love and emotional euphoria. Babies are cute and our brain loves cuteness.[2] Once in our arms, our babies transform us, and with that deepest of love comes the deepest urge to protect. Our softly spoken self is now ready to shout at anyone coming too close, the pacifist in us is now ready to take up arms to defend them. We feel that our love for them is such we could do anything for them. We discover that we could even kill because we love them so much. And that, too, can be shocking. But even in our deepest moments of love for our babies, we are already in touch with 'darker' feelings. Which perhaps makes it less of a surprise that these feeling can also be suddenly (or gradually) flipped. This is something we may be familiar with from intensely loving, and sometimes hating, our partners too. Who hasn't said (or at least felt like saying) 'I hate you!' to the people we most love in the world: our parents, our partners, our very best friends. So let's not be too alarmed, then, if the same feelings start welling up inside us for this new little person who we also love so much.

Let's instead brace ourselves for this other end of the spectrum, because there really is no doubt that our babies are also masters at eliciting some not-so-loving feelings. And we should not be too surprised to find ourselves sometimes feeling irritated by, disliking and even resenting them. I mean, have you seen how our babies treat us?[3] It is all about *them*! They are insatiable, and whatever we do it is never enough, they always want more, they have no consideration for our feelings, our needs, even our most basic ones, and they dictate everything, from when we go to the loo, when we shower, when we eat, when we see friends (and often don't), when we chat or make love with our partner, when we watch TV . . . And that's just the trivial stuff. Our babies' supreme crime, the one that really hits us in the guts, is that they deprive us of the two most fundamental things for our physical and mental wellbeing: our freedom and, even worse, our sleep.

The truth is that if any adult did a tenth of what our babies do to us, we would call them abusive, gas-lighting control freaks and our friends would beg us to leave them. When we look at it like this, it isn't so hard to think of our babies as detestable selfish little monsters and to start to resent them and dislike them. And once these feelings start to rise in us, it turns out there is plenty of things about our babies to fuel these feelings and make them worse: their crying irritates us, the smell of their poo disgusts us, their tyrannical schedule make us despise them, their weird enjoyment for repetitive games fill us with boredom . . . We miss our old life so much! Why did we even think we wanted to have a baby?

Luckily, for most parents, most of the time our babies are also carrying within them the sure-fire antidote to these intense feelings of irritation and frustration. Because suddenly they smile, look at us with their big beautiful eyes, kick their legs with excitement, put their arms out to us, gurgle, giggle even, and give us back the love we so desperately crave from them. If we are lucky, they may even yawn, close their eyes and eventually fall asleep, giving us our life back too, if only for a few moments.

And so, in response, we find ourselves bursting with love again – that weird and new kind of love that could make us murder anyone who dares to come too close. We are now well and truly caught up in what therapists call parental 'ambivalence', where opposite and conflicting feelings for our babies co-exists in our minds and our hearts.

What is often difficult about our mixed feelings is that they are frequently felt at the same time or in very quick succession.

Let's imagine it is 3 a.m. and we have just gone back to sleep after yet another endless feed. As we are starting to relax and enter a deliciously deep sleep, we are suddenly woken up by the screams of our baby, who is pausing from screaming only to vomit all over their cot.

In that moment we may very well feel extreme love, as we are worried about our babies' health, and so we start listing in our mind all the different reasons why they might be vomiting and what we could do to make them feel better and take away their pain and distress. But, at the same time, it's highly likely that we also feel extreme irritation, as we have just been woken up and are now fully aware of how much work and effort it is going to take to put our baby back to sleep and clean up the stinky mess.

This rapid journey between the two ends of the spectrum of feelings can be exhausting, as well as, at times, unsettling and even frightening. Discovering that we are not just the kind, gentle and generous person we thought we were can feel like a nasty surprise and leave us worried. But as this aspect of parenthood is still very much taboo and thus little talked about, we can then easily start judging ourselves very harshly, and a lot of us often enter the terribly lonely world of shame. We assume that we are monsters for feeling those strong feelings and so we keep quiet.

If this is where we are spending a lot of our time, mentally and emotionally, then it is time to give ourselves a break, to pause and reflect, to reach into our reserves of self-knowledge and self-care. We are *not* bad people and we are *not* bad parents just because these feelings visit us from time to time. Because these feelings are *completely normal*. But even more importantly, and perhaps surprisingly, though hopefully reassuringly and even excitingly, not only are these feelings normal, they are also completely healthy and absolutely necessary. Let's ask ourselves this: would our love be genuine, or real, or rewarding, if love was 'all' we could ever feel for our babies? Isn't it because we sometimes dislike them and find them insufferable that we also know when we are full of love for them again?

Feeling a wide range of intense feelings for our babies is part of the basic deal of parenthood, it is part of a *healthy* relationship with our babies, and it is genuinely ordinary, even if some of these feelings seem at times extraordinarily powerful and confusing, clashing and incompatible. We have already noted that this is a version of what happens with our partners, indeed with all our other relationships: we hardly have only loving feelings for our own parents, our siblings, our friends. So why should we only feel loving feelings for our babies? We know they are special, but they are also human after all, and so are we. Their very specialness, in fact, will just make the feelings at both ends of the spectrum even more intense, surprising, and sometimes a little scary.

So let's try to love and hate without embarrassment or shame and therefore fill in the list below:

My dearest baby,

Here are ten things I hate about you:

1

2

3

5

6

7

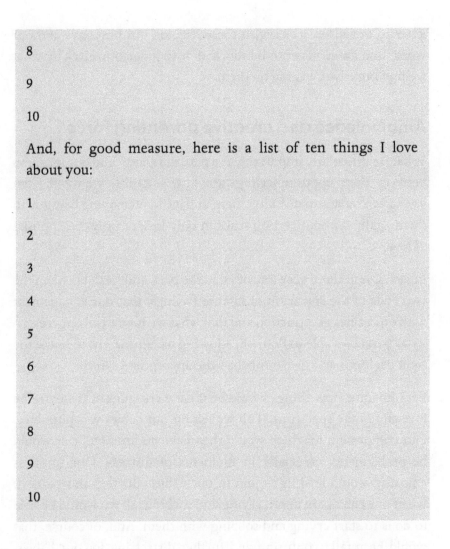

8

9

10

And, for good measure, here is a list of ten things I love about you:

1

2

3

4

5

6

7

8

9

10

Now, which one of the lists was quicker to write? Sometimes it is easier to write about all the things we find irritating about someone. But, as before, a balanced list, where we can keep in mind both the things we love and the things we dislike, where our babies are neither over-idealised nor dramatically demonised, is a pretty healthy outcome. But that won't always be easy or possible, and as with our letter to ourselves, let's revisit these lists, on our best days and our worst, and agree never to be shocked or to judge ourselves by what we find ourselves writing on them.

Ambivalence as a creative parenting force

What is particularly important, as a parent, is how fluid our journeys between these opposite feelings are, how smoothly we move from loving our babies to disliking them and back to enjoying being with them again, without getting stuck in only love or only the opposite of love.

In fact, it is in these very journeys, in the back and forth between the two ends of the spectrum of intense feelings, that our engagement with our babies gets traction and that what we might call our creativity as parents is able to flourish, allowing us, ultimately, to make the right decisions and give our babies the appropriate care.

Let's imagine how things would be if we were stuck at the extreme love end of the spectrum, if all we felt for our babies was pure love. Our compassion for them would then have no limit and this would be problematic, especially in moments of distress. Our limitless empathy would lead us to join in our babies' distress and sadness: when our babies are upset, crying and sobbing, all we would be able to do is to start crying and sobbing with them. And, of course, that would be totally confusing and further distressing for our babies, making things even worse for them, leading in turn to a vicious circle of spiralling misery and despair for both of us, rendering us completely hopeless at dealing with the situation and unable to make things better for our babies. (And where, you might reasonably ask, is the love in that?)

This is why a good dose of irritation, of feeling properly annoyed with our babies, is absolutely necessary at times. It helps us step back from that paralysing total love and compassion so that we are spurred into action in trying to find out what the matter is with our babies and so come up with a solution to their problems – and, in so doing, also bring our own frustration to an end. As in a well-designed seesaw, our love ignites our compassionate curiosity for our babies, whereas our irritation propels us to look for adequate solutions to their problems. Both have a vital role to play.

Being able to move swiftly and with awareness along the tightrope of our loving and not-so-loving feelings is what gives us the necessary liveliness and vivacity to make us curious, compassionate and creative parents.

Our babies' ambivalent feelings towards us

One of the many reasons why it is so hard at times to accept our own mixed feelings towards our babies is that it puts us in touch with our babies' own mixed feelings towards us. What?! Are you suggesting that, after all we do for them, day and night, they do not adore us all the time? Yes, that's maybe a big blow, but let's not delude ourselves: our babies, too, love us beyond measure and also – brace yourself again – hate us sometimes with a searing rage.

They love us when we get it right straight away, when as soon as they are hungry we give them some warm and delicious milk, when we change their nappies as soon as they have pooped. And they dislike us when we get it wrong: when we think they need a nappy change when all they actually want is food, when we put another layer on them when they are already too hot, when we put them to bed when they want to play, when we play with them when they want to sleep, and, of course, when we make them wait . . . Make no mistake: that furious crying, that screwed up face, the feelings they are expressing has to do with disappointment, annoyance, irritation, anger and even rage.

With young babies, in fact, the loving and the hating seem like such separate, distinctive states that some theorists have proposed that, for the first four months of their lives, our babies actually perceive us as two distinctly different people.[4] There is the good mum or dad who gives them pleasure by offering them warm milk, a soft voice, and gentle reassuring cuddles. And then there is the bad mum and dad (a totally rubbish one, in fact), who denies their needs, makes them wait, and fails to understand them instantly and completely.

However, as our babies grow and mature, they start getting a sense that perhaps the parent who deprives them of the delicious milk is the same as the parent who gives them so generously that very same delicious milk. And for a while this is quite confusing for them: how could we possibly be both a good and a bad parent at the same time? And as, slowly, the realisation dawns on them that, yes, the good and the bad parents are the very same person, they feel some sadness as they start, for the first time in their life, to experience some guilt and remorse for having treated us so harshly every time we got it wrong (I am sure their rageful screaming still echoes in our ears).

It must be quite a shock to realise that the person they were rightly blaming for getting it wrong turns out to be the same as the all-providing, ever-loving perfect parent. However, it is through this healthy process – of reconciling the good and the bad parent – that they can start loving us for who we really are, and that means with all our human imperfections. And that is good news for us, because it means that, as they grow, our babies become more tolerant and appreciative of our 'imperfect parenting': they are more forgiving when we get it wrong, more grateful when we get it right and, on the whole, less tyrannical; they are starting to be less impatient and so are able to wait a little longer for that delicious milk.

And as it is for us, for them, too, it is important and reassuring that they can move with fluidity between the extremes of emotions, and not get stuck in either all loving or not-so-loving feelings for us, so that when the warm milk eventually comes, they can leave their frustrated feelings behind and start to feel love for us again, and readily accept the milk we are offering and drink it with pleasure.

Let's try to imagine how they might feel about us as they experience our best and worst attempts to imagine what they are going through and give them what they need, and how this might translate to loving and not so loving feelings on their part.

List ten things our babies love about us:

1

2

3

4

5

6

7

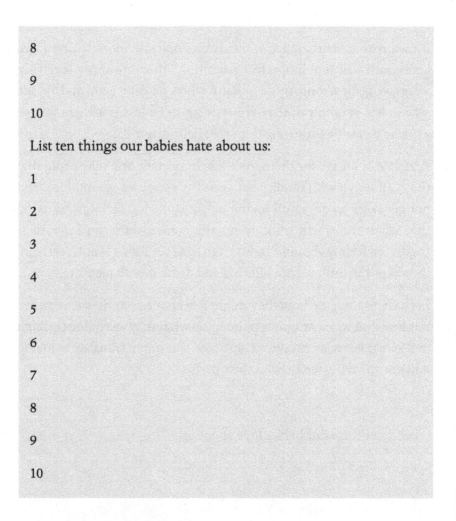

8

9

10

List ten things our babies hate about us:

1

2

3

4

5

6

7

8

9

10

Our imperfect parenting

These dilemmas and contradictions will certainly produce feelings that are not always easy to process or understand. We will often want to revert to the easy, simplistic notion that our babies could never have anything but adoring feelings for us. And this is partly because we want to think that we are perfect parents or at least that we are trying to be – surely that is what we must always aim for? But, actually, we should be consoled by the fact that our babies know very well, almost from the very beginning of their lives, that we are *not* perfect, and will never be so. And allowing them to remind us of that – by acknowledging their rage when we get it wrong – is important, as it makes it possible, then, for us to appreciate the full spectrum of our parenting, and that includes also the pleasure, satisfaction and love that we feel when we get it right.

Rohan (three months)

After changing his nappy, Lily gently lays Rohan on his tummy on his playmat. Lily watches him for a bit, but soon she says to Rohan that she needs to do something in the next room. Rohan watches her leave the room. When she has disappeared, he pushes up on his little arms and stays like that for a little while, trying to look around the room. As he lets go, his head falls on the cushion and he moves his head as if trying to suck the cushion. Soon he finds his bare hand and starts sucking it noisily instead. As nothing – milk, for example – comes out, he stops, but then starts again, putting even more energy into it. But, again, nothing comes out and he starts making a repetitive burst of high pitch sounds, as if calling someone. As nobody comes, he sucks his hand again, but with frustration, and then suddenly he starts screaming. The screaming builds up. Lily comes to pick him up, and now Rohan is crying furiously. She rocks him for a while, but the crying, if anything, intensifies. She tries to distract him by offering different toys. But again the crying goes up a notch, with Rohan tossing his head away from the toys. With slight exasperation, Lily says: 'Okay, I can see you are really cross with me.' After a further minute or so, Lily says: 'Maybe you are hungry? Do you think some milk will make you feel better? Shall we try?' With Rohan still screaming, she sits on the sofa and puts him to her breast. As his face is brought in contact with her nipple, he stops screaming for a second or two, but quickly the screaming resumes, somehow amplified, and he turns his head from side to side, as if unable to catch the nipple or even perhaps trying to avoid it. As Lily gently perseveres, patting his back rhythmically and saying softly: 'I know you are cross with me, I get it . . . I took too long to find you and now you are really angry with me . . . Hey, look, try eating a bit. I am sure you will feel better . . .' After more patting and reassuring words, Rohan eventually calms down just enough to start sucking noisily. Soon the room is silent and all we can hear is Rohan rhythmically feeding. Lily watches him carefully, caressing his forehead. After a few minutes of intense feeding, Rohan looks at his mother with the beginning of a smile, but as soon the nipple is about to fall out of his mouth, he grabs it firmly and goes back to feeding.

Rohan's understanding of the world is still very basic: as far he is concerned, he has a good mother who responds quickly to his needs, and a bad one who makes him wait. Because Lily needed to do stuff in the other room, she missed the cues that Rohan was getting hungry and did not see his sucking of his hand. So, for Rohan, the mother who took a minute too long to turn up and missed the cues was the bad mother and he was not shy to let her know his feelings towards her.

Luckily for Rohan, Lily was able to accept his upset and take responsibility for his screaming. Maybe making him wait a little was her way to express her own ambivalence about him and his constant demands – she had, after all, already fed him five times that morning. But what is important is that Lily did not take Rohan's rage as a hateful criticism of her mothering but as an ordinary way for a baby to express his ordinary anger with his mother for making him wait a little too long. This, in turn, allowed Rohan to move quickly and smoothly from angry feelings for his mother (and refusing to feed) to more loving and forgiving feelings (and being able to feed). Owning up to her own ambivalence also enabled Lily not to join in Rohan's panic but to be more creative in her search for a solution to his problem. She stayed relatively calm and tried a few different things before getting it right.

If all we can feel for our babies is love, if they never irritate us, if we never wish they would leave us in peace for a moment, if we always find their games funny, then are we really loving our real babies? Or are we loving an idealised version of our babies as well as a an idealised version of ourselves as parents? Our babies do not want us to see them as perfect, nor do they want us to be a perfect parent: they want and need us to see them in the glory of their imperfections as well as to accept and take responsibility for our own imperfections as parents.

It is only when we manage both to see our babies in all their humanity (with the loving and not-so-loving as well as the lovable and not-so-lovable parts of their personalities) and to let them see our own humanity (with the full spectrum of our feelings for them) that we will start forgiving ourselves for our imperfect parenting and become really brilliant (but not perfect!) parents. For our babies to flourish, we need to embrace and celebrate our own as well as their humanity with all its flaws and imperfections.

The big question: what to do with our ambivalence?

The significant question, but one we not surprisingly often shrink from, is what do we do with our ambivalent feelings? How do we express (or not) our loving and not-so-loving feelings towards our babies?

Thinking about how we communicate our love is fairly easy: we have many ways to let our babies know our pleasure, delight and joy and they often overlap with the ordinary things we all do when we take care of them. We feed them generously when they are hungry, we clean them tenderly when they are dirty, we soothe them calmly when they are upset, we smile warmly at them, we kiss them fondly, caress them gently, sing them songs, tell them stories, play with them . . .

It is often harder to think about how most of us express our ordinary irritation and annoyance with our babies. As with love, it often overlaps with our everyday care of them: the feeding, cleaning, soothing, playing. But when we do those things – even when we do it with love – we, at times, might also express our irritation by taking a second or two longer to respond to their upset or cry of hunger, we might hold them a little tighter when we soothe them, we might be a little brisker when we change them, our tone might be a little sharper . . .

Those expressions of our irritation are often hard to spot because they are usually subtle and quick, almost invisible, which makes it easier not to admit to ourselves that they are happening. But we know they are there – we can feel it in our body, in our voice – and they can leave us feeling a little confused and uneasy with ourselves. It can also leave our babies confused too and unsettle them further.

Because those feelings are often so fleeting, we need to pause a moment and turn a kind and judgement-free spotlight on ourselves in order to be more aware of how we are with our babies. By checking with ourselves how we talk to them, pick them up, hold them, how we feel when they cry, when they wake us up in the middle of the night or refuse to nap, then we can start noticing the subtle signs of our irritation.

And like little bubbles stuck at the bottom of the sea, we can let our feelings of irritation and exasperation rise gently and freely to the surface of our consciousness. Then, once there, once in the safe place of our mind, we can think about them rather than act them out through our body, which is important, because it means we are now in charge of our own feelings rather than them being in charge of us.

Indeed, if we pay attention to our feelings of annoyance, displeasure, boredom and anger, if we give them a voice rather than pushing them back down to the faraway corners of our minds, we won't have the (unconscious) urge to turn them into action by squeezing our babies a little too hard, making them wait longer than necessary, or using a harsh voice . . . Like bubbles gently bursting into the air as they reach the surface of the sea, our mixed feelings, once we have acknowledged them as not only worthy of our attention but normal and indeed important and necessary, can then dissipate and gently fade away.

One way to help us think about our ambivalent feelings, our annoyance, irritation, anger and/or boredom, is to give them some context, and the best way to do that is by tracking back to their origin: going back to the where, the when and the why we began to feel a certain way in the first place.

If we can say to ourselves: of course I am fed up with you, my baby, when I don't seem to be able to find the right way to soothe you, of course I feel quite bored to have to change your nappy yet again today (having already done it five times already), of course I'd rather do something else than clean all your dirty bottles, wash all your clothes (I have been working all day and the list of chores seems to have tripled since your arrival in my life), of course I am annoyed, and want to scream too, when you keep me awake all night with your cries (and I haven't had a proper night sleep in weeks), of course I am feeling rubbish and overwhelmed when I don't seem to be able to soothe you when you cry (and I've just got an email from my boss, who tells me the report I sent this morning needs to be redone), of course I find it hard to play with you today (I cannot stop thinking about how we are going to pay the rent this month or about the argument I had with your mum/dad) . . . then these feelings and thoughts, once put in their proper context, lose their alarming power to frighten us or to make us feel guilty. They can now be seen and felt for what they are: reasonable and ordinary feelings and thoughts for this extra-ordinary experience that is caring for a baby.

Acknowledging ambivalence

Let's try to locate these feelings of irritation. Do you feel them in our legs, arms, tummies . . . Can you remember when they started? Was it before your baby started crying or after?

Now, let's go a step further into the past: can you remember what happened just before the crying started? Were you having a cup of tea? Trying to rest or finish an important email? Having a nice chat with a friend on the phone?

Again let's go a step even further back: can you think of a significant event that happened several hours before the crying started?

You got a nasty email from one of your colleagues, perhaps? You dropped and broke something while tidying up the kitchen? You had a row with your partner or with your own parents? You watched/heard something disturbing on the news or saw perfect holiday pictures of some distant friend with their always happy and impeccable baby on Instagram?

If we feel that we have now managed to give some context to our irritation, by bringing it from our body to our mind, from a feeling to a fact, then let's imagine these feelings are little bubbles that were stuck and stopping the normal flow of things . . . Let them rise to the surface one by one and watch them pop and vanish . . . Enjoy the feeling and don't forget to breathe . . .

How to respond to our babies' own ambivalent feelings

By acknowledging and accepting our own mixed feelings rather than quashing them, we also become more available to accept our babies' own mixed feelings. Of course, receiving their loving feelings is fairly easy and pleasurable: we smile back to their loving smile, we coo back to their endearing cooing etc.

However, it becomes slightly more complicated when it comes to accepting their irritated feeling with us, when we feel we have turned, in their eyes, into bad parents. But whether it is a smile or a scream, it is best to understand these as healthy expressions and communications of their ordinary loving, and not-so-loving, feelings. They are certainly not personal attacks on you as bad parents!

And that's important, because what our babies need is for us to be able not only to accept generously their love but also sustain and bear their rage and angry feelings toward us. If we can see that the intention behind the crying and screaming is simply to communicate with us and let us know what is going on for them, then it is much easier to respond to our babies' needs with care and curiosity, rather than react irritably to their feelings toward us. If we can hear our babies' cries not as a personal attack on us but as a communication of their distress, then their crying loses some of its irritating power.

In other words, it is best for our babies if we don't take it too personally when they find us totally useless and imperfect. And it's better for us too! This is what unconditional love is: being able, as parents, to endure our babies' anger, rage and criticism without retaliating. Whatever they throw (metaphorically at the moment, at least) at us, we are going to resist the temptation to throw it back at them: if they scream, we are not going to scream back; if they kick, we are not going to kick back; if they bite us, we are not going to bite them back. Instead, by holding in our mind both their irritation with us (as their ordinary way to let us know that we have not got it right yet) and our own annoyance with them (for making us feel like terrible parents), we can stay curious about what their upset is about and hold them gently in our arms until we and they both feel calm and loving again.

By respecting and acknowledging our mutual loving and not-so-loving feelings towards each other, we parents and our babies will be able to feel freer, more creative and authentic with each other. And ultimately parenting will be more pleasurable and joyful. Plus it will be equally blissful to be the baby of such a brilliant (but not perfect) parent.

The rough with the smooth

I feel it is important to get our ambivalent feelings out in the open, because this is where they will cause the least trouble. For convenient reasons (Western) society prefers to see parenthood an idyllic journey that parents should be able to navigate smoothly without support, because if it did acknowledge parenthood as a multi-facetted experience, with its joyful moments but also its painful challenges, then the state might be forced to provide more adequate childcare facilities with therapeutically trained staff, more part-time and flexi jobs, longer and better financially supported parental leave and more easily available therapeutic support for the parents who feel stuck (just to name a few things).

Instead, society prefers to romanticise parenthood as a blissful time and tends to stigmatise the idea that parents might not just feel pure love for their babies. This means that, for us parents, it can often feel unnerving and very lonely to know that, at times, we find our babies more annoying than lovable and that we feel irritated by them. We may even feel ashamed and guilty and find it difficult to talk about it, as we worry that opening up may be risky. We might risk upsetting our partners, for example, or risk shocking our friends and disappointing our parents (who seem to have nothing but love for their darling little grandchild). Worse even than these fears, at the back of our minds is always the terror that, if we dare to share our ambivalent feelings towards our babies, then someone, somewhere might come and take them away . . .

So we bury these feelings deep and make sure nobody sees them, when in fact we, and our babies, know all too well that they are happening. But being able to be in touch with both our loving and our not-so-loving feelings for our babies and accepting them as ordinary and reasonable is a positive sign that we are able to appreciate our babies for who they are, neither idealising nor demonising them. And that is what our babies want us to be: curious parents who can acknowledge and be grateful for not only the lovable parts of their personalities and behaviours but also the less lovable and more antagonising ones.

It is only when we manage to see our babies in all their humanity (with the lovable and not-so-lovable part of their personalities), while also accepting, generously, our own humanity (with the full spectrum of our feelings for them), that we will start forgiving ourselves for our imperfect parenting and become really brilliant parents. For our babies to flourish, we need to embrace and celebrate our own as well as their humanity, with all its flaws and imperfections.

10
When we feel low

But what if the ordinary ambivalence becomes extraordinary? What if the movements between loving feelings and not-so-loving-feelings are not as fluid and effortless as we wished they were, or if feelings of irritation for our babies are not so much fleeting feelings that pass quickly but feelings that linger day and night? What if, perhaps even more painfully, we feel almost nothing for our babies, neither love nor annoyance, just indifference? What if instead of wanting to cuddle them when they are distressed, we want to run away from them? Or we feel more like a babysitter than a parent to our babies? What if uncomfortable and sometimes disturbing thoughts about our babies keep popping up in our minds?

Bonding is a process that is full of bumps and sharp turns, and for some of us the bumps can feel bumpier and the corners sharper. A recent survey has shown that more than one in ten women (11.5 per cent) struggle to bond with their baby in the first year.[1] Physically exhausted and emotionally vulnerable, new parents who do not feel a relatively immediate and strong sense of connection with their babies can quickly become very anxious and sad, and also full of guilt and shame that there is something wrong with them. Before we look at the most obvious signs that we are struggling, however, it important to be aware that some people (friends, family, even professionals) might try to minimise our difficult feelings by saying they are part of normal parenthood. Yes, parenthood is tiring and challenging, but there is a big difference between feeling exhausted and feeling low. So what follows is the list of the most obvious signs.

Signs that we are struggling with bonding

- We can't stop crying when we are on our own (but often put on a brave smile when we are with others)

- We find our babies more irritating than not, and we rarely feel like cuddling them

- We don't feel like picking them up when they are crying

- Our routine is largely reduced to feeding them, changing them and putting them down to sleep – basic physical care but very little emotional care

- We don't feel like meeting up with friends or other parents, or going to parent groups

- We begin to neglect our own care, eating irregularly and unhealthily; we find it hard to shower and get dressed

- We are struggling to sleep, even when our babies are sleeping

- We feel more like a babysitter than a parent; at times we feel that our babies are not really ours

- We have intrusive thoughts that we find confusing and maybe even scary*

* NB: A small number of women with very severe depression can develop postpartum psychosis. If you hear voices, behave in unusual and confused ways, if you have become fearful and suspicious, if you have thoughts of harming yourself or your baby, then ring 999 and seek help immediately.

If, while reading this (non-exhaustive) list, you went 'Yup, that's me!' more times than you wished to, then you might be among the 70,000 to 100,000 parents a year who, after the initial baby blues (which are often due to the hormonal changes in the first week or so), go on to develop a post-natal illness.[2]

Some mothers get better without treatment, and within three to six months these blank and negative feelings slowly pass and are over-taken by more positive feelings of connection with their baby. I hope this book may help some of these parents along that journey. Simply having some insights into, and information about, the ways you can connect and bond with your babies, and the processes that are in play, can be useful. It won't solve the problem at a stroke, but it may help you not to be too distressed and alarmed by your feelings and help you to continue looking after your babies in a caring way, even when you don't feel you are caring as much as you would like.

It will certainly help if you feel that you have some support in deal-ing with these feelings of isolation, loneliness and shame that your experience so far of parenting has brought on. The support can come from your partner, or family, a trusted friend or a local sup-port group.

But if your 'first stop' support network is either absent or doesn't seem up to the task of reassuring you, if you continue to be fright-ened by your feelings on a daily basis, then you really need to seek professional help to be assessed for Post-Natal Depression. When talking about their PND, parents who have sought professional help almost invariably say that they wished they had asked for help earlier.

What if other people know I am struggling to love my baby?

One of the biggest barriers for most parents in seeking support is the worry that, if they open up about their struggle, they are going to be judged and their babies taken away. It is as if their feelings about the problem have become way bigger than the actual problem. In their minds, their 'bad parenting' has become so disquieting that they cannot imagine that anyone hearing their story is not going to think of them as a monster and insist that their baby is immediately taken away. If this is how you are feeling, rest assured: professionals with experience in treating PND will not jump to conclusions or judge you harshly. They understand what you are going through and are there to provide a non-judgemental safe space where your stories, no matter how sad and painful, can be told and thought about and, from there, open up a pathway to change and release.

Parenting is certainly one of the hardest and longest adventures of our lives, and as I stated earlier, this adventure is often very bumpy. Here is a (non-exhaustive) list of some of the 'bumps' that mothers in my clinic have told me they have experienced, and which have contributed to them feeling very low:

- I was never completely sure I wanted to have a baby, or I felt the timing was detrimental to my life plan

- My baby came after a series of miscarriages or perceived 'failures' in conception

- I have recently lost a parent or other close loved one

- The pregnancy was difficult and scary

- The birth was traumatic

- I was instantly separated from my baby after the birth because they, or I, needed special care

- I wanted to breastfeed but did not manage to keep going with it, and so I feel I have failed

- I feel lonely and abandoned by my partner, who quickly went back to work

- I feel isolated and have little support from my close family or friends

- I am struggling with the new relationship dynamic with my partner

- I had a difficult childhood myself and still have negative feelings about the way I was parented

- I have suffered from mental health difficulties in the past

Reasons why bonding might be difficult

There is no single reason why some women struggle with bonding or develop post-natal illnesses. That is why, when I meet parents in my clinic – who tend to come to see me because they are worried about their babies, toddlers or teenagers rather than themselves – I always spend some time listening to the stories of the very beginning of their journey with their child. And while listening to their stories of the early years, I pay special attention to key moments such as conception, pregnancy, birth, feeding and sleeping. I want to know how their baby came about, how they felt after the birth, whether they have support from the other parent and wider family, and even about the parents' own childhoods.

How easily bonding can be disrupted

As a child psychotherapist, I have spent many sessions over the years talking to parents, some of whom have struggled with bonding and suffered post-natal depression, but also to many who have not, and I have found that, whatever our individual circumstances, we all leave the hospital carrying in one arm our brand new babies, but also, in the other arm, a certain amount of baggage from our past. And that baggage inevitably is going to impact, sometimes positively and sometimes negatively, on our bonding experience.

Bonding is a subtle physiological and emotional process and one, as we are about to discover, which can very easily be disrupted by not only external but also internal factors. If we could parent in a vacuum, a space where we could leave all our own emotional baggage behind, then bonding would be a whole lot easier (albeit perhaps a bit more boring too). But we all come to parenting with our own personal stories. A few of us may have managed to travel light, but most of us will have accumulated, over the years, rather a lot of emotional baggage, packed with varying degrees of neatness or disarray.

So what I am proposing is for all of us to stop for a moment and open our metaphorical suitcases and look inside. We will see that what is there can often come between us and our babies, not just impacting the way we feel as we do our best to care for them, but also, at times, getting right in the middle of things, interfering with our ability to bond. What is in these suitcases of ours can stop us seeing our babies for who they are and stop us responding to their needs with the right level of curiosity, care and love.

Marie Derome

The three big suitcases that every parent carries

While, of course, what is inside our emotional suitcases is unique to each of us, we all come to parenting carrying more or less the same three types of baggage. Let's even picture them in our heads as three different suitcases, just to get a better sense of how burdensome they may sometimes become. The first suitcase is full of the stuff related to our own journey towards parenthood, however planned or unplanned it might be. The second suitcase is like an old battered backpack, crammed with memories (some conscious, others unconscious) of our childhoods and the way we were once parented ourselves. And, lastly, there is the third case, filled with the stuff related to the actual birth of our baby and the extent to which it fulfilled or didn't fulfil our plans and expectations. (There may be less baggage in this particular suitcase if we feel the birth went well, or a lot of very heavy baggage if it was traumatic.)

Unpacking and repacking our suitcases can be a laborious and, at times, a painful task, but our babies will be grateful for our hard work. Indeed, by examining and understanding where our feelings for our babies – the positive but also the more negative ones – come from we will feel able to get rid of what is no longer needed and re-pack our stuff more neatly and efficiently, with mostly only what is useful for us and our babies. In turn, this will allow us to be freer in the way we care for them, and much more our true selves when we spend time with them. And, in the long run, we too will be grateful for the lighter load.

How our face becomes a mirror for our babies (and how what is inside our suitcases can impact on this)

As we have seen in Part Two of this book, one thing our babies love doing is simply looking at our faces. That is because, for them, our faces are where they get a sense of what is going on around them but also inside them. Indeed, as we are looking at our babies, imagining what's going on for them, the forty-three muscles of our faces kick into action, transforming our face into a mirror where our babies can see their own emotional reflection and so start learning about themselves and getting a sense of their own inner lives.[3]

For that to happen, we need a certain degree of self-awareness, a certain degree of insight about our own inner lives, about how we have come to be the way we are. What our babies need when we interact with them is for our faces to reflect what is going on for *them* rather than what is going on for *us*. They need our faces to be a mirror where they can see their joy, fear, sadness, irritation and confusion and so much more reflected rather than just our emotions.

Lila (two months)

Lila is looking at her dad intently with a big smile. He, too, looks at her with a big smile. Suddenly a police car with its siren going passes by. Straight away, Lila's face tenses, her eyes become enormous, and her big smile is now replaced by a mouth that is moving downwards as if she is about to cry. Alex, her dad, instantly stops smiling, his eyes widen, and his mouth follows his daughter's. He takes his daughter's little hands and moves closer to her, and says: 'I know it is scary – it is a police car, it is so loud . . . but don't worry, it is okay. They are on the way to help someone . . . I am here.' As Lila's face relaxes a little, Alex's face relaxes too. He strokes her tummy and then gives her little kisses. When he looks at Lila, she is starting to smile again, and he, too, starts to smile: 'Yes, that's better. We can play again . . .'

Lila enjoys seeing her own emotions reflected on her dad's face, because it makes her feel understood and safe. Her dad's face has become a true mirror where she can see her own reflection and learn about herself and the world around her. But for Alex's face to be that true mirror, he needs to put his own feelings and struggles to the side for a while, so he can be as available as possible to Lila's own experiences.

It is not always easy to be fully present and stay in the moment with our babies. Some of the stuff we carry in our suitcases from our past experiences, or indeed more recent worries about our lives or relationships since the birth, can come between us and our babies, preventing us from being truly able to allow our face to be a mirror of our babies' own inner lives.

Instead, our faces become a distorted mirror, where our babies no longer see their own reflection; rather, they see the expression of our inner lives, with their accumulated difficulties and distress. The feelings that arise from this can be very confusing for our babies. In the longer term, it may lead them to find it hard to be themselves. If they see only an expression of our inner experience in our faces, they will slowly learn to adapt their behaviour to the reflection they are given, i.e. to *our* inner world rather than *theirs*. And soon they will realise that, in order to survive, they need to adjust their ways of being to our desires and wishes rather than to their own. Then, when they are older, they risk being over-compliant, behaving in ways that they hope will please us (and subsequently their teachers, bosses, or partners) rather than in ways that truly reflect who they are and their own desires.

Therefore, for all of us, 'unpacking our suitcases' is helpful, as it will enable us get some insight into how and why we react in certain ways to our babies' needs and demands. With this new understanding we can start changing some of our behaviours, especially those that we feel are distorting our ability to see them, our babies, for who they are.

So let's be brave and look at some of the things that are most commonly found in our suitcases. And let's do that without judging ourselves. The temptation to blame ourselves will be great, but we must keep an attentive eye on that feeling, as it can easily get us stuck and stop the vital process of becoming more self-aware. We are here to try to understand ourselves, and the more we do that, the easier it will be to understand our babies and enjoy being their parents.

11
Letting go of the ideal baby

The first suitcase – our parental jouney

L et's unpack the first suitcase – our journey towards parent-hood, and how planned or not that may have been.

Each and every journey to parenthood is different, but in some way or another all of our journeys will have started with the idea of a baby in our mind. A fantasy baby, if you like. A baby we have not yet met, one on whom we can project our hopes and dreams and indeed fears about being a parent. Some of us hold this fantasy baby in our minds as a very clear and often idealised picture. Others of us may have a rather blurrier picture, so blurry, in fact, that we can hardly recognise it as a baby.

A clear picture

Let's start with those of us who feel we know what we are expecting. We have always known we wanted to be a mum or a dad. We know how many children we want, how many girls and boys; we are possibly already picturing what their eye and hair colour is going to be. We have names in mind, and a vision of family life with our babies that is sharp and coloured in.

Lucy (twenty-four weeks pregnant)

Lucy could not wait to get pregnant. Since her early teens she has known that she wanted to have at least three children. She has been toying with names for years and, at the first opportunity (her twenty-week scan), she wanted to know what she was having – and what she is having is a baby girl called Clara! Her husband, Mark, is very happy too. He himself cannot conceive of a life without at least two children. Since they got pregnant, they are both enjoying imagining their baby daughter. She will look like her mother, but with her dad's eye colour. They can picture her running (and maybe winning) the races on sports day. Clara will be an easy baby. She will be breastfed for at least a year. The birth is all planned. And they have already spent quite a few weekends preparing the nursery. Lucy and Mark do not believe in pink for girls, and Clara's nursery is all kinds of blue and yellow.

A fuzzy picture

For others of us, the picture of the baby in our heads is not nearly so clear cut. In fact, even our desire for a baby is not clearly defined. We can just about begin to imagine life with a baby, but then our projected images of that life start to fizzle out. Perhaps this is because we can also imagine ourselves continuing to live a fulfilled and interesting life *without* a baby. And we wonder, and worry about, how we will handle the obvious difference between life before and life after. It is as if a part of us wants a baby, but another part of us doesn't want one at all. And then, one day, we find we are pregnant, as if the part of us that wanted a baby has 'won' – it had the upper hand on the night we had sex . . . And yet nothing is resolved: just as our desire for a baby was an inclination, a vague hankering, our idea of our future, and our life with that baby, is hesitant and unformed too.

Johana (twenty-four weeks pregnant)

Jo became pregnant by 'accident' – although, if she looks back, she can admit to herself that, the night she got pregnant, she knew she was taking a risk . . . So when the test turned positive, it was – and wasn't – a surprise. It is hard for her to say how she feels about being pregnant. She had never really pictured herself having children, but she also never thought she *wouldn't* have children. It is as if, whenever she thought about the idea of having babies, she headed those thoughts off and 'changed the subject' in her mind. This is very different to the way she feels about her working life, where she often imagines what she wants to do next, how she can get there, and what 'success' looks like. She can certainly imagine a fulfilled life without ever becoming a mother. Her husband has always been keener than her to have a baby. But they haven't really talked through this discrepancy. They have begun to think about the birth and, of course, they are going to make a birth plan. But beyond the obvious steps of going to scans and telling their parents and friends, their plans are really quite vague.

Our journey to parenthood

Some journeys to pregnancy are straightforward, whether they are carefully planned or not. For others, the road to pregnancy might have been quite arduous and highly emotional. Perhaps the person who we thought was going to parent with us has left and we find ourselves on our own. Or getting pregnant has been hard – our pregnancy has finally come after one or several miscarriages, abortions, months/years of IVF or even the death of a baby. We might have had to use the sperm or egg of a known or unknown donor. And, for some of us, becoming pregnant just wasn't possible. After miscarriages and failed IVF, perhaps, we decided that adopting a baby was the only way to become a parent. While, for others, maybe adopting a baby was the only way they could ever imagine becoming a parent.

Our own unique journey to parenthood is going to affect how we imagine our unborn babies, as well as our capacity to see them for who they are once they are in our arms. And it does not necessarily follow that those who had the clearest idea about their baby, and becoming a parent, will have the most straightforward time of it. It can be hard to let go of the baby we fantasied about, and often idealised, and accept the real one. Sometimes the gap between the fantasy and the reality can feel so huge that we start feeling disappointed. Our babies are not how we dreamed they were going to be: wrong gender, too needy, not needy enough, too passive, too rebellious, too active, not active enough, too skinny, too fat, too much hair, not enough hair, too calm, not calm enough . . .

If we have twins (or triplets), we may find ourselves constantly comparing them to each other and one can easily become the ideal baby while the other becomes the difficult and annoying one. Learning to accept and hopefully, in time, to enjoy their differences is going to be important. In fact, we don't even need two (or more) babies to get into this potentially problematic comparison game. If we have fantasised in detail about the baby we are going to have, it is pretty certain that the baby that actually turns up will, in various ways, be different from that idealised baby. And if our imagined baby was close to being perfect, then the real one is inevitably going to suffer by comparison.

This issue of our real baby not 'matching up' may very well be compounded if we have had miscarriages or abortions or lost a baby in the past. We might easily imagine that the baby we lost would have been so much more beautiful and loveable than the baby we now have. If our babies were conceived from egg or sperm donors, we may at times catch ourselves scrutinising them, trying to spot the differences from or resemblance with us, worrying about whether they are going to look like us and maybe even feel like our *own* babies.

And if our babies have some unexpected feature, such as a mole, a birth mark, or a cleft palette – or even the 'wrong' colour hair – then we may find ourselves obsessing about this feature, so that it becomes all we see about our babies. And if our babies are not the sex we had hoped for, we can perhaps indulge in constantly wondering what it would have been like to have the boy or girl we were hoping for . . .

Margo (four months) and Emma

When Margo was born, Emma was shocked when she was told her baby was a girl. For some reasons she and her partner had always thought they would have a boy. When she imagined her baby, it was always a boy: he looked like a boy, he played like a boy, they only had boys' names on their list . . . She was so convinced that he would be this perfect and beautiful boy that she had not bothered with finding out the gender. She could not imagine herself loving a baby girl. So when she gave birth to a girl, she felt shocked and totally disappointed. She actually felt ashamed that she had let her partner down.

Then Emma found it hard and super painful to breastfeed Margo. She was a fussy baby and cried a lot. Emma genuinely felt she did not know how to be the mother of a baby girl, and all she could think was: 'I would be such a good mother if only Margo was a boy.' Even changing her nappy or giving her a bath was tricky for Emma, as she did not like being reminded that very definitely Margo was not a boy.

As the months passed, she felt more and more like a crap mum as she was struggling to feel any kind of love for her baby. Her partner did not seem to mind that Margo was not a boy, but she had never dared to talk about it with him. She was caring for Margo, doing all the right things, but it felt like a mechanical sort of caring, certainly not an emotional one. If someone had asked Emma if she loved Margo, her honest answer would have been 'No!! How could I love her? She is not the baby I spent months picturing in my head.'

At the local playgroup, Emma met another mum, and they quickly became quite close and, one day, the friend came to Emma's house with her little girl, who was generally, like Margo, quite a cranky baby. And then suddenly the friend said with some irritation: 'Oh, I so wish you were a boy . . . your high-pitched crying would be less irritating . . .'

Emma felt quite shocked when she heard her friend say that, but then she thought: 'Hang on, be honest here . . . don't I feel the same?' And without thinking, she said: 'Me too. I wish I had a boy.' Emma thinks her friend is quite shocked by what she has just said, but then they both started to share their feelings of disappointment about the gender of their babies, how it happened, and they both tried to understand why they felt like that. They talked, they cried, they laughed. And then, slowly, this heavy weight of shame and guilt lifted and Emma felt so much less lonely and so much lighter . . .

In the following weeks, when she was getting her little girl dressed after changing her nappy, she noticed afterwards that, probably for the first time, while dressing Margo she had not picked up on the fact that she was not a boy. Emma felt very strange that day, but she is convinced that her bond with her daughter grew stronger and stronger after that afternoon with her friend. She became more relaxed in her parenting, less critical of herself and her baby, and she started to enjoy being with Margo much more. Now she can honestly say that she couldn't care less that Margo is not a boy! And Emma and the mum from the play group have become really good friends.

Emma, like a lot of us, struggled to let go of her 'dream' baby. When she was with Margo, all she could see was what she did not have (a boy) rather than what she had (a healthy baby who was simply longing for her mother to love her). She got stuck in her disappointment, and this made it almost impossible for Emma to enjoy being with Margo, who became a constant source of irritation and dissatisfaction.

Unpacking her emotional suitcase suddenly became possible when she made friends with a mum from the same play group. This friend gave Emma permission to talk honestly about her feelings of disappointment, beginning the process of defusing a situation that had become toxic for her and Margo. Sharing our feelings with someone who we know is going to listen to us without judging us or making us feel ashamed can greatly help to deflate and reduce the intensity of feelings that have got out of proportion.

Most of us will, at times, feel a tinge of dissatisfaction, or more than that, with our babies, as, of course, they will never be the perfect copy of our dream babies. Acknowledging that this is the case helps us move more smoothly to a place where we are able to embrace our babies, with all their surprising, quirky personalities. Being honest with ourselves is a good place to start. And confiding in a friend, partner or parent may be hugely helpful in enabling us to do this, releasing us from the burden of shame and guilt that come with our feelings of disappointment.

But, of course, opening up to someone who loves you and your baby comes loaded with the potential risk that the person we choose to confide in doesn't quite hear us or support us in the way that we had hoped. If you are feeling particularly trapped or burdened by your feelings, and unsupported by those closest to you, then you should think about seeking some professional therapeutic help.

Saying goodbye to the ideal baby and welcoming your real baby

- List all the things you liked about your ideal baby and, in turn, all the things you might not have liked about your ideal baby

- In a moment when your baby is calm, observe them and list all the things you dislike about your baby and all the things you like about your baby

- Compare the two lists. Are they so very different? Is your baby that different from the ideal list? Perhaps, in fact, they have lots of the attributes of your ideal baby . . .

- Then take the first list, burn it or cut it up, and let it float away on a bit of running water/river/sea, or flush it down the loo.

12

The impact of how we were parented

Having a baby can feel like we are making a new start. We are embarking on a whole new chapter in our lives, in which we will be responsible for another human being. In all the excitement about this journey we are on, we can easily forget that we are making this new start with our 'old' selves, bringing with us a whole host of baggage from our past experiences – some of which will be helpful, while other bits may get in the way.

Our own early life

Among all of our experiences in our lives so far, one factor is going to influence our parenting more than any other, and that is how we ourselves were parented. As we hold our newborn baby in our arms, and look forward to our future life together, we need, sometimes, to remind ourselves that we too were once babies – we too were just as small, just as vulnerable and just as dependent on our parents – and that we carry on our shoulders a backpack full of stuff from our own babyhood and childhood. Our parents' particular way of bringing us up has had a big influence on shaping who we are; and now it is going to influence how we bond with and parent our own baby.

As we go through our lives, most of us will find ourselves talking to people at some point about our childhood: what it was like, what was good, what was bad . . . And, inevitably, with repeated retelling, our childhood 'story' can become quite hardened and set. This is totally normal, not least as a form of self-protection. But it can also be helpful at certain points in our lives to revisit the emotional legacy of our childhood and try to untangle the various strands in it, as there can be a lot going on.

Our inner parent and our inner baby

The way we were parented is going to impact on us in two key ways: firstly, there is how our parents related to us when we were children, and secondly there is how their behaviour and attitude towards us made us feel.

Let's think for a moment about what our parents were like. Were they attentive and kind, or mostly uninterested and sometimes critical? Whichever way they behaved will have imprinted itself deep in our psyche, leaving a kind of unconscious emotional memory, or 'inner parent', in us, which, when we grow up and have our own children, is likely to be reawakened and activated. And this inner parent can, at times, have a lot to say.

Now let's look at the way our parents' behaviour made us feel. Did they make us feel cherished and self-assured, or anxious and under-confident? Again, this will have left a strong impression: we can imagine this as our 'inner baby', a set of intense feelings buried deep within us from when we were tiny, which can be triggered when we suddenly find ourselves looking after a baby of our own. And as with our inner parent, our inner baby is rarely shy about speaking up.

So we have these two powerful and very active forces within us – our inner parent and our inner baby – and, as we become parents, these two voices can get horribly loud and competitive. They may be broadly supportive or broadly critical of our parenting. But either way they will affect how we see our real baby and can disrupt how we bond with them.

In fact, it is as if, now that we are parents or about to be, we have three different voices telling us all at the same time what to do: our I'm-a-grown-up-now-and-I've-got-an-important-job-to-do voice; our inner-parent voice, with its possibly critical background chatter; and our inner-baby voice, which may bring with it varying amounts of fear and anxiety. In many of us, these three different voices will compete with each other to be the most heard. And, unfortunately, with so much going on in our heads, it can be really hard to hear clearly what they are trying to telling us.

The Goldilocks Principle

One of our most important jobs as parents is to find the right emotional (and at time physical) distance between us and our babies so we can intuit their needs and respond to them appropriately: not to be so close that we become intense and obsessive and are anxious a lot of the time; and not so distant or disengaged that our babies do not get what they need from us.

Indeed, if we get too close emotionally, we will tend to see their needs in an exaggerated way, almost as if through a magnifying glass, which will make us feel anxious and worried and tempted to respond with an urgency bordering on panic. On the other hand, if we stay too distant emotionally, it is harder for us to stay tuned in to our babies and their needs can seem so far away and tiny that we might be tempted to dismiss and ignore them and eventually disengage with our babies.

The idea of 'just right' is known as the Goldilocks Principle. It is named after the story of Goldilocks and the Three Bears, and is used these days in the earth and life sciences to describe the habitable zone, an area of space in which a planet is just the right distance from its home star so that its surface is neither too hot nor too cold. It is a useful principle to apply to parenting as well. In essence, it's about putting just the right emotional distance between us and our babies.

By the end of this chapter, you will have a better sense of what this 'just right' emotional distance looks and feels like for you and your baby. And in order to get there, we are going to spend some time learning how to recognise, untangle and manage the two powerful voices that impact on our capacity to find the right distance: our inner parent's chatter and our inner baby's whimper or roar. It is only by untangling these inner voices that we will be able to free ourselves from their interference – they often bring us too close or push us too far from our babies – and begin to create the nurturing voice of the adult parents we want to be and find the emotional distance that feels right for us and our babies.

Parenthood: with awareness comes the power to make choices

This journey may seem a little alarming at times. As we realise the huge impact of our own parents on who we are and how we parent, we can easily feel quite deflated and disheartened. But the good news is that we also have an opportunity to turn these feelings around. The more we can look honestly at how we were parented and how it has impacted on who we are, the more we will be able to change our story. With awareness comes the power to make choices.

It's for us to decide how much or how little we want to repeat our past. Do we want our babies to feel the way we did as children, or do we want them to feel differently? Many studies have shown that it is not so much the way we were parented that impacts positively or negatively on our own parenting, but rather the way we make sense of it now, as adults.[1] This is where we now have a choice and are absolutely not destined to repeat blindly the mistakes or negative patterns of our own parents. Indeed, the more we can confront and relate to the pleasure or pain, confidence or anxiety, of our own childhoods, the more we can process these feelings and put together a coherent narrative about them. Which, in turn, will make it easier for us to create a nurturing relationship with our own baby.

There is an added bonus here: by making these conscious decisions, we are also able to repair to some extent the parts of our own childhood that we may feel were lacking or not as happy as they might have been. In nurturing our baby, we also get a chance to nurture our own inner baby selves.

So, although for a lot of us this chapter might stir up some difficult stuff, it will bring relief too, as we realise that not only are we not doomed to repeat the past, but also the past can be repaired, and our baby is actually going to help us to do this.

As we embark on this journey to get better acquainted with ourselves, it is important to try not to get into a spiral of blame. Let's remember that our parents had their own inner parental voice chatting to them when they parented us, and that their parents (our grandparents) parented them with their own inner parental voice ringing loudly in their ears, as did their parents (our great grandparents). And so the story goes on, back to the beginning of time. We cannot change the past, not even the near past, so blaming our parents, or indeed our grandparents, will not help us. What we can do is to try to understand and free ourselves from our childhood story, and thus be able to choose the way we behave with our own babies in the present and future.

Inner-parent chatter

All parents are different, of course, and there are many different types of inner-parent chatter. But if we allow ourselves to generalise, we might divide parents into two broad categories: the kinds of parents who made their children feel safe most of the time; and the kinds who were unable to do that. And we can then ask ourselves which kind of parents we had. If the former, then our inner-parent chatter is going to be largely kind, caring and reassuring, making us feel good about ourselves and confident about our parenting; and if the latter, it is likely to be mostly harsh and critical, making us feel anxious and generally unsure about the way we should be with our babies. For most of us, it is probably a blend of both, coming and going with varying degrees of emphasis.

In the next few pages, we're going to have a look at some real-life situations where our inner-parent chatter may be affecting our relationship with our babies and at times distorting our understanding of their demands and needs.

When our inner-parent chatter is supportive

Those of us who feel our inner-parent chatter is generally supportive are likely to have had parents who loved us unconditionally, and who looked at us with a sense of curiosity: intrigued by our emotions and behaviour, they could park their own needs for a while in order to try to understand ours. We grew up with an overall sense of safety, knowing that our emotions and feelings, and later our ideas and opinions, really mattered to our parents – that they could cope not just with our happy emotions and expressions but also with our more negative ones. They did not seem to have an agenda or a set road for our future; rather, they supported us on our own journey of self-discovery. As a result, now that we are parents ourselves, we have confidence in our ability to meet our baby's needs; indeed, we feel their needs are ordinary and reasonable, even when they are expressed at a high volume at 3 a.m.! When our babies make demands on us, rather than feeling anxious or rejected, we are motivated to discover and resolve whatever it is they are trying to tell us, even if it may be a bit of a conundrum, and we are able to respond to them with empathy.

Eva (four months) and Laura

Eva is lying on her back on the playmat. She is gently kicking her legs in the air. Her mum, Laura, is reading a magazine on the sofa not too far from her. Eva starts making whimpering noises. Laura glances at Eva and says: 'Hey, what's the matter? Are you a little bored?' Eva looks at her mum and the whimpering stops. She goes back to kicking her legs in the air. Laura goes back to her magazine. After thirty seconds or so, Eva starts whimpering again. Laura gets up and sits beside her daughter on the floor. She looks at her and says again: 'What's the matter?' She puts a hand on her baby's chest and rubs it gently. Again,

Eva seems to settle a little, but very soon the whimpering turns into crying. Laura says: 'Surely you can't be hungry – I fed you only ten minutes ago!' As she is saying this, Laura picks Eva up and holds her near her face. They both look at each other, but Eva's crying is getting louder. 'Okay, I will feed you again,' says Laura, while getting Eva's bottle. Back on the sofa, Laura gives the bottle to Eva, who starts sucking straight away. But after a couple of seconds, Eva spits out the teat, crying even louder than before. Laura tries to put the teat back in Eva's mouth, but Eva turns her head furiously, making it clear that is not what she wants. Laura puts the bottle away, saying, 'Okay, sorry, wrong guess . . . What is it, Eva? What is the matter?' Laura looks at Eva, who is still crying: 'Maybe you are not very well this morning?' She kisses her forehead, as if to check if she has a temperature. She then stands up and, holding her tight, walks around the room singing a lullaby in a soft voice. After a few minutes, Eva has settled in her mother's arms.

Despite Eva's upset, Laura stays calm and curious about her baby. She tries to imagine what is going on for her. Having had curious parents herself, she grew up feeling seen and heard. As a result, Laura's inner parent voice is mostly supportive, helping her to see her baby as separate from her, with her own specific needs and emotional life. When her baby gets fussy and refuses to eat, for instance, she doesn't take her fussiness personally, or as a criticism. On the contrary, she looks at it as an ordinary expression of Eva's emotional state, something she needs to try to understand and respond to to help her settle.

If, as a baby, we felt nourished in our relationship with our parents, it is much easier for us, in turn, to manage to keep a healthy emotional distance from our babies – not too close, not too far; to accept their dependence on us and see it as part of the normal process of growing up. Our inner-parent chatter is likely to be gentle and fairly quiet, which leaves enough space for the grown-up part of us to parent our babies without too much interference, even when they are being fractious and difficult to soothe.

When our inner-parent chatter is not so supportive

For those of us who were brought up more negatively, who never really experienced what it felt like to be loved unconditionally, or to be heard and seen whatever our state of calm or distress, our job as a parent, certainly to begin with, is going to be a bit harder. Our parents may have been more preoccupied with their own needs and anxieties than ours, and so struggled to be curious and interested in us. Whatever we did rarely felt exactly right, or enough, and our parents were perhaps quick to criticise us, ridicule us or ignore us, especially if we seemed to be 'behaving badly'. This has left us susceptible to hearing critical inner-parent chatter, so that more negative feelings can quickly come to the fore. When our babies are fussing, crying, struggling to feed or sleep, it is very easy to feel that they have turned into our critical, shaming, rejecting, uninterested parents . . . At these times, the inner chatter can be so intense that it can almost feel as if it is 'spoken' by our babies. This makes it very hard for us to see our babies and hear their cries for what they are: totally normal appeals for help and attention, and expressions of the need to be loved. Rather, we interpret any sign of our babies' discomfort or fussiness as a judgement about our parenting. For some of us, we might

188

feel a sense of rejection every time we cannot soothe our babies straight away or keep them engaged. In our mind, they make us feel the same way as our parents did when we were little: not valued, rubbish, incompetent . . .

Arun (five months) and Anna

Anna has been playing with her baby boy, Arun, for a while. Arun is enjoying his mum's attention, looking at her intently. She now moves her interaction with Arun up a notch and is blowing a raspberry on his tummy. With big wide eyes, Anna ramps up the tension, opens her mouth, and as she dives her head in his tummy, blows a loud raspberry.

To start with Arun is a little confused, but after the second go he relaxes and smiles widely at his mum, moving his legs quickly as Anna repeats the game, opening her mouth wide before diving again into his tummy. However, after another two goes, Arun is no longer smiling, and his look has become quite serious. Anna tickles him, saying: 'Come on, come on', and starts blowing raspberries again. Arun now looks uninterested and, as his mum tickles him again and brings her face closer to his, he turns away. Anna tries to bring his face back to the centre, but he turns it away instantly. Anna gets up and leaves . . .

When Arun initially shows delight in the raspberry-blowing, Anna feels like a good mum, relaxed and connected to him. But as soon as Arun shows the slightest sign that he no longer enjoys the game, Anna swings to the opposite extreme. Because of the way she was parented, Anna has developed, over the years, a hypersensitivity to criticism and rejection: it is as if Anna's inner-parent chatter is constantly pointing out to her all the potential signs of her shortcomings and failures: 'See, Arun is turning his head, which basically means he doesn't like you' or 'Arun is yawning, because he is bored with you'.

By putting a critical spin on everything, Anna's inner-parent-chatter stops her from being able to be curious about why Arun might be turning his head away and correctly interpreting his behaviour for what it is: that of a five-month-old baby who, after a lot of stimulation, needs a little rest. It is as if, when Arun turns his head away, Anna hears him saying: 'I don't like this game, and you are a rubbish Mum', when in fact he is saying: 'I love that game, Mum. It is a lot of fun, Mum, but can you stop for a minute . . . I need to catch my breath.'

Anna's inner-parent chatter interferes with her intuitive capacity to create the right emotional distance with her baby. Her inner-parent chatter either brings her too close or pushes her too far away from Arun, making it hard for her to really get to know him, and to respond to his needs appropriately. Instead of pausing, and patiently helping Arun to recover from a fun but very intense moment of connection, and perhaps putting into words what he is experiencing ('Oh, that was very tiring, all this raspberry blowing, and I can see you need a little rest'), or simply observing him kindly and silently, she insists – thus getting too close – that he carries on the game by trying to turn his face. When it is clear he doesn't want to do this, Anna cannot cope with the rejection. It makes her feel like a bad mum, and she walks away from Arun – becoming emotionally too distant from him. Over time, if this sort of communication failure is repeated, it can develop into a vicious cycle, with Arun gradually expecting less from Anna, who in turn will feel more and more like an incompetent mother and become less and less involved.

Turning the volume down

The best way to distinguish our inner-parent chatter from our own original thinking is to start consciously observing ourselves, and to notice how we react to our own babies – are we getting emotionally too close or too distant – especially when they are hard to soothe and we are feeling stressed. Indeed, it is when we are out of our comfort zone that we tend to go back to our default way of being, the one we learned with our parents when we were very little.

While we are observing ourselves being with our babies, as they use their voices and bodies to try to tell us what they need, we can begin to tune in to our internal chatter, and really listen to it and think about how it makes us feel. If we feel, for example, like we are being rubbish parents, being criticised, rejected, humiliated, we need to think about why this might be: is it really because we are getting it all wrong, or could it actually be that we are having an emotional reaction to negative feelings dredged up from long ago, now expressing themselves as rage, tears or anxiety? When we are irritated like crazy by our baby's cries, when we want to run away from them rather than pick them up, when we feel unloved by our baby, when we are full of anger and shame, we might ask ourselves: what is actually happening here? Where are these painful feelings coming from? Are they really being wished on me by this tiny little being? Or is it possible they are welling up from inside me, from a faraway place? Am I responding to my baby's cries right now, or am I hearing a version of my own parents' voice, telling me that obviously I am not very good at this?

As we become more aware of our inner-parent chatter, we can start to really notice how it affects the way we relate to our baby: is it bringing us too close to our babies or pushing us too far away? Of course, this is also going to vary, depending on how stressed or relaxed we feel, and what sort of night we have just had. The key thing is to be aware of it, and then, with patience and perseverance, and also lots of compassion for ourselves, allow our grown-up selves to start untangling what belongs to our chatter, and what is truly coming from our baby.

This untangling is an important and productive task for all of us, because it helps us realise that our babies are not our parents, obvious as that may sound. They see us with their own eyes, and they have their own voice, telling us over and over that they are hungry or uncomfortable, or maybe feeling lonely, confused or scared. They need our attention, our kind voice and our warm body to reassure them that we are here for them and love them even when they are yelling in the middle of the night.

So now that we have started to notice how much our inner-chatter could be affecting our parenting, let's try to turn its volume down. In an ideal world, of course, we would just tell our inner, critical, parental voice to shut up and leave us alone. But this is easier said than done, as we have been living with it for decades. That said, even as you have been reading this, perhaps you have begun to recognise your inner-parent chatter yourself, and how it can make you feel. If this is the case, then the process of managing it, of turning it down and tuning it out, is already underway.

And there is plenty more we can do that will gradually open up a space for a new nurturing voice, full of reassurance, empathy and warmth. Next, we are going to get to know our inner baby.

Inner baby

We have examined the voice of our inner parents, and already we have begun to recognise and address it, and turn it down a bit. Now let's look at that of our own 'inner baby' – an expression of intense feelings buried deep within us from the time when we ourselves were tiny. These forgotten feelings are inevitably stirred up when we have our own baby, and the strength and nature of them are likely to depend on how safe we felt as a child, which in turn connects with what our parents were able to give us when we were babies.

Most of us have generally managed to quieten our 'inner baby' as we go about our adult lives. We shut it up in the back of some deep mental cupboard so that we can let our grown-up selves be loud and in charge. But when our real babies enter our lives, and we have to face with such intimacy their extreme vulnerability and utter dependency on us (knowing that, without our complete devotion, they can even die), there is no more silencing our deep inner feelings. And as some of these feelings resurface – yes, we too were once that extremely vulnerable and utterly dependent – they can disturb us and disrupt our parenting. This is especially true if they have been locked away tightly, unaccessed for years.

Getting to know our inner babies

A good question to start with here is: how secure did we feel as we were growing up? For those of us who had parents who made us feel mostly safe, even when we were upset or cross, our inner babies are going to be pretty relaxed. This means that when our real baby starts crying or screaming, our inner baby will respond calmly and curiously. They will understand our real baby is upset and won't feel too threatened by it. This, in turn, will allow us to find the right emotional distance and respond to our real baby's distress in an ordinary and dependable way: not too fast or intensely so that we convey anxiety, but also not too slowly or reluctantly.

However, those of us who, as children, were parented in more neglectful, harsh or unpredictable ways, so that we rarely felt safe to be ourselves, may have developed a tendency to put a lid on our own emotions, especially the more negative ones. This will have left our inner babies full of unprocessed feelings of loneliness, fear, anger, confusion . . . And these unacknowledged, raw feelings in our inner babies can have two quite different effects on our capacity to find the right emotional distance with our babies. For some of us, our inner babies may feel so sorry for our real babies when they become distressed that an intense rush of compassion and concern for them pushes us to rush in and get too close to them. Alternatively, our inner babies may feel so upset and even alarmed by our real babies' distress that they cause us to panic and to pull back from them and become emotionally remote.

Let's look at each of these scenarios in turn.

When our inner babies make us get too close

Why is it that, in some of us, our inner babies find it so unbearable when our real babies show any ordinary signs of discomfort or distress? It is because our babies' cries remind us of a time when we too felt distressed, and our parents did not do enough to make us feel safe. In order to stop feeling the pain of this distress, our inner babies will demand that we intervene quickly and immediately. It's as if our inner babies become too friendly with our real babies, almost their twins, identifying very strongly with their feelings, and thus leaving little space for our grown-up selves to look at the situation objectively. Being too close, we see our babies' distress magnified and we try to take on their discomfort as if it were our own.

In the first days and weeks, this 'super-close' parenting is hardly going to be a problem for our babies. But if the 'rapid response' intensity continues for months and years, it can become unhealthy. As our babies develop, it is useful for them to gradually learn how to wait a little, so they can start to deal with some of the ordinary discomfort and distress of life on their own. We are not always going to be there for them, and we certainly cannot make the world a pain-free place for them. The process of learning to cope with the inherent difficulties of everyday life starts early on, as we saw in Chapter 7 – How do we know what our babies need? Our babies, ideally, will learn from experience that they do not need to shout for an instant response to their every fear or discomfort, and that if they trust and wait, then most of the time all will be well.

So if we notice that we feel a sense of intense anxiety when our baby cries, and an unstoppable need to rush in as soon as they make the faintest of noises, if we cannot bear watching them deal with the slightest struggle, if we catch ourselves always wanting to make things better, perfect even, then it is important to pause and acknowledge the part that our inner babies are playing in this. It is very likely they – and not our adult selves – who are really calling the shots!

Felix (six months) and Lisa

Lisa came to see me when her son, Felix, was six months old, because she was totally exhausted. She blamed her exhaustion on her son's lack of sleep and her having to constantly attend to his needs during the night. After exploring this during a couple of sessions, it became clear that it was not just during the night that Lisa was doing so much for her son. When Lisa related what she did for Felix, it was as if she were describing looking after a baby of six days old, rather than one of six months. Lisa was totally focused on making sure that her son did not experience any sort of discomfort. She still rushed to him as soon as she heard the first grizzle. It seemed she had not learned to distinguish between his different cries yet. To her they all sounded the same: sounds of distress that needed immediate attention.

Lisa explained that she grew up in what she thought was a happy but chaotic family. When we explored this further, Lisa acknowledged that while, yes, there were lots of happy moments, in fact the chaos was such that she never completely felt safe. Her parents had been very busy with their business, working long hours even at weekends. Her dad was quick to shout at everyone, especially after a few drinks, which would sometimes kick off huge rows between her parents. As a child, Lisa often felt scared and tried to appease her dad and to cheer up her mum.

It was hard for Lisa to remember moments when she had felt her parents were really interested in her. Instead, she spoke of how she felt she could never talk to them about her difficulties (she was bullied at school) and soon she learned to keep her problems to herself and put a lid on her emotions.

So now, when Felix is upset, Lisa's inner baby, still full of all those painful feelings of being ignored, takes over, and gets so close to her baby that she can no longer see him objectively and calmly assess his needs. Everything he does, especially when he is crying, becomes so magnified in her mind that it is as if her own anxious, unsafe inner baby and Felix have become one.

Working with Lisa meant trying to help her hear and listen to her inner baby's story of fear and confusion, so that she could see it as something completely separate from Felix's experience. By allowing herself to step back a little, and with her inner baby soothed by our sessions, she could slowly put a bit more distance between her and her real baby and start to distinguish his different cries and respond to them more fittingly. Lisa's relationship with Felix soon became richer and more enjoyable: instead of seeing Felix in such a black and white way, either upset or happy, she could now see him in colour, with many different shades of emotion and behaviour. Instead of responding urgently to his upset in a frightened and anxious way, she was curious about Felix's feelings and would try to understand what he was trying to communicate before stepping in. This also meant that Felix was allowed to experience a much richer spectrum of emotions. Knowing her son better, Lisa could help him to learn more about himself and better deal with the ordinary upsets and difficulties of life.

Most of us will not need to enter the therapy room to make progress in hearing and nurturing our inner baby. We can progress through increased self-awareness and a gentle commitment to 'observe and notice' what is happening between us and our babies. By engaging in this process, we will start to recognise that our reaction to our baby's discomfort is in fact coming from our own inner baby – our long-held memory of how it was for us. We can also begin to understand that our response is disproportionate – too close – to our real baby's level of distress. As we become aware of this repeating pattern, we can slowly let our grown-up selves be in charge and put more distance between us and our babies. And it is in this space that our grown-up selves can talk kindly to our inner babies, reassuring them that they have been heard and we are looking after them, and they can now go back to sleep.

When our inner babies cause us to turn away

Some of us, when confronted with the vulnerability of our babies and their complete dependence on us, will go in the very opposite direction. Instead of feeling sad and sorry for our real babies, we struggle to cope and get really panicky and upset and just want to run away.

Be reassured: this urge to run away is highly unlikely to make us abandon our babies, but it will put some unnecessary distance between them and us. In this case, when we are faced with our crying baby, we are unable to see their distress as simply their way of alerting us to some discomfort or fear; instead, we see it as something seriously alarming that requires a level of attention that overwhelms us and that we feel ill-equipped to provide. Emotionally and even intellectually, perhaps as our parents did with us, we 'minimise' our baby's distress and then rationalise our own minimal response. For instance, we might let our babies cry on the grounds that 'it's good for their lungs' or 'they can't be that upset, as they have just been fed' or 'they are just trying to get our attention . . .' Our inner babies effectively stop us from seeing our babies' ordinary needs with clarity and prevent us from connecting with them.

Soothing our inner babies

As we learned in the section above about getting too close to our babies, if we make a commitment to 'observe and notice' our tendency to be irritated by our baby's crying, and to be inclined to delay picking them up, we can start to recognise our minimisation of our babies' needs.

Remember that when our real baby is hard to soothe, when they cry and scream, our inner baby is very likely to wake up, metaphorically speaking, fussing, crying or screaming too. And suddenly we have not just one but two babies crying to be looked after. In the same way that it is important not to ignore our real crying babies, it is also important not to ignore our emotional inner babies. It is a good opportunity, now that we are parents, to attend to them and listen to what they have to say too, to let them tell their story, which now needs to be heard.

Indeed, the more we can be attentive to our inner babies' stories – and, as I've mentioned, some of those stories may be sad – the more power it will give us to decide how we want to parent. Do we want to repeat the past and parent the way we were parented? Or are our inner babies telling us that we felt a lot of pain and uncertainty when we were tiny? The great news is that now we have a chance to do things differently. We can choose to parent in the way that we wish we had been parented.

When we do this – when we give our own babies the sort of love and care we wish our parents had given us – then we not only provide them with what they need, we also soothe and comfort our own inner baby. When we pick up our crying babies, when we hold them tight in our arms, when we tell them kind words, we also metaphorically pick up our crying inner babies, holding them tight in our arms, and sooth-ing them with kind words. And so we create the ultimate virtuous cycle: once reassured, our inner babies can support us with our par-enting, and so help us to make our real babies feel safe and loved.

Finding the right distance

As we have seen throughout this book, there is no such thing as per-fect parenting. All of us will experience some degree of critical inner-parent chatter, and, even in the best of situations, our inner

babies will often have been left with some feelings of ordinary dissatisfaction from time to time. Now that we are parents, these two inner
voices may be keen to air those grievances, whether moderately or
intensely, more or less loudly. So, when we are stressed and tired, it is
easy to get lost in the cacophony of voices, and not hear what our real
baby is really trying to communicate. We may find ourselves sleep-
walking in our parenting, repeating easily and unconsciously the
mistakes of the past, and the way we were parented ourselves.

But this can all change when we turn up our awareness and hear the
critical chatter of our inner parents, and feel the intense emotions of
our inner babies, and recognise where they are coming from. Most
importantly, we can begin to see clearly that these emotional prompts
are not coming from our real babies.

Our real flesh and blood babies, with their real noises, and real needs,
will undoubtedly awaken voices and feelings from our past, and in so
doing they give us a wonderful opportunity. It is a chance to turn
things around. By really 'hearing' the voice of our inner parents, we
can choose a different, more compassionate voice. We can forgive
our inevitable, run-of-the-mill parenting mistakes and attend to the
inevitable, ordinary distress of our babies with love and compassion
instead of anxiety and self-judgement.

As for our inner babies, by paying attention to their feelings, we get
a chance to separate their needs from our real babies' needs. Our
competent adult self can thus tune into our real babies' needs,
making us better at soothing them and keeping them happy. With a
more contented real baby, our inner baby can relax a little, which in
turn gives our adult self more confidence and authority to tune out
our inner critic and turn the volume up of this new nurturing voice
of our own.

And remember that we have created our new nurturing voice with our babies' help: this is the one they are asking for, and because we are now hearing them, with less interruption from other, conflicting inner voices and past feelings, we can tune into it more easily. We can better negotiate the emotional (and physical) distance with our babies with freedom and creativity. Now we are not too close, not too far. We have found what is just right for us and our babies.

13

Healing from a traumatic birth

Giving birth (or being present at a birth) will be one of the most formative experiences of our lives. Our memories of it fill up our 'birth suitcase' and stay with us for weeks, months, even years. These memories can remain vivid and intense. And will often have a significant impact – whether positive or negative – on how we feel about ourselves and the people around us. Even more importantly for us here, and depending on how heavy or light our birth suitcase is, these memories will have a huge influence on how we feel about our babies, and how we interact and bond with them in the weeks and months ahead.

All births are, of course, dramatic and in some ways shocking; but what matters is how that drama and shock makes us feel. The majority of women in the UK report having good memories about giving birth. But a large cohort of around one in three mothers leave the hospital with anything from negative to traumatic memories, which means that a lot of us start our parenting journey with a heavy birth suitcase, feeling anxious, sad and angry, and with our confidence severely knocked.[1]

Negative memories and painful feelings are very likely to cloud our vision of our babies, and make it harder to enjoy being a parent to them. It is as if, after a difficult birth, we are also given a pair of glasses with 'trauma lenses', all fuzzed up by painful feelings. And from then on it is almost impossible to see our babies for who they are. Instead, we see a distorted version, which leads us to interpret and decode their behaviour and demands through the prism of trauma. We may, for example, attribute a meaning to their crying that has nothing to do with what our babies are trying to communicate, but rather with the legacy of our terrifying experience. Happily, as we will see, it is most definitely possible to clear these lenses so that we can see our babies for who they truly are – vulnerable little people who need us – and start enjoying being with them, and feeling fulfilled.

Of course, our babies have also got their own story of their birth, one they cannot put into words, and one that we often struggle to try to see from their point of view. Towards the end of this chapter we will see how thinking about our baby's experience of birth, and talking to them about it, can be highly restorative for us both.

No matter where we are in our parenting journey, whether we are just starting it, already deep in it or if it is a distant memory, we need to be mindful when unpacking our birth suitcase as we will all – mothers and birthing partners – find bits and pieces in it that will remind us that giving birth is not just physically demanding but emotionally complicated. So go carefully, at your own pace, pausing to breathe.

The roots of birth trauma

In Part One, we saw how helpful it can be to find out as much as possible about our potential birthing options in order to decide what an emotionally safe birth might look like for us, so we can hopefully put as many measures as we can in place to create that safe environment.

But we also have to face the uncomfortable truth that, no matter how much research and preparation we do, there will be aspects of the birth process that we will have no control over. And this is often where trauma takes root, because the sensation of not being in control can make us feel anything from discomfort to outright terror. So let's take a deep breath and look at where that loss of control is likely to occur.

The main thing that we have little or no power over is the progress of our labour and delivery. A labour that's going well can suddenly run into trouble, or be stalled by an unexpected medical complication that puts our own or our babies' health at risk. We may need to be rushed to an operating theatre, or find our babies being taken away to Neonatal Intensive Care Unit within minutes of being born. We may even have to face that our babies' lives, or our own, are in danger. Not surprisingly, during such a medical emergency, maybe even a life-or-death situation, we will experience alarming feelings of powerlessness and shock.

Thankfully, these unpredictable situations are the exception rather than the rule. But even in a situation where our birth is progressing 'normally', there are aspects that we cannot control. We live in a culture where we have largely handed over the management of the birthing process to others, in the medical profession, and unfortunately this does not always produce a good experience. Research shows clearly that it is more often the poor quality of the care mothers receive, rather than the birth itself, that leads to their feeling of having had a traumatic birth.[2] Indeed, the majority of women who remember giving birth as a traumatic event describe not a medical emergency or physical distress, but a range of negative experiences, from feeling unsupported by medical staff to being humiliated by them.

We will look at this particular aspect of the birth experience in more detail shortly. For now we just need to take on board the fact that, because we have so little control over our labour, and the quality of our care is often the luck of the draw, many of us end up not giving birth the way we hoped we would. We may start our labour with an idea, or even a plan, and then have a very different birth than the one we had hoped for or imagined, and that can leave us feeling hugely disappointed, with a deep sense of failure. Unless we have been receiving supportive care and attention, and, crucially, some reassurance that this divergence from our idealised plan is really not our fault, then it is very likely we will end up blaming ourselves.

If you are reading this *before* you have given birth, you may already be feeling a sense of mounting anxiety: please don't worry! Remember that most women have good birthing experiences. And the last thing I want to do is make anyone feel anxious or afraid. That said, those who report having had a traumatic birth make up a significant minority and I also believe it is important that we look at the positives and negatives in the round. It may seem counterintuitive but, by confronting some of the things that can go wrong, we are more likely to come out with a positive experience, if only because we have prepared ourselves for potential problems and so will better manage them if they do arise.

You may wish at this point to look back to pages 33–37 to remind yourself that you already have a plan and a sense of what your safe space might be. Remember that, while there are some universal features that generally enhance our sense of safety (low levels of light and noise, having people we know and trust alongside us . . .), the core of what makes us feel safe is highly personal to each of us and depends in large part on our personal history and circumstances.

In the rest of this chapter we are going to explore further what feeling emotionally safe means for us. And then, armed with a better sense of what the real obstacles to feeling safe while giving birth are, we are going to be able to refine our plan and put in place more strategies to help us deal with some of these aspects that we have so little control over.

If you are reading this *after* you have given birth (maybe shortly after, but also maybe months or even years after), and you have a persistent feeling that you are among the one in three women who were traumatised, whose birth did not go according to plan and who did not get the right support, and if you are still feeling anxious, sad and angry about the experience, then now is the time to bring those tormenting feelings to the fore and acknowledge them. No one should suffer these feelings in silence or alone. I hope that reading the rest of this chapter will help you put words to your painful feelings, and alleviate that sense of loneliness and kickstart your healing journey. Having our experience thoughtfully described and explained, and having our painful feelings compassionately acknowledged and validated, can help us to slowly accept and process them and gently put them to rest. Recovering from birth trauma is not only possible, it can often also be surprisingly quick and relatively simple. It can even turn a negative into a positive, leading to a process that is sometimes called 'post-traumatic growth'.[3]

However, if the thought of having to confront the past feels too frightening – studies suggest that between 4 and 5 per cent of us are so traumatised by the birth of our babies that we develop PTSD (in real numbers it means 30,000 mothers every year)[4] – and if what you have read so far is making you feel super anxious, I would urge you to try to work through your story with some professional guidance. There is some helpful information on how to seek help on pages 369–371.

Giving birth in the Western world: idealisation and minimisation

Although there are some positive signs that the culture is slowly changing, talking about traumatic birth is still fairly taboo in our society. Even just talking about birth in any honest way at all is taboo. Rather, we idealise the experience, both before and after it actually happens. We idealise it in conversation with friends or family, even at antenatal courses, or during consultations with our obstetrician or midwife. Images of the 'perfect birth' are everywhere. We see them in glossy magazines, on social media and in TV shows and films, where the arrival of our babies is generally presented as a quick and relatively clean event, with mum glowing and very little blood and certainly no poo or fluids, tears and stitches. We don't get to see babies with wonky heads because of the forceps; or scenes in which women look terrified because they think their baby might die.

Where did it begin, this concept of the 'perfect birth'? The answer is probably after the Second World War, when, with the advent of the NHS and advances in obstetric medicine, having a baby in hospital became the norm, and the 'perfect birth' became a medicalised one. In the 1950s, with the invention of synthetic oxytocin, medical induction became possible and gave us (or at least the doctors looking after us) the ability to decide when we would have our babies. Then, in the 1960s, with the advances in anaesthesia, having an epidural to eliminate all pain was the new big thing.

The idea of the perfect, pain-free medical birth has, of course, been challenged, and rightly so. But it is now being replaced by another idea of perfection. In the last decade or so, there has been a push back regarding the medicalised experience, with bestselling birth books and the most popular antenatal courses promoting the idea of a 'natural birth', with minimal intervention. And this, too, it is alleged, can, if all goes according to your perfect birth plan, be almost completely free of pain.

These books and courses are generally trying to empower women by helping them to be more in control of their minds and bodies, for example with the practice of hypno-birthing techniques. But, unfortunately, they often also imply that a successful natural birth is all down to the strength of one's commitment to and mastery of these techniques, which puts a lot of pressure on women to invest time and effort (and often plenty of money) in order to achieve one. Many women who have followed this path embark on their labour feeling that the responsibility for the success of their birth rests entirely with them: giving birth becomes an exam that they will only pass if they have prepared in the best possible way.

This approach is flawed on two accounts. First, it ignores the fact that, as we have started to explore, there are aspects of the birthing process that we cannot control. Second, it often skirts around the fact that, no matter how much prenatal exercise, controlled breathing and visualisation we do, giving birth is and will always be a painful physical process. And if we end up being one of the 40 per cent of women whose birth was meant to be 'natural' but turns out to be medicalised, or if we scream in pain, begging for an epidural, we are much more likely to berate ourselves, feeling that we have failed the 'natural birth exam' and let ourselves, our partners and our babies down. If, on top of this, we believe that most of our friends have 'passed' the natural pain-free birth exam – because that's how it seems when they talk about their experiences – this will further undermine our confidence and self-esteem.

More than just a physical event

Of course, society, and the medical profession, do not completely deny that there can be pain and anguish in childbirth. But even when the notion is exposed to the light of day, it is often 'minimised'. The extremity of the experience may be dismissed on the grounds that it is 'natural' (which is quite ironic, when it is the medical profession doing the dismissing!). Giving birth is somehow put in the same category as the things we do without thinking: sleeping, eating, digesting, passing bowel movements . . . By putting all the emphasis on the physiological aspect of birth, society and medics tend to minimise and diminish the vital fact that giving birth is always a hugely emotional event, with a deep and lasting psychological impact on our sense of selves. Research shows that if we feel the birth of our baby has been overall a positive experience, this helps us grow emotionally and be more confident. But if, on the contrary, our birth experience has been traumatic, we are likely to regress to a more anxious and fearful state. And to go on to have confusing and ambivalent feelings about our babies, and struggle to interpret their needs.

This minimisation of birth is magnified by the fact that the medical profession sees it as a contained, clinical event, which starts with our first contractions and ends with our babies coming out. And, as such, the only meaningful measure of success is whether mother and baby are alive and physically healthy. Women are made to feel that if they can walk out of the hospital with a healthy enough baby in their arms, they should be thankful, and should certainly not question, let alone complain, about what happened during the birthing process and how they might have been affected by it. Of course, we all want to leave the hospital carrying in our arms our healthy babies, but, with the emotional and psychological impact of giving birth being ignored, a significant proportion of us also leave the hospital with an unacknowledged sense of confusion and a whole range of painful memories that we feel we'd best just bury in the hope they will fade and eventually go away. In this way we can quite often be involuntarily complicit in the minimisation of our own experience.

Sue

I was hoping to have a natural birth with a healthy baby. In the end, after a failed induction, a failed epidural, hours of back-to-back harrowing labour pain, and blood pressure going through the roof, I ended up terrified of dying during an emergency caesarean section.

I often have scary memories of the birth of my daughter and feel really bad about it, but I try really hard to remember that, at the end of the day, she is a healthy and happy baby . . . So it doesn't matter how she came out.

Sue is right: it doesn't matter how her baby came out. But what does matter greatly is how *she* felt during the birth of her daughter. Feelings – especially about the big things in our lives – always matter, as they impact on our mental health and wellbeing, which in turn influences our relationship with our babies and the people around us. But, like many mothers, Sue has hung on to the idea that as long as her baby is alive it doesn't really matter that she felt disappointed and terrified. She is minimising not only what she felt at the time but also her residual 'bad' feelings about what happened, and has been left to start her parenting journey with her baby girl in quite a fragile position.

Let us please get something straight right now: we feel the way we feel because of what has happened to us. If we had a birth that had complications, we have been in a very scary situation, one that completely undermined our confidence, and perhaps even challenged our sense of self. And this all happened as we brought a new life into this world, and so all these frightening feelings about ourselves were mixed with fears for the safety and sometimes the survival of this new little person. That is certainly a recipe for trauma.

It may be helpful at this point to remind ourselves that we are not alone. I mentioned earlier that one in three women in the UK report having traumatic births. Well, around 600,000 women give birth every year in this country, which means that more than 200,000 women are traumatised every year. So there are thousands of women who are experiencing very much the same feelings as us at exactly the same time – somewhere else in our street, city, country or the world. Indeed, connecting with some of these other women might be an important part of our recovery journey.

Giving birth: a subjective experience

The experience of birth is very subjective, and what might feel traumatic for some mothers might feel fine, or even positive, for another. A super-quick home birth might feel quite scary for some, whereas for others it might feel like an exhilarating achievement, or the dream scenario. The same is true for the emergency caesarean section: some women find that, by the time this is decided upon, it's a huge relief, whereas others find the experience utterly terrifying. So it is the perception of what is happening at the time, and how we remember it afterwards, rather than the birthing event itself that often determines whether giving birth is felt to be traumatic or not.

Below are two very different experiences:

Esther

I knew that the all-natural birth was not for me. I was keen to be in the labour ward so I could get an epidural as soon as the pain became too much. I hoped there would be no tearing. However, when I was one week overdue, I was advised to be induced, and consented to it. This was straightforward and the contraction started five hours later. It felt that all was going to be fine.

But then we discovered that the baby was back-to-back and suddenly I was in complete agony – it was total torture for the next eight hours until, at last, I was 2 cm and could get my epidural. The next five hours were amazing, as I was very relaxed. But when I started to push, my baby got stuck and her heart rate became totally erratic . . . They tried everything: ventouse, forceps, episiotomy . . . the whole lot. I lost several litres of blood due to a postpartum haemorrhage and I ended up with a second-degree tear. The medical staff were incredible. I felt so looked after and involved that I managed to stay calm during the whole time and, despite everything that happened, I did not find the birth traumatic. And now I have my amazing little boy.

Natalie recalls a much less obviously traumatic birth, medically speaking, but from a very different perspective:

Natalie

I think I was really naive when I went to hospital with my first baby: the whole birth felt like a horror show from beginning to end. The only things I did not want – and said so clearly on my birth plan – was an epidural, forceps or ventouse. Sadly, the medical team did not seem to care much about the birth plan and even less about informed consent! What was traumatising was not the birth itself, which was, in the end, quite straightforward – it was the feeling that I did not matter. Things were done to me in such a way that I felt violated by the very people who were supposed to make me feel safe and care for me.

Esther describes a very long and painful labour followed by several invasive medical interventions, and yet she says she did not find the experience traumatic. In stark contrast, Natalie says that the birth itself was not particularly difficult, yet she felt traumatised. So what is it that made Esther feel good and positive about her extremely complicated birth and Natalie traumatised by a relatively straightforward birth? The main difference between these two mums is that Esther felt emotionally safe and actively involved in her birth, whereas clearly Natalie did not. Respect, nurturing and positive feedback from the medical team around Esther made a medical drama into a positive birth experience for her. And the complete lack of all those things made a comparatively simple birth seriously traumatic for Natalie.

The importance of good care

The act of giving birth puts us in a physically precarious situation but also in an emotionally vulnerable one. One thing that is particularly at risk – an important facet for our mental health – is our dignity. Most of us give birth in rooms we have never been in before, surrounded by unfamiliar smells and noises and by medical staff we have never met. In this strange place, generally at least half naked, we may be in terrible pain, very often moaning and groaning, crying, sobbing at times, shouting, screaming, swearing even, throwing up, possibly pooing . . . all in front of strangers who we have allowed to prod and poke us, and look at our most private parts . . .

Little wonder, then, that the strongest factor in determining whether we are going to perceive our birth experience positively or negatively is how well we are looked after by the medical staff. Our wellbeing, in this moment of complete vulnerability, depends hugely on whether the staff are making this awkward situation more or less awkward than it needs to be, whether they are compassionate or not with our pain, whether they take the time or not to explain and reassure us about what is happening, even whether they close the door or leave it open for everyone passing in the corridor to see and hear us . . . We need to feel that the medical staff are not only medically competent but also kind; that they are listening to us, taking our concerns and our pain seriously, answering our questions clearly and reassuringly. In other words, if we feel treated with respect and are able to trust the people looking after us, then even the most complicated and medicalised birth can leave us with very positive feelings. If we are a fully active participant in the birth process, it becomes easier to see labour pain as a sign that the process of giving birth is progressing well. It doesn't mean it is pleasant – and we might still want an epidural – but we know the pain means our babies are on their way and that helps to give us a sense of agency over the process.

If, however, we feel unsupported, unheard, belittled and patronised, that our concerns are being dismissed, our pain minimised or even ignored, that our behaviour or call for painkillers is judged, criticised, or mocked even, our bodies exposed unnecessarily, even the most straightforward birth is going to leave us with extremely negative feelings. In this instance, we will start to attribute a very different meaning to our painful contractions: no longer seeing them as part of the normal process of having a baby, but rather as a sign that something is going wrong and that we or our baby might be at risk. If this experience continues without reassurance, or gets worse without explanation, if we feel coerced into agreeing to interventions or procedures are performed without our consent, then the pain of labour is likely to become entirely associated with fear and a sense of having lost control. It will cause our mind and body to go into fight, flight or freeze mode, and giving birth will be marked in our memories as a traumatic event.

In a study where women were interviewed fifteen to twenty years after the birth of their babies about their experience, most of them could recall vividly what the medical staff were like.[5] Those who recalled the birth as a positive event, even if it had been clinically difficult, remembered being surrounded by a supportive, kind and compassionate medical team. Some women remembered almost word for word what the doctors or midwives had said to them, and how it changed their whole experience of the birth from negative to positive. But for those whose memories were traumatic, they recalled feeling criticised and undermined by the medical staff – some of the crushing remarks they received still ringing loudly in their ears.

We are touching on controversial ground here, of course. We are blessed with an amazing health service in the UK, which brings huge benefits to our lives. And when I share research about poor treatment by medical staff in birthing units, I do it mindful that many of them are working in a system that is run down and under-resourced. But it also needs to be said that the protocol of care they offer takes its cue from a deeply traditional, male-dominated system that has never sufficiently prioritised women's needs. And that a lot of the distress that mothers suffer could be avoided if the system of care in our Western countries was more compassionate in its whole approach to pregnancy and childbirth – more respectful of women's bodies and minds and more appreciative of the emotional complexity of giving birth. This is too big a conversation to be pursued in this book, however. The positive news, as we shall see, for those of us who have had a bad experience, is that we can recover from it, especially if it is acknowledged as such and not minimised or, worse, ignored.

Impact of birth on our sense of self

Those of us who have already given birth know that childbirth has a long-term impact on many different aspects of our lives. After a positive birth we are liable to look back and feel astonished that we managed to accomplish something so extraordinary – a feeling which leaves us with added confidence in our physical and mental strength. Thus we start our mothering journey more confident in our competency as a mother. In the longer term, the memory of the birth can even be a regular source of comfort and reassurance, not just in our parenting but in life in general.

By contrast, a traumatic birth often leaves us feeling defeated and bewildered. Why did nothing go as we expected? We struggle to recognise ourselves, and quickly start blaming ourselves (often as a desperate and clumsy attempt to keep a bit of control over our own story). We go over the event and start thinking that if only we had done a better birth plan or no birth plan at all, if only we had done more breathing exercises, if only we had paid for the premium ante-natal course, if only we had been more quiet or more loud, if only we had managed to control our distress better, if only we had pushed harder, if only . . . This self-blame leads us to feel guilty and think that we are in some ways responsible for the 'bad' birth. And, feeling perturbed about our physical and mental strength, we start our mothering journey unsettled and apprehensive.

This sense of failure on our part is often exacerbated if we have been separated from our babies straight away, either because we have been taken to ICU, or because our babies have been taken to a special care unit. Such separations generally happen when either the life of the mother or that of the baby are at risk, and they can be very frightening and brutal. There is rarely time to discuss or prepare us for this, and mothers and co-parents are often left in the terrifying situation of not knowing how their babies are for a long time. These early separations are especially likely to impact on a mother's ability to bond with her baby but also on the other parent's too.

I have been describing so far birth events that have been upsetting and traumatising for many thousands of women. Indeed, you may already be one of these women. And this may be the first time that you have had some of your frightening experiences described back to you. Reading about a past trauma can feel very powerful. If your heart is pounding, your breathing short and fast, do take a pause, and perhaps come back and read this at another time, when you feel a little more relaxed. You might also want to have someone you trust not too far away or even reading this chapter with you. Hopefully, thinking about your experience, how it has impacted on your sense of self, will also be helpful – it may even be the first step to letting go of any self-blame and bringing in more self-compassion. Try gently and kindly reminding yourself that, yes, what you went through was very frightening but you had no control over it and you are not responsible for it. Remind yourself that you and your baby survived it. Your physical and mental strength made it possible for you to withstand the experience. And that is something you should be proud of and that you should celebrate.

The impact of a traumatic birth on bonding

Bonding, as we have seen throughout this book, is a complex process. Despite all we have read on social media or in glossy magazines, it rarely starts with love at first sight, even for those who have experienced a positive birth and are full of oxytocin. For most people, falling in love with their babies takes time and effort and it is usually in the minutiae of caring for them that we get to know them and slowly but surely fall in love with them. It is therefore particularly important to appreciate how easily this subtle process can be disrupted by a difficult birth – especially if it's unacknowledged and unexplored.

Remember those distorted trauma glasses we were handed at the beginning of the chapter? It is time now to go a bit deeper, and look at the effects those glasses may have on us as we take our first steps with our babies. And as we go, we'll polish them up a bit, until hopefully they'll start to seem a little less fuzzy.

Meeting our babies for the first time after a traumatic birth

Meeting our babies for the first time after a traumatic birth may give us some very mixed feelings. It can feel like a huge relief that the birth is over; if we have our babies in our arms, it means that at least we and they do not have to suffer any more of the physical pain of labour and delivery. But it can also be quite a shock and a disappointment: totally exhausted and still in survival mode, bewildered by what has just happened, our mind often fuzzy with drugs, it can be hard to feel much for our babies. And it can be very distressing, particularly if what we do feel is very different from what we hoped and imagined we would feel.

Brace yourself for two upsetting words: indifference and rejection. Feelings of indifference towards, or even an impulse to reject, their new baby are quite commonly reported by traumatised mothers when they first meet their babies. It can be hard to grapple with those two words – or even to see them printed on this page. If either word resonates with you, you might straight away think of yourself as an unfit and bad parent and be overwhelmed by a debilitating sense of shame. But let's for a few minutes suspend our judgement about our own emotional fitness and try to understand just how we have ended up feeling like this about our babies.

Of course, feelings of indifference or aversion when we first meet our babies are immensely painful. But if we are still held in trauma, then they are not really surprising ones. We have just had a very frightening birth, and our bodies and minds have had to use all their incredible resources to survive the ordeal. So right at the time when we are handed our babies, we are in 'survival mode', not in 'falling-in-love mode'. Indeed, at a physiological level, we are very likely to be lacking the bonding hormone oxytocin, which is released most freely when we feel safe. Instead, we are primed for indifference or aversion/rejection, being full of cortisol and adrenaline, hormones which are more conducive to fighting and running away than to cuddling our babies.

In some cases, we may not even have had the chance to meet our babies after their birth, because they were taken straight away to Neonatal Intensive Care Unit (NICU). We all hope and expect that, at the end of our pregnancy and labour, we will have a healthy baby. So, if our babies need to be taken to NICU because they are born prematurely or need immediate medical intervention to save their lives, we are likely to feel totally unprepared and in shock. We are often left not knowing how they are doing for a long time, perhaps several hours, or even a day or more. Our fear and anxiety rise as the minutes pass, and there's very little chance that won't affect us deeply, and continue to do so over time.

Inevitably, we start blaming ourselves: if we had worked less, if we had worked more, if we had done less yoga, more yoga, if we had slept less, slept more, if we hadn't had that glass of wine on our birthday, surely our babies would not have problems. By the time we are finally able to go and meet them, which sometimes might be after several days, we may find them alone in their transparent cribs, attached to feeding tubes and noisy life-saving machines. Of course, we are thankful they are alive, but we have maybe, by then, and without much effort, managed to convince ourselves that it is all our fault.

Whatever the circumstances of our traumatic birth, if we do not feel that rush of intense warm feelings, if instead we feel nothing, or even some sort of aversion, let's remember that it is because of what has just happened to us, that we had no control over it, we are not responsible for it and we certainly should not blame ourselves. There will be a right time to fall in love with our babies – maybe this will be in a few minutes or hours, maybe in the days, weeks or even months to come.

Starting our mothering journey with a feeling of incompetency

Once home, and with our new trauma lenses fuzzed with the memories of our traumatic birth and already scratched with our newly acquired guilt and anxiety, we are liable to start our mothering journey with a nagging feeling of incompetency. Convinced that we have 'failed' the birth and that we have let down our babies, we may question our capacity to parent and even to keep our babies alive and well. As we find it hard to trust our instincts and intuition, we struggle to create the right distance between us and our babies, and can easily become either too involved with them or too detached from them.

Henry (four months) and Anika

After a traumatic birth – having felt a complete loss of control during her labour and thought her baby, who had to be taken straight to NICU, was going to die – Anika has become anxious in a way she has never experienced before. Now home, she finds the idea of leaving Henry alone even for a few seconds unbearable, so she carries him around in her arms all the time. When he is asleep, even though she has bought all the latest baby-monitors, she cannot stop herself from checking on him every few minutes, constantly worrying that something bad is going to happen.

As a result, she is totally exhausted. And it seems no amount of reassurance from her consultant that Henry is a healthy baby and completely out of danger can help her relax. She struggles to let anybody else look after him, even her own mother or Henry's dad. This puts a huge strain on her relationship with her partner, who feels undermined by Anika and sad that he is not 'allowed' to bond with his baby. But every time Henry is out of her sight, Anika is filled with fear and she is quickly taken back to those terrifying hours and days at the hospital. It is as if, by clinging on to Henry all the time, she can avoid being taken back to those dark times.

Sadly for Anika, the people around her are struggling to empathise with her. In fairness to them, they don't really have any idea what she has been through as she has not really told anyone in detail about the birth and the painful following days. Full of shame, she cannot bring herself to talk even to her partner.

And now everyone around her is starting to voice opinions about her parenting, and to make 'helpful' suggestions about what she should do: surely, now that Henry is four months old, it is time for her to put him down for a nap instead of keeping him in her arms? As a result, Anika feels criticised, which reinforces her feelings of incompetency and guilt, and gradually she has withdrawn increasingly into herself, preferring to stay home alone with Henry.

For Henry, having his mother on tap all the time means that he is developing well, smiling and enjoying interacting with his mum and other people. However, he is also a very anxious and clingy baby who cannot settle on his own and rapidly panics if he is away from Anika. Which only adds to Anika's belief that Henry cannot be left alone and needs her 24/7. And quickly a vicious circle is established, with Anika's trauma feeding into Henry's, and vice versa.

This is by no means the only story of how parents react to trauma. At the other end of the spectrum, instead of being too close to their babies, some mothers may keep them at arm's length, blaming themselves for the disappointment and terror they experienced, and doubting their ability to care for their babies. So they end up providing a very mechanical sort of care, finding it almost impossible to engage emotionally with their babies.

George (5 months) and Sarah

On the few occasions Sarah reluctantly sees her friends and family, they all think she is doing really well as a new mum. She and George are always dressed in spotless clothes, Sarah is always smiling and George quiet in his car seat. However, when Sarah is back home alone, she spends her days in a daze, often forgetting to wash and dress, living off crisps and biscuits. She goes through the motions of being a 'good' mum: washing, dressing and feeding George. On occasion, she even tries to coo to him – although she soon stops this, feeling self-conscious, as if she is being fake in some way.

She says she feels numb and has no warm emotions towards George even when he tries to smile at her or catch her attention. The worst times are when he cries: her body tenses, and she becomes frozen, unable to move to pick him up and comfort him; instead, she stays still on the sofa, watching him cry and cry. When George screams, she feels he is telling her off for being such a 'rubbish mum'. And within seconds she is overwhelmed by the same debilitating feeling of humiliation she experienced during his birth. She remembers one of the many midwives who looked after her telling her to stop being a drama queen, and that if, instead of screaming, she had got on and pushed, the baby would have been here by now. Not surprisingly now, all she wants to do is run away and hide rather than cuddle George when he screams. And as soon as George's dad is back from work, she hands him over and goes to her room to cry.

To cope with his mum's difficulties with engaging with him, George has started to learn not to expect much comfort from Sarah. Even when he is upset, he has stopped trying to get her attention and tends to avoid looking at her, moving his head from side to side when she is talking to him. This unfortunately reinforces Sarah's belief that George wishes he had a different and 'better' mum and that he doesn't like her and doesn't need her.

Both Anna and Sarah are looking at their babies through lenses fogged up by their birth trauma, so the perception of their babies is very much distorted. Anna sees Henry as a weak and vulnerable baby and cannot leave his side, whereas Sarah sees George as a highly critical baby and stays away as much as she can from him. These two mums have responded to their traumatic birth with very different strategies, but neither is enjoying their time with their baby. Sarah is parenting reluctantly, and Anna anxiously. They are both struggling to see their babies for who they are: two strong, healthy little people who are simply craving their mother's love and attention.

In some cases, our reaction to birth trauma may be more drastic. Whether the feeling starts as soon as we meet our babies or develops later on, some of us can feel unmanageable amounts of anger and resentment towards our babies, perhaps unconsciously blaming them for the 'failure' or terror of the birth. Witnessing their utter vulnerability triggers frightening memories of our own vulnerability during the birth. And this is unbearable . . . So to ward off these feelings, we shout and scream at our babies, we might even handle them in brusque and harsh ways. In this case, seeking professional help is essential and urgent.

Most mothers who feel they are not acting in their babies' best interest are extremely anxious about being judged and labelled a 'bad mother' and terrified that they will be reported to social services and have their babies taken away. They may want to go to great lengths to hide both their feelings and their behaviour. If you feel like this, it is vital that you seek support from a therapist who understands birth trauma. There, in a non-judgemental space and with someone who understands the impact of birth trauma, you will be able to tell your story and explore safely where your scary feelings about your baby come from. By acknowledging these feelings, you will start to make sense of them and finally be able to let go of the pain and self-blame that is tormenting you. Gradually, your trauma lenses will clear and you too will be able to enjoy your baby for who they are.

The impact of traumatic birth on our babies

It is often painfully hard to acknowledge our own birth trauma and its impact on our parenting. But it is even harder to bear the idea that our babies, too, could have been affected by their birth. Being born is a stressful event, even when all goes relatively smoothly: being pushed, by the force of our contracting uterus, through the narrow space of our pelvis, out of the five-star self-sufficient floating palace that we described in the first part of this book, to enter a world of gravity, noise and hunger, is bound to be quite a dramatic experience. So births when babies become stuck for a long time, or have the umbilical cord wrapped around their neck, or are delivered with a forceps or a ventouse to pull their head, or by an emergency C-section, are going to be an even more dramatic and probably traumatic experience for our babies (and, indeed, for us).

Some studies have shown that the way babies are born is likely to affect their physical health. Those born with the kind of problems and medical interventions described above are more likely to develop both short- and long-term health problems (jaundice, feeding difficulties, hypothermia, asthma, respiratory infections eczema, gastrointestinal disorders . . .) than babies born by spontaneous vaginal birth.[6]

However, it is the short-term emotional impact of a traumatic birth that interests us most here, and how the way our babies are born might impact on the way they relate to us. It would be reassuring to think that, even though we have been feeling intensely distressed during the birth process, our babies have remained oblivious to our trauma, and have been spared going through some similar feelings of anguish. Unfortunately, it would also be unrealistic. As we have seen

226

in the first part of this book, by the time they are born, our babies our sentient beings, very capable of experiencing emotions as well as physical sensations.

What they lack is the words to describe these feelings, so we will have to use our curiosity and try to imagine what it was like for our babies when they were born. To do this, we simply need to do what we do all the time when we interact with them, as we have explored in Part Two, and put ourselves in their place so we can attempt to understand what is going on for them. By paying attention to our babies' reactions when we talk to them, feed them, play with them, as well as to what is going on around them, we can begin to understand what makes them tick, what makes them happy or sad, what seems to make them anxious or agitated. And it is thanks to this carful observation of our babies that, gradually, we will start recognising a pattern in their emotional reactions to different situations and, by extension, perhaps begin to intuit how they might have experienced their birth. This will help clear our lenses a little more by allowing us to understand some of their trickier behaviour more objectively. It will be reassuring to realise that behaviours that we might otherwise interpret as a personal rejection or a proof of the failure of our parenting are much more likely to be rooted in our babies' experience of trauma during birth.

Before reading the next few paragraphs, remember that examples I have included are to illustrate my point about the behaviours of babies who have experienced a difficult birth, and not to be taken as general principles. If, for example, our baby got stuck in the birth canal, having an elbow in the way or facing the wrong direction, it might have felt very frightening and claustrophobic for them. And now they might show a real dislike when we cuddle them, especially if we hold them tight. This can help us understand better why some of our babies find being cuddled not such a soothing experience as we would hope.

Similarly, if they were born by ventouse or forceps, we can easily imagine that it must have felt intrusive and unpleasant to suddenly have these cold, hard objects grabbing their heads and forcefully pulling them. Perhaps now they show strong signs of irritation and distress when we touch their heads, and this might also explain why they are struggling with feeding: their skulls can get quite squashed and bruised by these harsh instruments during the delivery, which can affect their facial nerves and muscles, making the process of latching on physically painful (I will explore this further in Chapter 14 – Feeding).

Babies who were born by emergency caesarean will certainly have experienced a real sense of stress – a feeling that will have been compounded by suddenly being pulled out into the bright light and noise of the theatre room. These babies might now seem quite easily distressed and hard to settle, especially in loud, busy places, and need constant reassurance that things are okay.

A baby who ended up being taken to NICU (Neonatal Intensive Care Unit) straight after their birth, meanwhile, will very likely have felt lonely and somewhat abandoned. Some of these babies might now be quite anxious and struggle when they are left on their own, while others may be wary and reject our care. And some of our babies might even, like us, feel somehow responsible for the difficult birth and appear quite withdrawn, perhaps not feeling that they are worthy of our love and care.

Of course, we will never know for sure how our babies felt during their birth, and how that has shaped their feelings about being parented. What we can be sure of is that the feelings they have are intense and real. And it is important that we try to use our imaginations to consider things from their point of view. This will help us to exercise compassion for both them and for ourselves. And, if things are difficult, the feelings are painful and the interactions between us seem complex and confusing, then at the very least we can try to understand and to remind ourselves that we do not need to ascribe blame, either to our babies, or to ourselves.

Just by acknowledging the importance of their distressing birth experience, by trying to empathise with them, we are likely to become gentler and more forgiving towards them; and this gentleness, in turn, will help them with their feelings.

As we have seen throughout this book, the interaction between parents and babies is extremely intricate. And it is often hard, especially when trauma is involved, to determine the direction of causality: is it our behaviour that causes our babies' behaviour or their behaviour that affects ours? It is a classic chicken and egg story. And we and our babies can easily become stuck in a vicious circle of misinterpreting each other's reactions. One way to turn this vicious circle into a virtuous one for both us and our babies is to 'tell' each other our stories. We will learn more about how to do this in the pages to come.

Recovering from birth trauma: wanting to be seen and wanting to be heard

Although there are often commonalities, every traumatic birth story is unique. However, I hope that by sharing the story of one young mother I worked with, and how she and her baby recovered from their traumatic experience, I can help show that it is possible to lift the shadow of a difficult birth – even to do so fairly quickly – and that we can ultimately find ourselves feeling we are stronger parents for it.

Clara came to see me when her baby girl, Izzy, was five months old. She was feeling very low and distressed and worried that her difficult birth and sudden separation from Izzy just after she was born were impacting negatively on her bonding with her baby. As is usual with this sort of presentation, I offered six initial sessions.

Izzy (five months) and Clara

Clara and her partner got pregnant easily and, generally, Clara enjoyed her pregnancy. However, Clara was diagnosed with gestational diabetes and was told she would need to be induced. Deeply disappointed, Clara had to let go of her dream of a home birth, but carried on nonetheless with her hypno-birthing classes.

At thirty-eight weeks she was induced, and at first the labour seemed to be progressing well, if quite slowly. But then her baby got stuck in a back-to-back position, which was extremely painful for Clara. She was offered an epidural, which she reluctantly accepted. She is not sure why, but it took nearly two hours for the consultant and his team to find the right spot in her spine. Not surprisingly, Clara found the experience very stressful. From then on Clara's recollection is quite hazy . . . All she remembers is the feeling of panic that overtook her when, as Izzy was still not turning and her heart rate was becoming very erratic, the medical team tried without success to deliver her by ventouse. Eventually, Izzy was born by forceps, but with her umbilical cord around her neck. As she was struggling to breathe, she was rushed straight away to the Neonatal Intensive Care Unit. In the meantime, Clara, who had suffered extensive tearing, was starting to haemorrhage and was herself rushed to the operating theatre for surgery.

It would be several days (she couldn't remember how many exactly) before Clara would be able to meet her baby, as she had to stay in the maternity ward to recover. There, surrounded by other mums and their newborn babies, Clara felt extremely sad, lonely and abandoned. She felt that no one had really explained to her what was happening and could not understand why her partner was spending all his time with their baby. Alone on the ward and watching the other mums, Clara became painfully aware that she was missing the first days of Izzy's life. When, finally, she was allowed to go and see Izzy, Clara's dad had to take her in a wheelchair to the Neonatal Intensive Care Unit. There, Clara became very distressed when she saw Izzy with all the tubes and drips attached to her little body. Izzy was being tube fed and receiving antibiotic drips. But things got worse when Clara, who was determined to breastfeed her baby, struggled to get Izzy to latch on. For Clara, still trying to recover physically from the aftermath of the birth, bewildered by the lack of support, this sad first meeting with her baby daughter felt like just the latest calamity in a succession of disasters: why was this happening to her? What had she done wrong? If only, if only everything could have been different . . .

Therapeutic work

When I first met Clara, Izzy grabbed my attention straight away by making very confident eye contact and smiling widely at me as we were walking down the corridor to the consulting room. It was impossible to ignore her. She wanted to be seen and, as we found out later, she also wanted to be heard!

During our first session, Clara sat Izzy on her knees facing me, holding her tightly on her lap. As Clara explained that she was coming to see me because she spent most of her day crying and was not sure she was bonding with her daughter, Izzy stayed very quiet. She had somehow lost her earlier liveliness and she looked quite withdrawn. However, when Clara described the birth in more detail, she became quite agitated. And so did Izzy, who started to wriggle on her mum's lap. Then, as Clara explained how Izzy was born with the cord wrapped several times around her neck, she burst into tears; and Izzy started kicking her legs quite strongly and making very loud sounds. I pointed this out to Clara, who bent slightly sideways to get a better look at her daughter. I started to talk to Izzy, saying: 'Mummy is telling me that it was very scary when you were born. You had your umbilical cord around your neck and it must have been hard to breathe . . .' Izzy made more loud noises, looking at me straight in the eyes. I carried on: 'Yes, that must have been so scary for you, Izzy . . . It was scary for Mummy and Daddy too and the doctors . . . But they took the cord away and you felt better, didn't you? . . .' Izzy listened attentively and calmed down quickly.

During the session, it was obvious that Clara was finding it difficult to recollect coherently what had happened during her birth and the subsequent days spent at the hospital. It was hard for me to follow her story and many times it made me feel as if I was on a boat in the middle of a storm, and I had to concentrate very hard in order to hold on to all her words and not get lost. I wondered if, when describing her birth, Clara, too, felt that she was being tossed about at sea? We explored how it might be helpful to her recovery if she had a better understanding of what happened at the hospital, as this might make her feel more in control of her birth story. I suggested that she could perhaps book a birth debrief appointment at the hospital to go over her notes with a midwife. She said she could not imagine going back there yet and suggested instead talking to her mum, who had been at the birth.

In the second session, two weeks later, Clara came in and sat Izzy on her knees facing me, exactly as she had done in the first session. Again, Izzy was lively to begin with, but then became quiet and rather detached. Clara started the session by talking about the experience of visiting Izzy in the care unit, how noisy it was and how upsetting to see Izzy attached to all those tubes. At that moment, Izzy, looking intensely at me, started to make very clear and loud sounds, to the point, again, that we could no longer ignore her. As we listened to Izzy, Clara, again moving slightly so she could see her daughter better, said: 'I think she's got a lot to say about this.'

I agreed with Clara, and as I had in the previous session, I talked directly to Izzy, trying to imagine what it must have been like for her and acknowledging how frightening this must all have been, but also reaffirming her parents' love and concern: 'It must have been so scary for baby Izzy to be all alone in this big room full of noisy machines and with people you did not know . . . You must have wondered where Mummy and Daddy were . . . But Mummy and Daddy were not far, and they came as often as they could, because all they wanted was to be with you, Izzy, with their little baby girl . . .'

Although Izzy was unable, of course, to understand the meaning of my words, it was evident she was picking up on the mood of the story, and responding to my interaction with Clara as well as Clara's lessening anxiety. As we have seen in Chapter 7 – How do we know what our babies need?, communication between parents and babies has nothing to do with language, but more to do with the emotionality of our interactions. Now that Clara had been able to bear hearing, in my words, what Izzy must have been feeling, she was more at ease and Izzy was responding to this change.

Later on in the session, Clara explained how Izzy suffered from reflux and spent most days and nights crying. She said that when her partner came home he often found them both crying. Clara described how powerless and completely rubbish she felt that she could not make Izzy better and stop her crying. She had tried everything: feeding her, rocking her, singing to her, everything . . . nothing worked. All she wanted in those moments was to run away from the house and Izzy. But she knew she couldn't leave Izzy alone. Now in tears, Clara admitted to me that she ended up screaming at Izzy, telling her how she hated her . . . She knew she shouldn't shout at her baby, but she said she couldn't control herself. I gently asked what sort of thoughts and feelings went through Clara when Izzy cried: she said she felt that Izzy was shouting that she did not love her, that basically she was telling her off for being such a bad mum. Sobbing, Clara said that Izzy deserved a better mum. Together, Clara and I were able to link those feelings of not being valued and of being criticised to her huge disappointment around the way Izzy was born and the way she was treated by some of the medical staff, who she felt had implied she was not making enough effort to push Izzy out. Slowly, Clara could see that it was her trauma that was distorting her perception of Izzy's behaviour. And that her anger had little to do with Izzy, but rather with her unhappy experience at the hospital.

Clara then talked in more detail about Izzy's reflux and we were able to link Izzy's extreme reaction – of crying inconsolably – whenever the milk came out of her nose to her experience of being tube fed through the nose while in the NICU. As Clara was describing the milk coming out of Izzy's nose, Izzy again picked up on her mother's heightened emotion, and started to become very agitated, making high-pitched shouty noises, moving her arms and legs as if wanting to run away, yet looking intently to me. As I pointed out this change in behaviour to Clara, Clara said: 'Gosh, I can see that she has a lot more to say on this as well . . .' And I added: 'That's right, Izzy. You have a lot to say . . . And I think you are telling us that, yes, it was horrible and very painful when the doctors put all the tubes in your nose, that you felt very scared . . .' Izzy quietened straight away, her legs and arms now immobile, but she was still listening to me intently, her eyes wide open. I carried on: 'Yes, you had all these tubes in your nose and now every time the milk comes out of your nose it reminds you of the tubes and the scary time you had away from Mummy and Daddy at the hospital . . . And that makes you cry and cry . . . And sometimes Mummy thinks you are cross with her . . . But I think you are telling us that when you cry it is not because you are cross with Mummy, but because you are very sacred, maybe you think you are back in the hospital . . . But Izzy, you are here now with Mummy, and you don't need to go to hospital, you don't need tubes in your nose, you and Mummy are safe and all well now.' Responding to the gentle assurance in my voice, Izzy now became calm and looked relaxed.

Three weeks later, Clara and Izzy came for their third session. Clara came in and sat Izzy on her knees facing me as before. She explained she had talked quite a lot with her mum and her husband and now understands better the succession of events. She said that talking to them had helped her make peace with what happened at the hospital. She also said she was starting to feel more confident and was now taking Izzy to a baby group every week. She had even been able to go out for dinner with her two best friends, leaving her husband to look after Izzy for the whole evening.

Clara was now approaching the end of her maternity leave and was feeling very nervous and anxious about going back to work and leaving Izzy in a stranger's care. But as she had no choice, she and her husband had been meeting several childminders and felt they had found one they trusted and who seemed to share their views on parenting. Izzy had already had a few mornings there and seemed happy. Clara explained how guilty she felt about leaving Izzy with the childminder, but she also described how excited Izzy was to see her every time she picked her up. We explored together how these short separations from Izzy seemed to be helping Clara to take the measure of Izzy's love. Izzy's excitement when reunited with her mum became a tangible proof for Clara that Izzy loved her and enjoyed being with her.

Although Clara wanted to end our work then, I persuaded her to come for one more session. I still had not witnessed much eye contact or interaction between Clara and Izzy and wanted to explore that with Clara. However, when Clara and Izzy came for their fourth session three weeks later, Clara sat as usual with Izzy on her knees, but this time Izzy was facing her! I knew then that this would be our last session.

As Clara took her coat off, I could see she was wearing a black t-shirt saying 'I [HEART] my Mum' in big red letters. Clara explained that she felt that a cloud had been lifted and how she was now feeling her old self again. She said that coming to see me had allowed her to look at her experience from a different perspective. Not only was she more at peace with what had happened, she could now see it as a more positive experience for both of them. Clara explained how she felt stronger now, maybe more confident than before she had had Izzy, and how she could even cope with the idea of having another baby.

Every time Clara spoke to me, Izzy tried to grab her mother's attention back by looking intently at her face and making sharp and short vocalisations, as if calling her. Clara could not ignore her for long, and quickly intuited what was going on for Izzy: 'You're finding it annoying, Izzy, aren't you, when I talk to Marie . . . you want to be part of the conversation too . . .' Holding her little hands and shaking them gently, she added: 'Hey Izzy, what is it you have to say now?' Izzy, locking her eyes with her mother, wriggled her legs and arms, clearly delighted to have managed to gain her mother's full attention. I commented how I thought Izzy just wanted to say how happy she was to be on Clara's lap, how she was enjoying her chatting. I told her I thought she was saying: 'I love being with you, Mummy.' Clara agreed that she could now see that Izzy enjoyed being with her and she felt confident about their relationships and proud to be her mum.

Clara spent most of the last session interacting with Izzy, smiling at her and kissing her, laughing and cooing with her. Even if at times I felt a little redundant, it was a real pleasure for me to witness how much Clara and Izzy were now enjoying each's other company.

I don't know how Izzy and Clara are now. But what is clear is that carefully unpacking her birth suitcase helped Clara to get back on track with a bonding process that, because of the traumatic birth, had started on the wrong footing. It only took four sessions for Clara to feel her old self again, but it can take other parents longer; and, of course, parent-infant psychotherapy is not a magic lenses-cleaning tool, and it is not for everyone. For some parents, just making the difficult and courageous choice to come and seek professional help is hard enough. When we feel like a bad parent, that is a brave decision, and I am sure every time Clara drove to my consulting room she felt nervous and anxious.

When Clara first came, she was feeling very low, spending most of her time crying and wanting to run away from her daughter. She was in the midst of her trauma, which clouded everything she did and felt. Having a therapeutic space where she could tell her story and feel that someone was listening not only to the meaning of her story but also to the emotions carried by her words, silences, slight movements of her body, tears and smiles, meant that Clara felt heard but not judged. This empowered her to replace her self-blame about the difficult birth with self-compassion for herself and her baby.

Working with a therapist also meant that Izzy could now tell her mum her side of the story. She too had been traumatised by the process of being born, which often made her overreact to some of the ordinary sensations she felt, and, in the safety of the therapeutic space, Clara learnt how to 'listen to' Izzy's difficult story. Indeed, although intimately linked by their shared birthing experience, Clara and Izzy had drifted apart because they could only see each other through their own trauma lenses. By telling and listening to each other's story, they could again be united and enjoy each other.

The healing journey

The first step towards healing is to acknowledge how what has happened is making us feel: to put words to these feelings, share them if we possibly can, and certainly spare ourselves from any blame. It is helpful to do this with a therapist. But finding a therapist who can appreciate the impact of a traumatic birth is not always possible and is by no means always necessary. Rather, we can try to find our own way to clean our trauma lenses. Hopefully what you have read in this book so far has already helped you on the path to healing. Let's now see how we can take the process further, using some specific tools.

Talking to someone who can validate our feelings

Central to the recovery process is feeling able to talk to someone who can take our feelings seriously and hear them out. Indeed, in this situation, it can be more helpful to simply be listened to, and feel heard, than to be given actual 'advice'. So it is important to think carefully about who we are going to talk to, as a lot of people find it hard to listen to someone's difficult feelings; they may struggle to empathise, and therefore be inclined to minimise our feelings, or be in a hurry to help, quickly offering solutions without really hearing us. You will probably know instinctively which friend, sibling, parent or colleague has the best temperament for listening patiently. And when you think you have found the right person, perhaps explain to them why you need this conversation and how you need them to listen to you.

Choose a moment when you (and your interlocutor) are feeling as calm as possible. Doing some grounding breathing can help with this. It is also best to choose a moment when neither of you have to rush somewhere afterwards. Remember that you don't need to talk for hours. In fact, putting a time limit (you could set an alarm on our phone) on how long you are going to talk about your traumatic birth can be really helpful: twenty, thirty minutes can be a good start. Generally, it is best not to talk for more than hour. Feel free to stop at a moment when you feel a little bit better (even if it is only after a few minutes). You will probably need several conversations. Some of you might want to plan and agree on those 'talking' times and put them in the diary. Others might prefer the spur-of-the-moment approach. Also, do not forget that it might take time for your 'listener' to get it right. So be patient.

If you choose to talk to your baby's other parent, it is important to acknowledge that he or she could also have been traumatised by the birth. So having a conversation around how they, too, feel about what has happened is essential. And you might end up realising that you are far less alone in your distress than you thought. Talking about your shared experience of the birth will help you both process the difficult memories.

Regaining control of our stories

As we have seen, it is largely the overriding feeling of loss of control that makes us experience the birth as a traumatic event. Therefore, finding a way to take back ownership of what happened to us, even after the event, will help in the healing process. And a good place to start is by trying to put the details of it in some sort of chronological order.

As with most traumatic events, it can be hard to recall them in a coherent way. We are left with a sense of chaos, uncertain what exactly happened or when it happened, and full of unanswered questions. This is especially true if the medical staff were not able to explain calmly and clearly at the time what was going to happen next and why. The birth process can then feel like a long list of sudden, random and even unnecessary interventions. And our rigorous brains do not like fuzzy stories: we like stories to be coherent and logical, with a beginning, a middle and an end. So finding a way to put the story back together can be hugely therapeutic.

Comparing notes with your birthing partner(s) is often the most helpful way of doing this. They might not only be able to validate your feelings but also to confirm that what you thought might have happened really happened: 'No, you are not mad, that is exactly how it went. And, yes, it was scary . . .' With time, this might pave the way for a mutual validation of your shared experience: 'You are right, it did seem outrageous; they really did talk to you like that!'

Either way, once the frightening and confusing events are ordered and make more sense, and as we gradually see more clearly the possible rationale for some of the decisions taken during our labour and delivery, it is easier not to worry so much about them. For instance, all the interventions leading to an emergency caesarean or the use of forceps, which felt random and terrifying at the time, can start to be understood and finally accepted as necessary lifesaving interventions.

Changing perspective from victim to survivor

Bringing some order and logic to our birth, reclaiming the narrative, can help us gradually shift our perspective from that of victim to that of survivor: we are no longer just the person to whom things were done, but the person who survived it, who is very much alive and well with our baby.

When we are still in the grip of trauma, all those nightmares, flash-backs, all the ruminating thoughts about the birth that seem so constantly present in our mind, can make us feel like we are still stuck in a terrifying loop that's repeating itself all the time. Talking to someone can help us bring meaning to the event and can grad-ually help us let go. Slowly, steadily, as we sift through the memory cards of our experience, and process the emotions they provoke, we can start to push those traumatic events back to where they belong: in the past.

Birth notes

Another way of regaining some control over our narrative is by accessing our medical birth notes, either directly or by booking an appointment with the debriefing service, something that most hospitals now offer. It is an opportunity to share our perceptions of the birth and to hear the other side of the story, the medical one. When this is done well, it can be extremely therapeutic – with parents either perceiving the process as an apology, or getting an actual apology from a midwife or consultant on behalf of the team for the way the birth turned out.

Joining a therapeutic group

For those of you who feel that your closest and dearest are not the right people to talk to, joining a support group might be the right step. Listening to their stories, empathising with other parents who have had scary experiences of birth, even if they are very different from yours, and watching them interacting with their babies, can help lessen your feeling of self-blame and be more compassionate with yourself.

Resolution – writing it down

As the 'true story' of your birth experience starts to come together, it may be a good idea to write it down. You don't have to do this in one go. You can always come back to it and edit it and then write more as you gain greater clarity. This work in progress may take weeks, months or even years, and you may never feel it is completely finished. But at whatever stage it is, whenever you return to it, it will hopefully act as an anchor and reference point for your emerging truth about the birth. This can be a hugely helpful therapeutic tool.

Talking to our babies

Finally, as we saw with Clara, having a conversation with our babies, telling them our stories and, crucially, listening to theirs, will provide a great source of mutual healing. Indeed, when the time feels right, this may be the most therapeutic and healing thing of all. It is probably best not to rush to this exercise: better to have the 'what really happened' conversation with your chosen talking partner first, and also, ideally, be some way into writing down your story, and only then find a time to gently share that story with your baby.

Choose a moment when you are both calm at home, perhaps with someone you trust not too far away. As with talking to your partner or other chosen person, you don't need to talk for hours – a few minutes' conversation will be more than enough. Holding your baby close to you, so that you can easily observe their reactions, tell them just as much as feels right.

'You know, it was so nice to have you in my tummy . . . I could feel you kick and kick . . . and then, one day, it was time for you to be born. I couldn't wait to meet you, I was so excited . . . maybe you were excited too to meet me? I thought everything would be okay, but things went a bit wrong and I got really scared . . . There were doctors everywhere and I couldn't understand what was going on . . .'

While you're talking to them, some babies might stay quite passive (although it doesn't mean they are not listening) or, like Izzy, they might display an obvious reaction, verbal and/or physical. Some babies might even cry. Observing these reactions is crucial, as it is our chance to 'hear' their stories. And by putting simple words to their experience, we can let them know we have heard them:

'I imagine that for you, too, it was quite scary . . . Do you remember when all the doctors came in and there was a lot of noise . . . You must have been so frightened when they put the ventouse on your head . . .'

It is very important to try to finish this conversation with our babies on a positive note, as neither of us should ever forget that, even though our birth was scary and painful, we have both survived all the difficulties and we are now very much alive and together.

'I am sorry things happened the way they did, but you are here with me now, in my arms, and we are okay, we have made it, we are very strong, you and me: we are a good team.'

As we have seen throughout this book, to be seen and to be heard are two of the most important experiences for us all as human beings. It is vital for us as parents, and vital for nurturing the healthy development and emotional growth of our babies. First, we as mothers need to make sure that the true story of our birthing experience, and the painful feelings it may evoke, both physical and emotional, have been heard and witnessed by an adult who listens and cares. And then we need to share that story with our babies. However strange it seems to be talking about hospitals and procedures and fears and anxieties to a tiny person who cannot yet speak or reply with words, sharing all these gnarly facts and feelings with our baby is perhaps the most important act of all. Everything they need to understand will be communicated in our tone, our eyes and our body contact. And, in return, they, in their own way, will tell us what we need to hear: their story.

Four

What we do with our babies

14
Feeding

F eeding our babies and putting them to sleep can quite quickly come to seem like rather mundane, even boring, activities – the daily parenting tasks that just have to be done. And yet, feeding and sleeping are so obviously essential to our babies' well-being that the stakes, both physical and emotional, can run high. No wonder that these tend to be the two undertakings that parents and babies most struggle with. As for playing, you will by now have gathered that this, too, is an activity that is equally vital in its way . . . and one that does not always come naturally.

So, let's take the time to explore what exactly is happening between us and our babies when we feed them, play with them and put them to sleep. These activities may seem routine to us, but for our babies they are extraordinary emotional experiences – and hopefully, as the next few chapters progress, we will begin to understand that they can be so for us too.

Feeding . . . the ultimate moment of intimacy with our babies

Since our babies left the snugness of our tummies, we have engaged with them in a never-ending dance of both togetherness and of separation. It is a dance we perform throughout the day and night: we bring them very close to us when we feed them and let go of them when we put them to sleep. And this is why feeding and sleeping can get so tricky. Managing a fluid movement between being very close, almost physically merged with our babies when we feed them, and then being totally separate from them when they sleep, can be challenging both for baby and for us.

It is easy to think of feeding our babies as an activity with a purely physical purpose, i.e. to make them put on weight and grow. But there is another way of looking at it: as we hold our babies in our arms, close to our bodies, and give them some milk from our breast or a bottle, we are not only giving them plenty of protein and nutrients for their physical development, we are also giving them plenty of emotional food to feed their mind and grow their brain.

When we feed our babies, the thoughts we have, the way we hold them, look at them, talk to them: all of this allows us to pass on an incredibly rich and nourishing 'mind-milk', which helps them develop their consciousness and sense of self, just as much as the breastmilk or formula provides fuel for their bodies. As with all aspects of the dance we are dancing with our babies, this activity helps lay down new neural pathways: some of the foundations of the all-important Feeling Safe Roundabout (see Chapter 6 – Building our babies' brains).

And the nourishment is mutual. When feeding goes well, we too are emotionally sustained by the physical closeness and calm that we experience with our babies. It is a privileged and special time, an opportunity for deep bonding and rich communication, whether we are offering them milk from our breast or from a bottle, or from a combination of the two.

The more we can make ourselves aware of the intensity of this inter-action, the more we will be able to make the most of the experience. We are going to explore how to do this in the next few pages. How-ever, feeding isn't always straightforward. And later on we will look at some ways of helping to keep the emotional nourishment flowing, even when the practicalities of delivering the milk, by breast or bottle, are not going as smoothly as they should.

Rosie (four months)

Rosie is lying on the sofa, kicking her legs and moving her arms around. Elena is talking to her: 'I know you are hungry . . . just a minute . . . I am getting all the things I need.' As soon as Rosie hears her mother's voice, she turns her head towards the sounds and then follows her with her eyes as her mother goes around the room collecting her things.

Elena is now sitting on the sofa with a glass of water, her phone and a muslin next to her on the little table. Rosie's legs and arms are moving a little faster and she is making louder little 'O' sounds and putting her hand in her mouth. As Elena bends sideways to pick her up, their eyes meet and stay locked for a long time. Elena smiles a big wide smile. 'I am here now,' she says, as she lays Rosie on her lap and starts unbuttoning her bra. Rosie is now making continuous gurgly sounds, kicking her legs even more vigorously and stretching her arms towards her mother and pushing into her breast. Elena says softly: 'Yes, it is coming . . . I know you are hungry . . . just be a little

patient . . . one more popper and that's it . . . here we go . . .'
Rosie's leg-kicking reaches a new level of intensity.

Rosie latches on to the breast. Shutting her eyes, she starts sucking with great vigour, her whole body going almost stiff. After thirty seconds or so she relaxes a little and her sucking becomes slower and more regular. While Rosie is feeding, Elena looks at her baby, half caressing with her eyes, half inspecting her, scanning slowly from the top of her baby's head to her feet. Every now and then she stops and strokes Rosie's cheeks with her fingertips, scratches her skull, or holds her hand, letting Rosie fold her little fingers around her index finger. Gently, Elena opens Rosie's hand, admiring each tiny finger. She looks down to her toes, and rearranges Rosie's socks, one of which has almost come off with the kicking, and tucks her babygrow more neatly around her nappy. The 'inspection' over, she looks at Rosie's face. After a while, Rosie opens her eyes, searching for her mother's face. Their eyes meet, and mother and daughter are again looking at each other.

Ten minutes into the feed, Elena's mobile phone pings. Elena and Rosie jump a little bit, and Elena picks up the phone and checks the message. Rosie has not stopped looking at her mother's face. While she is reading the message, Elena frowns a little. Rosie, as if in imitation, frowns a little too and stops sucking, but keeps the nipple in her mouth. With one hand, Elena types a quick reply and then puts the phone away. She turns back to Rosie, who is now looking at her mother with a very serious look on her face. Elena smiles to her and, as Rosie smiles back at her mum, the nipple slides out of her mouth. But with a quick and almost invisible little push, Elena helps Rosie to get hold of the nipple again. Rosie starts feeding once more, pushing with her hand into her mother's breast.

She feeds for another few minutes while looking intently into her mother's eyes. Elena smiles softly, nodding a little: 'Yes, I love you . . . do you think you have nearly finished or you are still hungry?' Rosie smiles again at her mum and lets go of the nipple. 'So you are full now . . .' says Elena, while clipping her bra back. She sits Rosie on her knee facing her. Rosie looks so full of milk, her lips slightly distorted by all the sucking, that Elena cannot help but smile. 'You look drunk, Rosie,' she says. Rosie blinks her eyes a few times, as if trying to focus again on her mother's face and, after a short moment, she looks very alert and intently at her mum, then smiles wildly.

Elena now lays Rosie on her knees. She bends down a little and she and Rosie start playing: Elena holds Rosie's hands, wrapping them around her index finger, then brings them towards her tummy. 'Is this tummy full? Yes, it is full . . . !' Each time Elena brings Rosie's hands down to touch her tummy, she gives her a little tickle. Rosie opens her eyes wide, full of expectation, and then laughs, kicking her legs. This goes on for a little while, until Rosie makes a sort of grimace. Then Elena wonders aloud to Rosie if maybe they should stop that game, as it might be a bit too much for her tummy after such a big feed. She puts Rosie on her shoulder, patting her back gently. Rosie emits a big burp and Elena seems delighted. She then takes Rosie to her playmat. Kneeling in front of her, she offers her different soft toys . . .

For Elena and Rosie, feeding is a time of great physical and emotional closeness. Observing them, we get a strong sense of the connection that allows Elena's invisible emotional 'mind-milk' to pass from her mind to Rosie's. In this moment of relative stillness, as she holds her baby in the crook of her arm, gently caressing Rosie with her thoughts as well as her hands, Elena loses herself in a sort of reverie, during which the warp and weft of her relationship with her baby gets tighter and more intricate.

As for Rosie, feeding is a multi-layered experience that engages all of her senses. She hears her mother's voice, she looks at her face, and as Elena brings her closer to her body, she smells her mother's delicious smell, the smell she began to know while she was still in her tummy and that since birth she has been able to easily differentiate from any other person's scent. With her lips, she touches and feels her mother's nipple, and with her fingers, once the feeding has got going, she feels and caresses her mother's skin, pressing on her breast every now and then. Finally, of course, she enjoys the taste of the warm sweet milk, a food that she senses is the perfect nourishment.

Rosie, like all babies, will have practised feeding in utero. On scans from as early as the twelfth week of pregnancy, we can see babies sucking and swallowing, some even sucking their thumb. Consequently, as with all infant mammals, within minutes of being born, our babies have a pretty good idea of what they need to do (see Chapter 3 – At last, we meet . . .). But it is still quite a complicated task that they have to accomplish. In fact, it is a remarkable physical feat. They have to root, suck and swallow, and for that they need to work the muscles of their jaws and mouth, while also timing their breathing to be in tune with their sucking and the contraction of their tummy muscles. In all, they use six out of the twelve cranial nerves, twenty-two bones and sixty voluntary and involuntary muscles to suck, swallow and breathe in a coordinated activity that occurs at forty to sixty cycles/per minute, ten to thirty minutes at a stretch, up to sixteen times a day! Which is one of the reasons, along with the intense emotional component involved, that it plays such a key role in the development of a baby's brain, mind and body.

Snuggled up close to her mother, Rosie is learning about both her mother's body and her own, about their similarities and their differences. For instance, they are both warm, but Rosie's skin is softer than her mother's, and less hairy. This gives Rosie a chance to sense where her own body starts and where it ends. And, in turn, this helps her to gently and slowly discover that she is separate from her mother – close, but no longer physically connected. Each time she feeds, she feels a sense of reconnection, and then, when it finishes, disconnection again. This coming together and pulling away provides an intense emotional and physical education.

Along with learning about her mother's physical form, Rosie is learning about her mother's emotions and mood. She studies her mother's face so carefully that she notices all the tiny movements of her different facial muscles. When Elena frowns – her face changing from relaxed to slightly stern – Rosie imitates her facial expression and frowns too. In this moment, Rosie, by imitating her mother's facial expression, is starting to learn that other people have a mind that is different from hers, a key milestone in her development of her sense of self, and of her empathy with others.

She is also learning about expectation and communication, and how certain behaviours induce particular responses in her mother. When she gets hunger pangs in her tummy, if she makes certain noises and movements, her mother is going to respond in a certain way, and pretty soon the pangs in her tummy will disappear. This gives Rosie a great sense of potency. Her capacity to communicate her needs to her mother makes her feel strong and powerful. And thanks to Elena's attuned response to Rosie's signals of hunger, Rosie experiences the all-important feeling that there is a grown-up close by who is looking after her and making sure that she is okay. By feeling understood by her mother, and gradually more sure about what she can expect, Rosie feels safe. Over time, as the experience is repeated, this gives her the capacity to wait for her mum to get ready to feed her, even while feeling the uncomfortable sensation of hunger in her tummy. This acceptance of a little temporary discomfort is the beginning of learning patience.

Through feeding, Rosie also gets to experience that things have a beginning, a middle and an end. The sensation of being full at the end of the feed is very different from the hunger pangs she felt at the beginning. And it is this feeling of being satisfied that helps her stop feeding, to let the breast or bottle go, and enjoy the special feeling of closeness that persists afterwards. For Rosie, the end of feeding is an uncomplicated event, as she has learned, thanks to her mother's consistent love and care, that next time she feels that emptiness in her tummy, Elena will magically appear with more warm milk that will make her feel better. So, she doesn't need to hang on to the breast for ever: she feels able to let go of it, safe in the knowledge that it will be there for her again when needed.

Nestled in the crook of her mother's arm, filled with a sense of safety, Rosie now has all she needs to explore the world a little further. And playing, as we will see in the next chapter, will be one of her favourite ways to do that.

First, though, let us look at what happens when feeding does not come easily, when it can feel like anything but a bonding experience.

Feeding: a question of life and death

Although Rosie and Elena have together managed to create a harmonious feeding routine, it may not have been like that at the beginning. Even for the most experienced (or luckiest!) parents, feeding, especially in the first few days and weeks, can be accompanied by practical difficulties and a trail of anxious questions. Am I producing enough milk? Is my milk good enough? Is the formula I have chosen the right one? Am I using the right bottle, the right teat? Am I holding my baby in the right position? Is my baby feeding too often, not often enough, too fast, too slow . . .?

If, within a few days or weeks, we manage to successfully establish a good feeding relationship, these doubts will quickly lessen in intensity. When breastfeeding is relatively comfortable, i.e. not painful for the mother, or stressful for the baby, and the baby puts on weight, then feeding, as we have seen, has the potential to become a privileged moment of intimacy where we not only nourish our babies with actual milk but also our emotional 'mind-milk'. As we watch our babies calmly enjoying the food we are offering them, we, as parents, cannot but feel a sense of pride. Our confidence grows, which in turn allows us to produce more nutritious 'mind-milk' to give to them. Physiologically, our newfound positivity also keeps our supply of actual breast milk going too. Feeling self-assured and relaxed, enjoying having our baby against our skin, helps with the release of two key hormones: prolactin, which encourages the production of milk; and oxytocin, which causes the muscles around our breasts to contract, allowing the milk to flow. Accessing this virtuous circle of breast and brain, food-milk and mind-milk, is a great boost to the bonding process and to our confidence as a parent.

Of course, as with most virtuous circles, there is a contrasting vicious one waiting in the wings . . . If breastfeeding is difficult, if it is painful, if our milk production is low, if our baby struggles to latch on and is not putting on weight, or, even more worryingly, loses weight, then those life and death questions can easily become very real. As parents, we quickly lose any confidence in ourselves. Filled with worry and guilt, instead of feeling close to our babies, we feel emotionally distant from them, which affects the supply of both our mind-milk and our breast-milk. Our cortisol level increases, which means that our milk production diminishes and our level of oxytocin goes down too, making it really difficult for our babies to take what milk we have, as our body is too stressed to let the milk flow. This vicious circle can lead us to feel very low, and is a fairly common factor in the onset of post-natal depression.

As parents we all, at times, doubt our capacity to do a good job. And feeding, because it is so essential to the very survival of our babies, can often come to encapsulate all these doubts, channelling our anxieties into this one, crucial area. The key thing is to find a way to mitigate these fears. And that starts with confronting our deepest feelings and understanding where they come from.

Breastfeeding: a learning process for mother and baby

In the last few decades our society has put more and more pressure on mothers to breastfeed. It has become accepted wisdom that babies should be breastfed until their first birthday, and, ideally, exclusively for the first six months. The rationale is that breastmilk has all the nutrients necessary for the long-term healthy physiological and neurological development of our babies and is the best thing to support their immune system and also our own physical and mental health.

As things stand, about 80 per cent of new mothers give breastfeeding a go. However, after eight weeks, less than half are still breastfeeding (and, after six months, this proportion goes down to around 16 per cent).[1] So, what has happened in the meantime? A handful of mothers will have planned to breastfeed for only a few weeks, mostly because they have to go back to work. But the vast majority will have stopped breastfeeding earlier – sometimes much earlier – than they planned to. For these mothers, the decision to stop is rarely taken lightly. On the contrary, after hours of trying, often suffering unbearable pain from cracked nipples and sore backs, and burdened with the huge worry that their baby is not thriving, many women feel they have no choice but to give up.

The ubiquitous idealised image of mothers blissfully breastfeeding their babies unfortunately sets many women up for failure. It leads to the misleading belief that breastfeeding is instinctual and should just happen like magic. But between the instinct of placing our babies close to our breasts and our babies' instinct to suck, there is still plenty of learning to be done, both for mother and baby. Our babies are born a little more ready than us – they have all the reflexes necessary to feed – but it doesn't always mean that they will know how to latch properly on our nipple straight away. And it can take a lot of practice for both our babies and us to learn together how to establish a good feeding relationship. In fact, for the vast majority – around 70 per cent of us – learning how to breastfeed our babies is difficult, slow and painful. Let's look at these widely variant experiences in more detail.

Breastfeeding after an uncomplicated birth

Birth and breastfeeding are intimately linked, as they happen in quick succession, with the nature of the birth inevitably impacting the first experience of feeding. Generally, after a relatively uncomplicated spontaneous vaginal birth, babies are very alert and keen to have their first feed within the first hour of their lives. If they are then gently placed on our tummies or in our arms, they quickly start rooting, using their super-sensitive lips to seek out our breast. Following our smell, and the smell of our milk, which may even be leaking in anticipation of their need, and encouraged by the contact of their skin with ours, they will push on their little legs or move their head around until they find our breast with their mouths, and can latch on and begin to suckle. This first feed kick-starts a complex set of hormonal reactions that are going to be supporting us throughout our breastfeeding journey with our babies.

When our newborn babies start sucking on our breast, it triggers a strong burst of oxytocin, which has multiple effects on our body and mood. Firstly, it encourages the colostrum, our super-rich first milk, to move towards our nipples. Secondly, it helps our cortisol levels (which have increased with the stress of giving birth) to return to their normal levels, so that we feel calmer and ready to get to know our babies. Lastly, it stimulates our uterus to contract and deliver the placenta, indicating to our bodies that the pregnancy is finally over and that it now needs to change gear and focus on milk production. Once our babies start feeding properly, a system of supply and demand is established and our bodies know when and how much milk to produce. This makes breastfeeding a truly collaborative adventure between us and our babies.

However, even when the first feed has been successful, it doesn't mean that feeding is plain sailing. Most of us need some support to help us find the best positions in which to feed our babies, to be shown how to help them to latch on properly, especially in the first week, as the colostrum slowly gets replaced by milk and our breasts get fuller. But, generally, within a week or two, we have usually managed to master the technique, and we are beginning to understand our babies' different feeding cues. Whether it be with their pouting mouths, their waving arms and kicking legs, or with little cries or big screams, our babies have lots of ways of telling us they are hungry.

Once we are settled into a comfortable and collaborative routine, we should be able to carry on breastfeeding for as long as it suits us.

Breastfeeding after a difficult/traumatic birth, and other physical difficulties

As we saw in Chapter 13, giving birth for a lot of us is not a straightforward affair, and this can have a significant impact on our breastfeeding journey.[2]

After a difficult or traumatic birth, many mothers and their babies are often too drowsy (either from the effect of the opioid painkiller, or due to stress and exhaustion) or unwell (some babies need to go straight to Neonatal Intensive Care Unit, while some mothers need urgent medical intervention) to be able to spend that first hour close together, where the possibility of a relatively unproblematic first feed is optimised. Some mothers and babies might have to wait several hours or even days before they can be together.

This delay in the kick-off of the feeding journey does not mean that breastfeeding will fail, but it makes it much more challenging. And, sadly, this is often exacerbated by a tendency among medical staff – worried that the mother is going to give up breastfeeding – to take an 'over-optimistic' approach, in which the physical impact of a difficult birth is not fully acknowledged.

Indeed, even though there is plenty of research explaining why and how anaesthesia, strong sedation, prolonged labour, surgical intervention, and other sources of stress impact a mother's capacity to produce milk and a baby's ability to latch on, this information is rarely shared with parents. Rather, many staff offer the same advice and support on breastfeeding to all women, regardless of their birthing experience.[3]

As a consequence, unable to make sense of their struggle with breastfeeding, mothers are often inclined to blame themselves and eventually give up.

With the right support, however, difficulties with breastfeeding can generally be overcome, and a good feeding relationship established. This might involve careful, targeted techniques and plenty of practice to resolve specific challenges. Or it might just require some patient therapeutic support from trained staff, who are able to appreciate the importance of the personal circumstances of each mother and baby and are willing to explore the difficulties they are facing, rather than deny or minimise them.

So, if you are struggling in your feeding relationship with your baby, it's vital to find someone, whether a breastfeeding counsellor, a lactation specialist, or a local support group, who can listen to your birth story, explore the issues you are having and apply their professional knowledge to the situation. As a new mum, you need a gentle space in which you can be clear and honest, about how much pain you are in and how worried you are about 'failing' your baby.

As we become parents, our sense of responsibility increases dramatically, and with it our capacity to blame ourselves for things that go wrong. Our birth and breastfeeding experiences are generally fertile ground to kickstart that self-doubt and potentially make us feel extremely low. This is why it is so important to seek help, to try to resolve any physical difficulties that might be slowing down the establishment of a good breastfeeding experience, and from there either move forwards with breastfeeding, or proceed to bottle feeding – thereby maintaining the physical closeness that will ensure the 'mind-milk' can flow and increasing, in the long term, our confidence in our parenting and our capacity to be close to our babies.

The great divide – bottle or breast, breast or bottle?

The question of which is best – breast or bottle – has been a matter of vexed debate for decades. First, obviously, breastfeeding was king. That was all there was. And if a mother's milk supply was sparse or she chose not to breastfeed herself, the family often employed a 'wet nurse' to breastfeed the infant. Then, in 1865, a German chemist called Justus von Liebig developed and marketed an infant food, first in a liquid form and then in a powdered form that could more easily be preserved. During the late nineteenth and early twentieth centuries, nutrition scientists continued to study human milk and to make infant formulas that more closely matched it. And bottle feeding really took off in the post-war years, when formula started to be seen as a safe substitute for breastmilk, encouraged by aggressive advertising campaigns from the manufacturers.

The 1970s saw a resurgence of breastfeeding, after years of decline, along with a renewed interest in natural birthing techniques, as part of a backlash against the medicalisation of birth. And since the early 2000s, there has been a worldwide trend to promote breastfeeding, spearheaded by the World Health Organization (WHO), whose official advice is that babies should be put to the breast within an hour after birth, be exclusively breastfed for the first six months, and where possible continue to be breastfed up to the age of two.

Although well intended, the WHO promotion of breastfeeding has unfortunately not been supported by an increase in government funding in the healthcare profession. Nor is it reflected in how our societies regard and support breastfeeding in public places. We regularly hear of breastfeeding women being asked to leave buses, trains or other public spaces. Meanwhile, in the workplace, where statutory maternity leave is still only six weeks on 90 per cent of your pay (before tax), and then £184.03 or 90 per cent of your average earnings (whichever is lower) for the next thirty-three weeks after that, there are very few protected spaces to express milk or part-time job options for breastfeeding mothers.

The 'breast is best' stance has also inevitably ramped up the pressure on mothers who find, for whatever reason, that they can't make breastfeeding work. While a minority of women are adamant that breastfeeding is not for them, and they are all set up to bottle feed before their babies are born, most mothers arrive at bottle feeding not by choice, but after having tried breastfeeding and reluctantly being forced to give it up.

What is often forgotten in the debate about breastfeeding/bottle feeding is how struggling and 'failing' to breastfeed impacts on the mental health of mothers and on the bonding process with their children. Just as with the exemplar of the 'ideal birth' we discussed earlier, the standards for 'successful breastfeeding' can seem so impossibly high that a lot of mothers are likely to feel that they have, at some point or another, 'failed' their babies. In the same way that, for example, women are made to feel guilty for having chosen to take painkillers during the birth, they are apt to feel judged according to their ability to breastfeed, and even for the length of time they manage to keep it going before introducing formula milk.

Too often I have seen in my clinic parents who are still grief stricken, years after formula-feeding their babies. When I ask them about their experience of feeding their now spotty teenager, they often burst into tears and are able to recall their struggle as vividly as if it was yesterday – the pain of cracked and bleeding nipples, the extreme exhaustion they experienced, other worries about their baby's weight, or immunity, or intelligence, and finally the shame they still feel after all this time in admitting that they eventually gave up.

These parents can feel that perhaps their determination to breastfeed had a negative impact on their relationship with their babies – because feeding had come to feel like an endurance test, and instead of looking forward to their babies waking up and being hungry, they maybe just wished they would stay asleep as long as possible. This unhappy cycle led them to feel very anxious and low and even to fall into postnatal depression. They feel that it 'spoiled' their first weeks, and wish they had introduced mixed-feeding or given up breastfeeding altogether much earlier. But, most of all, they all wish they had been better supported, with more consistent care and advice.

If only they had. Because, yes, breastfeeding is great when it works out, for all the reasons outlined above; but, truly, what matters most when we feed our babies – more than what we give them to drink – is our emotional state. It is what our mind-milk is made of that is going to colour our babies' feelings and help them to develop a bond with us. If we tense our whole body every time we bring our babies to our chest for a feed, cringe and recoil when they latch on to our sore breasts, twist our face in excruciating pain, maybe even cry when they pull on our cracked nipples, this is inevitably going to impact on our babies' feelings. Imagine how much more comforting it will be for them to feel their mum is calm and relaxed as she snuggles them into her body, smiles at them, gently talks to them, caresses their cheeks, plays with their little hands and feet . . . while giving them a warm bottle of formula.

To get our emotional milk flowing from our mind and nourishing our babies' mind, giving them a feeling of being loved and an increasing sense of safety, we need, as parents, to be feeling a certain degree of confidence and enjoyment in the process. This is why parents/mothers should get all the support they need and feel they can experiment freely with different feeding options to see what suits them. No parent should have to worry that they are going to be judged harshly for choosing how they can best feed their baby.

Mixed-feeding

Mixed-feeding is where you partly breastfeed and partly bottle feed, whether with formula or expressed milk. And a huge bonus of this method is that you can share feeding with your partner/co-parent and get a much-needed rest while they bottle feed your baby. Even when it goes well, feeding babies can be so relentless and shattering that, for some mothers, the first couple of months are often a bit of a blur. So any chance to get some rest, to feel reinvigorated and relaxed, can make our time with our babies much more enjoyable and memorable.

Sharing the feeding also allows our fellow parent to experience that special closeness and intimacy that comes with feeding their baby. They too have a mind-milk they can share with their babies. And, of course, this more inclusive approach to feeding gives our babies a different experience – another flavour of mind-milk, if you like – and this will be very enriching for them.

Dylan and his partner, Alisha, decided early on to mix-feed Sam: Alisha would breastfeed three quarters of the time and Dylan would top up with bottle formula the rest of the time.

Sam (four months) and Dylan

Dylan is sitting on the floor in front of Sam, who is in his baby bouncer. Each time he gently pushes on the bouncer, Sam opens his eyes wide and takes a deep breath. After a few minutes, Sam gets tired of the game and Dylan picks him up, saying: 'I think you have had enough and maybe you are a little hungry now. Let's make a bottle.' Dylan, carrying Sam in his arms, goes to the kitchen to warm up the bottle, giving Sam a cheerful running commentary about the whole process. After a few minutes, Dylan, grabbing a muslin that has been lying on the table, sits in an armchair, saying to Sam: 'We'd better have a muslin in case you spill some milk like last night.' With Sam on his knees, and looking at him in the eyes, Dylan says: 'Are you ready, my little boy? Shall we eat?' Sam looks intently at his dad, then at the bottle, then at his dad again, wriggling his legs and flapping his arms a little: he seems ready and excited. Dylan then nestles Sam in the crook of his arm, with his head turned slightly towards his chest. He checks the temperature of the bottle and, as he brings the teat towards Sam, Sam opens his mouth wide and latches on with great vigour. 'Oh, yes, you were really hungry . . .' As Sam is gulping his bottle, Dylan who has not stopped looking at his baby, says: 'Hey, we've got all the time in the world, you don't need to drink so fast.' Sam's hands are now closed fists, so tight that the knuckles are nearly white. While holding the bottle, Dylan manages to take his right hand, saying, 'It is okay, you can relax. I am not going to take the bottle away . . .' As Dylan takes a big breath, Sam relaxes, opening his hand and curling his little fingers around his dad's index finger. They stay like that, looking intently to each other for a while. Although Dylan is not saying anything, he keeps gently moving his head as his eyes are scanning his baby, as if in deep conversation with Sam. Eventually Sam turns his head to the left and lets go of the bottle. Dylan says: 'Oh, you have had enough? There is a tiny bit left.' As he offers the bottle to Sam, he says: 'Do you want it?' But Sam turns his face away and makes it clear that he is not hungry anymore. Dylan puts the bottle away and gently lifts Sam, sitting him on his knees for a bit. Sam is all wobbly, looking slightly drunk. Suddenly, he does a big burp. 'Is that better?' asks Dylan. He puts Sam on his shoulder, and gently taps his back. After thirty seconds or so, he lifts Sam off and puts him back on his knees. This time Sam is wide awake, looking alert and ready for the next adventure. 'What shall we do now?' says Dylan. 'Shall we play?'

Both Dylan and Sam are enjoying this intimate moment. And it is clear when watching them together that what is most important is not what type of milk Sam is being given but the emotional connection between him and his father as he is being fed. When we feel physically at ease with feeding, we are more likely to be relaxed and connected. In turn our babies, feeling full of our love, drink in our positive mind-milk, and will be soon be ready to leave the crook of our arms and explore the world a little further away from us.

When breastfeeding is technically going well, but still feels hard . . .

For a lot of us, the experience of breastfeeding – even when we have mastered the technique – can feel all-consuming and leave us at times overwhelmed, maybe even resentful and confused. Our babies are putting on weight, everything seems to be going fine, but we still worry that our milk supply is not adequate to satisfy their seemingly voracious hunger.

Behind this worry is perhaps a more existential one that strikes at the heart of our sense of self: with our babies constantly on our breast, it easy to feel that we are being depleted. With every feed (and there are so many, especially in the first few weeks), with every latching on, with every suckle, we can feel that our babies are drain-ing us of all we have got: our mind, our soul, our very identity. And after yet another broken night, or a day when we have hardly left the corner of the sofa that has become our feeding station, it may seem that we have turned into a feeding machine, our body hardly feeling ours anymore, and we may well wonder how much of ourself, if any, is going to be left by the end of the process. In these moments, it is hard to imagine regaining a life without a baby attached to our breast.

If these overwhelming feelings linger too long, if even after a good night's sleep they are still there bothering you, you might want to explore them a little further. It is likely that you will find that those feelings have to do not just with our ravenous baby, but also with buried emotions from our own childhood. Examining those feelings, knowing perhaps that our parents were in a stressful situation as young parents, we might wonder how much mind-milk we were given as a baby. We might even feel jealous of our baby – resentful that they are getting so much more than we were offered. Maybe we don't know much about how we were fed, as we have never been told and we feel loathe to bring it up. This sense of not knowing can add to the confusion. And it is easy for our tired mind to catastrophise, turning our hungry babies into 'greedy monsters', who want more than we feel we can give them, and to be resentful that they are taking so much out of us.

It is not unusual for parents, especially if they have had a difficult and traumatic childhood, to worry that what we have to give our babies might simply not be good enough. And, of course, this applies especially to the quality of our mind-milk. Are we going to be like our own (critical or neglectful) parents? With this anxiety in the back of our mind, we worry that we might 'damage' our babies, making it extremely hard for us to relax into the peaceful reverie of mutual gazing while we feed them. In an attempt to distract ourselves from the overwhelming worries about the quality of our mind-milk, rather than looking at our babies' faces while they feed, we jump at the easily accessible opportunity to watch the TV or scroll on our phone. Even when the feeding is ostensibly going well, we may constantly fiddle with our babies' position, rearranging it, stopping the feed in the middle to make them burp, or to check the speed of flow of the milk . . . Doubting the quality of our mind-milk, we are afraid of getting too close to our babies. Instead of making feeding a warm moment of emotional connection, we turn it into a purely functional session, which can leave us feeling confused and sad.

The very act of developing an awareness of these difficult feelings, and admitting them to ourselves, is an important first step in overcoming them. Sharing them with our partner, or a close friend or a family member, may bring more relief, and 'disarm' their intensity or toxicity. We can start to step back a little, and be more realistic about the situation, and see our babies for who they are: hungry little things whose only chance to grow is to drink our milk.

In some cases, particularly if we are unable to confide in family or friends, it may be helpful to see a therapist. Opening up, whether to a loved one or a professional, can help you get some perspective, and focus more on the positive: realising that your baby is putting on weight and getting plenty of that physical closeness that is so important for them. Seeing the situation in a different/more positive way can slowly help you replenish your depleted self and increase your confidence in the quality of your mind-milk, reminding you that actually you are doing a pretty good job. We will then start to find it easier to connect with our feeding babies, through skin contact and eye contact, and may soon access the virtuous circle of mind-milk boosting food-milk, and vice versa.

Taming the greedy monsters

One of the biggest quandaries, especially for first-time parents, is when and how much to feed our babies. For some of us this question hardly registers, as we find it relatively easy to follow both our intuition and our babies' rhythm, no matter how inconsistent that rhythm might be. We tend to go with the flow, adopting the 'on demand' style, and feed our babies as often as they want, whenever and wherever they want.

However, for a lot of us, the ordinary unpredictability of our babies' hunger, which they often express with poignant but also startling crying or screaming, can leave us feeling anxious and exhausted: how can we get into a routine when we never know how long we have before they will need to be fed again? For some of us, it can be a real struggle not to know what is going to happen next.

There is a whole genre of parenting style that tries to help new parents deal with the unpredictability of their babies by suggesting that, if they follow rigid routines of when and how much to feed their babies (and when and for how long to put their babies to sleep), they will, in no time, make their babies eat (and sleep) at regular hours. This parenting regime may even insist that our babies' displays of their needs are to be minimised and ignored and their signs of hunger (and distress) not to be trusted, to the point of suggesting that letting our babies cry without comforting them or feeding them is, at times, a 'healthy' thing.

Even if this feels like the best approach in the short term, helping us with our tiredness and giving us a sense that we are regaining control, it is doubtful that it is really the best way of responding to our babies' needs. Being fed when they are not hungry and ignored when they ask for food will be confusing for them, to say the least. And this confusion will have an impact on them over time. Their developing brain is likely, in the long term, to register that crying and asking for help or food is a hopeless proposition and that their needs are not important to us. And soon enough some of our babies will stop crying and comply with our routine. But this is not necessarily because our routine is making them feel good and looked after; it may simply be because they have given up the hope or expectation that we will respond to their crying with the care and reassurance they need. And some of our babies may also be highly resistant to this type of training. This can ultimately leave parents whose babies 'fail' to be trained into scheduled feeding feeling that they are doing a bad job at parenting. Or, worse still, that they have 'bad' babies.

Greedy monsters or just hungry babies?

As soon as babies have left our tummies, they intuitively know that they have to do whatever it takes to survive. And their best and only option is to connect quickly with us so that, thanks to our incredible empathy for their vulnerability, we give them as much breast or formula milk as they need to grow their body, and generous amounts of our mind-milk to grow their brains.

Babies are not factory-made; they come from two different people, so they all come with their unique genetic makeup and their unique set of circumstances that are going to create a unique physiological and emotional being. And it is all these singular characteristics that are going to dictate when they, personally, are hungry and how much milk they as an individual need. And, depending on what else is happening for them (playing, sleeping, pooing and noticing the world), they may not be hungry at regular intervals. It is that simple – and we have to trust that they know when they are hungry and how much they need.

For some babies, especially at the beginning, this might mean feeding them as often as every twenty minutes. For others, whose metabolism is a little slower, it might be every hour or more. Generally, newborn babies, with their tiny stomachs, eat little but often (just watch young lambs or puppies at their mothers' teats). To survive and grow out of the helpless state in which they are born, they need to get as much of our nutrition as they can. So instead of trying to train them and impose our grown-up schedule, why not simply observe them with our curious and generous mind and, as far as possible, follow their lead. Then the all-consuming feeding adventure might become a much more enjoyable experience for both of us.

Feeding for comfort

At the other end of the spectrum, some of us find it almost too easy to run to our babies and feed them as soon as they express signs of hunger or indeed of wanting any attention at all. This means we will often be feeding our babies even when they are not hungry; and soon putting to the breast or giving them a bottle will become a way not only to feed them but also to stop the slightest sign of discomfort or irritation that they may be trying to express.

If we look more closely, we should soon begin to discern the difference between the 'I'm hungry' signals and all the other gestures or noises that are aimed at getting our attention for other kinds of interaction. If we struggle to make this distinction, it may be helpful to think why this is.

Our rush to feed them might, for example, be hiding an anxiety about our parenting: when we hear our babies begin to cry, we may take it personally and understand their cries as a criticism. And, this being really hard to bear, we will quickly give them a feed to 'shut them up' and effectively silence the demons that are taunting us about our parenting. However, the other side of that story is that our babies miss the chance to fully express their emotions and quickly learn that there is little point in sharing their feelings.

If you feel you have a tendency to offer your breast or a bottle perhaps too quickly, try to imagine other ways to comfort your baby. You could, for instance, cuddle them and talk to them about what might be going on for them, acknowledging their feelings and putting them into words.

Using feeding as a first-and-only response to all their cues stifles our babies' attempts to communicate with us about other things. In so doing it also deprives us of an opportunity to be curious about our babies, to try to understand what they are really trying to communicate to us, and hugely limits our opportunities for the many important and varied interactions that will develop our bond, and indeed their brains: cuddling, playing, exploring, even sleeping.

Breastfeeding as a way to 'repair' trauma or loss

Breastfeeding can be a great source of strength for mothers who have suffered a traumatic birth, and who view that experience as being somehow a failure on their part. They can end up putting all their energy, sometimes quite obsessively, into breastfeeding as a way to 'make amends' and 'be forgiven' for not having been able give their babies the 'ideal birth'. Breastfeeding becomes a way to prove to their babies (and also perhaps their family, friends and themselves) that they are good mothers. It is also a way to prove that their bodies are working well and that they can be trusted to look after their babies.

But, of course, the more meaning and importance we attribute to breastfeeding, the higher the emotional stakes. Some of us can indeed get great strength from successfully breastfeeding our babies. This becomes a way to repair the difficult experience of the birth and helps us make a positive transition to a place of calm and confidence. However, it is important to be aware and mindful of the emotional risks if, despite all our best efforts, we do not manage to get breastfeeding going. This can leave some mothers with a double sense of failure.

For some women, the fear of failure can simply become too much to bear. Having 'failed' at the birth, what if they 'fail' at breastfeeding as well? In these instances, they may decide that, for their own wellbeing and their relationship with their babies, it would be better not to risk even trying, and to bottle feed them straight away. And they should be given every encouragement in this. For recovering mothers, the closeness and intensity of breastfeeding can feel quite daunting and threaten to trigger traumatic memories. Having a bottle between them and their baby creates a small but helpful physical distance, which enables them to manage their feelings and to slowly begin to trust themselves and get used to the intimacy and healing that feeding affords.

This can also be helpful for those who have experienced important losses – such as the recent loss of a parent or another child. Indeed, these losses can make the intimacy and intensity of breastfeeding feel quite daunting. We might also worry that the possibility of 'failing' to breast-feed, and that the inevitable weaning of the breast, would be too closely associated with a loss and trigger unbearable pain. Sometimes we find that using a bottle makes it easier to manage the closeness of feeding our babies, making it a little less intense but yet still very intimate.

Weaning

For months, perhaps even a year or more, we have held our babies in the crook of our arms to feed them. But as they grow and develop and gradually get interested in solid food, the way we feed them changes. Now they are no longer in our arms, but sitting on our knees as we give them little bits of food with our fingers or spoonfuls of puréed vegetable and fruit. Soon they migrate to a highchair at the dinner table, perhaps eating at the same time as us. We can start feeding them mashed-up versions of what we are eating ourselves. As solid food slowly replaces milk, some physical distance is emerging between us, which is healthy both for us and for our baby's growing sense of independence.

For some parents, weaning happens seamlessly, with their babies becoming more and more interested in the solid foods offered to them, and in what their parents are eating. Soon breast/bottle feeding is relegated to a morning and evening feed, and maybe a top-up before an afternoon nap. And then, as if parents and babies had tacitly agreed on the timing of it, it is no longer needed at all. Often these parents feel some pride and maybe also a bit of relief that their babies are gaining some autonomy as they are learning to feed themselves.

For those who have to go back to work rather than choose to go back, weaning can feel like a rather brutal separation, a milestone imposed rather than naturally reached. Faced with this, a lot of parents try to keep the morning and evening breast or formula feeds going, hanging on to those valued moments of closeness that feel all the more precious after they have returned to work.

And for yet other parents, weaning can bring up a whole host of complex feelings. Although, of course, they want their babies to grow and develop, they are also acutely aware of the time passing, and so they try to postpone weaning for as long as they can, and letting go of the special closeness that comes with breast or bottle feeding their babies.

Feeding our babies is such an intense start to our relationship with them that it can be hard to imagine other ways in which we might ever be as close to them again. But have no fear: weaning tends to spur our babies' development. It is not unusual, after saying goodbye to the breast or the bottle, to find that their talking develops quite suddenly. And, soon, it is no longer our milk-feeding that brings us close to our babies but our ability to share words, opening the door to a new lifelong conversation with them. We have learned the art of feeding them our mind-milk, and this will continue long after we stop giving them our food-milk. In some ways it may never stop.

15
Playing

I n our adult life, it's easy to think of play as that special thing we do when we have freed up some time after crossing off the chores on our to-do list: our luxury 'me time', or perhaps when we get on with a hobby we are pursuing. For our babies, however, playing is an essential activity and one that they will pretty much insist on doing quite a lot of the time.

As a new parent, you might wonder how you are supposed to play with your tiny baby when they cannot talk, walk, make jokes, or even hold a toy. Don't worry too much about that, because at this stage in their development playing is simply what we do most of the time without even noticing it. It is all those effortless moments we spend with our babies because we enjoy being with them, when we have nothing else in mind but just the pleasure of being with them, observing them and interacting with them. And if, occasionally, it does take a bit of effort to get in the right frame of mind for playing, well, that's fine too.

The great thing is, our babies are going to help us with how to play. And a little understanding of what is happening, both for them and also for us, when we play will serve us well, making playtime more fun, and hopefully even more interesting.

Babies are born (just as we were) with the need and urge to play, an urge that is buried deep in the most ancient part of their brain.[1] They share this need with all animals: think of baby lambs in the spring, playing rough and tumble together in the fields, or kittens and puppies running after a ball . . . Why do all baby animals share this primitive instinct to play? Because there is no better and safer way for them to learn about themselves and the world around them – for a lamb to learn how to be a lamb and live in the world of sheep, for birds to learn about a life on the wing and life in a flock, and for babies to learn how to be themselves and live in the social world of human beings.[2]

It is through play that our babies are able to explore their emotions and feelings. Not just the feelings they are comfortable with, but also new feelings, ones that seem more risky and frightening. It is through play that our babies discover what they enjoy and what they can tolerate (or not) about other people, and vice versa. In other words, play is one of our most ancient tools for discovering how to be ourselves among others.

So playing with our babies is key to their healthy development and key to the building of our relationship with them. It is while playing with our babies that we learn about them, about their personality, what they like and dislike, what makes them laugh or makes them sad, what makes them feel safe and what makes them feel scared. By letting our babies take the lead and following them in their play, we are given a unique entrance ticket into their world.

But, for this to happen in an optimal way, play has to be *pleasurable*. When playing is interesting and fun, it sets off a whole physiological reaction in our babies, as their brains are flooded with the most amazing cocktail of happy hormones. And it is partly thanks to this incredible play-cocktail (a subtle mixture of oxytocin, endorphin, dopamine and serotonin) that our babies have the time and space and energy to explore their creativity, their emotional and physical limits, and express and communicate what is going on inside them. These events are helping both to build our babies' brains, and create that lasting bond between them and us.[3]

It doesn't mean play always has to be safe and cosy – being challenged, solving problems (what does that face mean?) and even being a little frightened (as long as they are quickly made to feel safe again) can all be enjoyable for our babies and for us too. But when play becomes stressful, or even boring, then the emotional learning and growth that are at the core of our play are no longer there. This is something we will feel, and which may add to our stress and compound it. What's important is to be able to get things back on track.

Let's look at different vignettes of babies playing with their parents to help us understand the emotional experience of the babies.

Look at me!

When our babies are tiny, we are their favourite toy. All they want is to be close to us, with our delicious smell and perfect warmth. This physical proximity helps them to feel relaxed, regulating their heart rate and their body temperature. Luckily for us, they think everything we do is quite amusing – even the most mundane tasks are a fascinating, eye-popping mystery to them. But what they particularly enjoy is watching our increasingly familiar faces. Their favourite game is to watch us watching them. They find every movement of each of the forty-three muscles of our face endlessly riveting. Very soon (within three months of birth) they will have mapped our unique facial features, and the way we move them. And when they look at us looking back at them, with our unique lovely smile, they get a rush of oxytocin, making them feel good about themselves and excited about our relationship with them.

Poppy (two weeks) and Liam

Liam puts Poppy carefully on his lap and moves his face towards hers. As he does that, Poppy opens her eyes quite wide. Liam's eyes widen as well: 'Hey, it is okay. It's me, Daddy.' He waits a little, watching Poppy constantly. Poppy is now looking at him a bit more intently, as if trying to figure out who he is. As she moves her arms, he offers her his index fingers to hold on to. Bringing both her hands towards each other, he rests them on her chest, then stretches them open again. Poppy's mouth now makes what looks like tentative attempts at a smile. Liam slowly smiles at her. Her eyebrows move up and down, and Liam asks her: 'What is it? What are you trying to tell me?' As Liam speaks, Poppy's attention intensifies, and her mouth starts to move as if she is trying to say something . . . She shuts her eyes for a few seconds and opens them again, scanning Liam's face. Liam makes an O shape with his mouth, saying 'oh, oh, ooh'. And Poppy slowly makes a sort of O shape too. Liam's face lights up and Poppy's legs move a bit faster. Liam makes an O shape again and again. Poppy imitates him . . . this happens a few more times. Then, as Poppy turns her head to the side, Liam moves back a little, still watching her. After a few seconds, Poppy looks at Liam again and he gives her a gentle kiss on her forehead.

There is nothing Poppy enjoys more than looking closely at the people who love her and care for her – really inspecting their faces for signs of that love (their smiling mouth, dimpling cheeks, and widening eyes).

Liam instinctively knows he needs to bring his face closer to Poppy's for her to see him in focus, as for the first few months after birth she is near-sighted and can only clearly see objects, including faces, that are no more than 30–40 cm away. In those playful moments when her dad copies her facial expression, Poppy is starting to get a sense of what being connected to someone feels like – and for Poppy right now, it feels incredible. Her dad's face has become this funny mirror where she can see the reflection of her own emotions. She is starting to learn about who he is, but also about who she is.

Even though Poppy is still only a few weeks old, she has the capacity to observe and imitate her dad, and by copying what her father does (making an 'O' shape with her mouth), she is also signalling that she wants to play a game with him – asking Liam if he is up for it. These early imitation games are the precursors of more sophisticated turn-taking games, using toys and words that Poppy and her dad will be playing in a few months' time.

Play: a mind-to-mind game

As our babies' bodies grow and develop, so does their curiosity and their appetite for exploring the world. Although our faces are still the main attraction, with their improving eyesight they are starting to look around them, and it is by following their gaze that we can join them in their next adventure.

Eva (eight weeks) and Joe

Eva has just finished being fed by her dad, who has put her down on her back on the sofa while he takes the bottle back to the kitchen. On his return, he sits on the floor next to the sofa. Usually, Eva would then turn her face towards her dad, but today she doesn't. Joe watches Eva for a few seconds and says: 'What is it you are looking at?' He then looks in the direction she is looking in. There doesn't seem anything obvious. 'What is it, Eva? What are you looking at?' Then Joe gets it: there is slight breeze outside, and through the window he can see the leaves of the tree in their garden catching the sun as they gently move . . . 'Ah, you are looking at the tree in the sun. Yes, it is lovely, isn't it? Shall we have a look?' Joe picks Eva up. They go outside and the bright light makes her frown. Every now and then Joe looks at Eva's face to see what she's looking at. When they get to the tree, Joe rustles some leaves a little with one hand. He looks at Eva and says, 'Look, they are moving . . . lots of little green leaves.' Eva looks enthralled by the movement, the light. After a pause, Joe takes her hand and gently moves it towards the leaves. 'Look, they are all soft.' As Eva lets the leaves caress her hand and arm, her eyes slightly widen, her mouth opens as she wriggles her legs with excitement. Joe noticing this, and says: 'Yes, they are very soft. It is nice, isn't it? All soft, and a little bit tickly.'

Joe now puts the leaves in between his face and her face and, as he moves the leaves to the side, says: 'Peekabooo!' Eva's eyes are now so wide open that they look like they might jump out of her face. Joe smiles and adds: 'Here is Eva.' Eva's face relaxes a little.

Joe waits a few seconds and then again puts the leaves in between his face and her face and, as he moves the leaves to the side, says: 'Peekaboo!' Eva seems to hold her breath, but when he says, 'Here is Eva,' she smiles widely and wriggles her legs and arms, as if saying, 'Again, Daddy, again . . .' Eva and Joe play this game several times, each time with Eva getting more excited, opening her eyes wide in the expectation of her father's face reappearing. Until, eventually, Eva turns her head to the side. She needs a rest . . .

Joe had not necessarily planned that, after feeding, there would be play time. He is simply taking the time to be with his daughter, to notice what is important to her – by noticing what she is noticing. He is allowing himself to be curious about her, to understand what is it that has caught her attention and what she finds so fascinating. By following her gaze and trying to look at what she is looking at, it is as if his mind is meeting her mind. And that is something that Eva relishes and needs more than anything. Initially alone in her experience of looking at the tree and the shiny leaves, she is soon joined by her dad and, together, they are able to share the experience, go on the same adventure. This gives Eva a sense of being together with her dad, of being understood by him, of being connected. And, right now, there are no better feelings for Eva: this sense that the adult in charge of her survival is interested in her world and sees it through her eyes is the beginning of a deep trust.

And something else is going on in this particular playtime: novelty. After agreeing to follow Eva on her adventure, Joe now adds a brand-new adventure of his own: he encourages her to touch the leaves. And as Eva enjoys this, he even plays a simple peekaboo game with her . . . a new experience that Eva finds very pleasurable and exciting. Feeling safe in her father's arms and knowing she is held securely in his mind, she is ready for something new, something she has never done before . . .

Thus, without even being aware of it, Joe is slowly helping Eva's ability to deal with unexpected things, which will be a very useful tool as she grows up, as life is full of uncertainty and surprises. Over the next weeks and months, Eva and Joe will play many more peekaboo games and in many different ways, with their hands, blankets, hiding behind sofas and walls. And Eva will slowly learn that she can be okay even when she doesn't know exactly what is going to happen next.

Sometimes these kind of games and adventures, initiated by us, parent or carer, are quite unplanned, flowing naturally in the moment, arising from what we might call maternal or paternal instinct. But on other occasions, when we are busy and seem to have too many things on our minds, we might need to remind ourselves to put in this playtime. Of course, we don't need to go as far as noting it in our diaries, or setting the alarm on our phone. Although, actually, that's no bad thing! The play that follows can be just as much fun, just as much of an adventure, just as nourishing for our babies and just as bonding for the two of us. The more we do it, even if it is planned, the more we are likely to do it by spontaneous instinct.

Play: a body-to-body game

As our babies develop their muscles and their coordination improves, they enjoy spending more and more time on their backs, moving their arms and legs, turning their head from side to side . . . This might be a good time to introduce a little more distance and movement into our games.

Arthur (four months) and Louise

Arthur is lying on a blanket on the floor, looking around him and stretching his legs and arms. Louise, as she lies down on her back beside him, says: 'Let's see how it is down here . . .' After closing her eyes for a few seconds, she turns her head towards Arthur, who has been watching his mum all the time. 'Yes, it's me,' she says to him. As he smiles at her, he stretches his arms above his head. Louise smiles back and stretches her arms above her head. As Arthur brings his legs toward his tummy, Louise does the same. As he lowers his arms, she too lowers her arms. Now he is stretching his arms again above his head and Louise follows suit. As he stretches his legs, she stretches her legs . . . This imitation game goes on for several minutes. And, over time, as Arthur notices that his mum is copying him, he makes an excited high-pitch sound.

Turning his face properly towards his mum, he stretches his arms and reaches out towards her face. Louise shuffles closer to Arthur so he can touch her face. As he puts his hand on her mouth, she pretends to eat it, gently putting her lips around his fingers, saying 'Yum yum yum . . .' Arthur pulls his hand away, not too sure about this. Then, as Louise smiles gently to him, he reaches for her mouth again. Again, she pretends to gently eat his little hand, and he pulls it away, but this time with a little laugh. When he reaches to her face again, and she again pretends to eat it, making delicious yummy sounds, Arthur widens his eyes and now laughs properly as he pulls his hand away. Louise is laughing too as they carry on the game a little longer.

Suddenly, Arthur decides to touch his mother's face with his other hand, crossing this arm right over his body to do so. As he does this movement, he starts rolling onto his side, his eyes open wide with alarm, and he quickly goes back to his initial position on his back. Louise looks surprised too, but she carries on copying her son and rolls gently to her side and then back on her back. Arthur, after kicking his legs vigorously, tries again to touch his mother's face with the opposite hand. This time the movement is vigorous enough that he manages to roll onto his tummy, and once on his tummy, he wobbles a little. Louise now moves closer and says: 'Arthur, you have rolled on your tummy all by yourself – that's amazing! Let me take a picture . . . I will send it to your daddy . . . It is your first roll. I cannot believe it!' Arthur is now smiling, looking quite proud of himself.

By lying next to her baby and imitating his movement, Louise is learning not just to see the world from her baby's point of view but also to physically feel the world in the way that he is feeling it. This shared experience between Arthur and his mother is not just a meeting of minds, but also a co-ordination of bodies. Louise may not necessarily be conscious of it but, by imitating Arthur's movements, she is creating a new body-mind-body connection that allows her to imagine just how Arthur is experiencing the world, and, in so doing, she feels even closer and more connected to him.

A bonus with this sort of play (and again, perhaps, an unconscious reason why she chose to engage in it) is that Louise is also getting some rest. After hours of feeding, it can be extremely relaxing and restorative to just lie on our backs and imitate our babies. In these early months of parenthood, being able to switch into a different mode and get any sort of respite is hugely valuable! So, like Louise, try lying on your back next to your baby and copying them, adding your own extra bit in every now and then . . .

By seeing his movements being reflected in his mother's body, Arthur is learning something about his own body, how different movements feel, what he likes doing and what he doesn't like, what he can and cannot do. On this occasion, having his mother observe him and follow his lead allows him to feel he can be more adventurous and creative with his body, can try things he has not done before. And so, all by himself, Arthur manages to roll on his tummy, suddenly reaching a new milestone in his development.

Playing/Training

These 'firsts' in our babies' behavioural progress are exciting to watch, especially if they have arisen in our most intimate playtime. But we should be a little cautious about wanting them to happen too much or too quickly. With so much information out there about babies' developmental milestones – in books, videos, and so on – it is easy to get disconcerted, and feel that your baby is somehow getting behind. Perhaps you have just come back from your weekly baby group, where you couldn't stop yourself comparing your baby to the others. Try not to let these feelings get to you. And don't, whatever you do, feel tempted to try to get your baby to 'catch up'. This will turn your playtime from fun and exploration into a 'training' session. Of course, encouraging our babies to do things they cannot yet do can be a good thing if it is done sensitively and occasionally. But directing our babies' play, with our own hoped-for outcomes in mind – say, putting their favourite toys slightly out of reach to nudge them to 'practise' rolling over or crawling – can be very stressful for them. And if this is the main form of play they encounter, it will quickly drain the pleasure out of the experience. Nor is it likely to bring them closer to those milestones. Instead of encouraging their development, it might actually hinder it. When a baby is forced into a frustrating and therefore stressful situation, it is likely to increase their cortisol levels, which will displace the feel-good chemicals that they should be getting during play and, in turn, undermine the accompanying feelings of pleasure and safety. If this is repeated often, it can even lower a baby's immune system, and their general sense of wellbeing.

Experiencing pleasure while playing is fundamental to the healthy development of our babies. When our babies are enjoying life, their bodies and brain function at their peak. And in this happy state, our babies' development will forge ahead, boosting their capacity to be curious and to learn new things. So, the best way to keep our babies' body and mind healthy and growing is simply to have fun with them, being led by their curiosity rather than our own hopes or ambitions for them. Let the milestones come as unexpected gifts, not sought-after prizes.

Fortunately, this way of being with our babies is also very good for our own tired brain and exhausted body. Playing with our children boosts our own production of oxytocin, and relaxes and supports our immune system. Every time we make our babies laugh, or have that special eye contact with them, or get the smile that means we cannot help but smile back, our body can be relied on to reward us. We might not always remember this, when we are away from our babies, and thinking more about the undone washing and tidying. When the demands and responsibilities of 'real life' push themselves into our minds, playing with our babies might seem like a frivolous or even boring activity. Or a derogation of our domestic duties. But in truth it is probably just the tonic we need. The feeling that we are at the very least on top of our parenting might help offset the anxiety of that ever mounting pile of laundry or our less than spotless kitchen.

When playing does not come easily

For most of us, playing with our babies is quite intuitive and can quickly become something we enjoy and do without needing to think too much about it. Knowing how much good it's doing will simply reinforce our pleasure and excitement. But for some of us, play does not come so naturally. I talk to many parents who find it difficult just to hang out with their babies, to relax and let their babies take the lead: what are they supposed to do? They feel awkward, watching other parents making funny faces, perhaps talking in a special voice, and it makes them feel deeply self-conscious. When I ask them to think back to how they were parented, they often struggle to remember anyone really playing with them. It wasn't that their parents were ogres, or did a bad job; but they perhaps weren't able to easily stay in the moment or empathise with the childish need to explore the world through just . . . messing about. In their experience, there was more emphasis on formal learning, achievement and success. This being the case, it is not surprising that engaging in baby-play does not come naturally to them. These new parents might be able to absorb all the messages of the above, take on board intellectually the importance of play both for their babies' development and for their mutual bonding, but still find the idea of it daunting or nerve-wracking. Indeed, knowing just how important it is may only make them feel more stressed or anxious.

There are always reasons for these kinds of feelings, and it's important to realise they are not our fault. Our memories of how we were parented provide the model for much of our own parenting instincts, but there is much we can do to override these memories and build new pathways of being. Those of us who struggle to sit back, observe our babies and follow their lead, might have to make a more conscious effort to play with them. As I mentioned above, we might even have to set aside some special playtime, where we try to just do that. And when we do, tempting as it is to come armed with a bunch of pre-formed ideas of games and even props and toys to make them happen, we really don't need to do that. Babies are very good at setting their own learning agenda – and there's a very good reason for that. They don't want to be babies for ever. Driven by their endless curiosity, they know intuitively what they are able, physically and emotionally, to do next.

As we have been witnessing, simply taking the time to observe your baby, taking an interest in their movements, and particularly their eyes, will show you the way. There is a therapeutic phrase that can be very helpful in these sorts of situations: 'Act, and the feelings will follow.' So banish the self-consciousness, and try to let yourself go with the flow – there is no one out there judging you. Just try to follow your baby's lead, and their gaze, and imitate them imitating you. Trust that they know what they are doing and let them be in charge, and respond to their play rather than imposing your ideas and targets. Offer back to them their own expressions and gestures, with perhaps a little bit of exaggeration or emphasis, and occasionally something ever so slightly different to draw their attention, and you won't go far wrong.

Look, I can play on my own . . .

As we have seen, playing face-to-face with our babies, and exploring the world alongside them, is fundamental to their physical, intellectual and emotional development. The next step for them, as they grow more confident, is to start to play and explore not only with us but with the other trustworthy humans in their circle – and from there progress to playing on their own, especially if we are not too far away. But play can only really become a productive, beneficial solitary activity if it has been a social one first. Indeed, all the playing we have done with them in the last few weeks and months has been laying the groundwork for this shift – gradually building those pathways to the Feeling Safe Roundabout (see Chapter 6 – Building our babies' brains).

Igor (three and a half months)

Igor is lying on his back on his playmat, looking excitedly at all the toys dangling above him from the portable mobile. After a little while of just kicking his legs and looking around, he moves his right hand to grab the star toy above his head. But as he touches the star, he knocks it rather than grabbing it, and it slips away from his fingers. Igor kicks his legs even more vigorously and tries again to catch the star. Again, it eludes his grip and swings off like a pendulum. Bringing his legs up over his tummy, he kicks out and knocks one of arches of the mobile with his toes. This makes all the dangling toys move, and the more he kicks the arch, the more they move. Igor's face is lit up with pleasure. He is now using both his legs to make the whole frame of the mobile shake, and all the toys are shaking. As some of them have rattles, they are making quite a loud noise. And then, suddenly, he stops kicking his legs and looks a little shocked by so much movement and noise. He stays relatively still for a few seconds and then goes back to trying to catch the star above his head. Looking quite serious, as if designing the best way of catching it, he launches himself with a roll and swing of his arm, and this time manages to grab it. Igor looks incredibly proud but also not too sure what to do next. He looks around and catches his mother's eyes. She is smiling at him and Igor smiles back at her. 'Wow,' she says, 'that was fun. You caught the star. It was hard, but you managed it.' And as she moves closer to Igor, she adds: 'That was so good, Igor. What are you going to do next?'

While he plays on his own on his mat, Igor is developing his muscles and his motor skills, but most of all he is enjoying noticing how well his body is working and discovering all the things he can (and can't) do yet. He may seem to be kicking his legs randomly, but he is noticing that it is his actions that are making the toys on the mobile swing – he is getting a vital sense of his own agency, learning that he can have an impact on the objects around him. Excited by this new discovery, he also gets a little overwhelmed by it. He is taken to the edge of his excitement and realises that he has gone a little too far. All the mobile toys dangling, swinging and rattling all at once is a little scary for him, so for a moment he needs to go back to where he feels safer. This is a huge developmental step: learning how to regulate his own emotions as he impacts the world around him. And because he is still so very little, meeting his mum's eyes when he is a bit unsure is extremely reassuring for him. He settles quickly back into the space of feeling safe, the extra reassurance from his mum further boosting his oxytocin level. And soon it is time to start playing again . . .

Igor is also building up in himself his all-important capacity for resilience. Before managing to catch the mobile, he fails several times. But instead of feeling defeated and giving up, he is actually rather excited

292

by his near-misses, and stimulated by the accidental wobbling of the mobile toys that he has caused with his kicking. The pleasure he takes in the game he has invented helps him to bounce back each time, and to try again a little harder. All the love and care and fun and play he has enjoyed with his parents have given him the confidence that he can do it . . . and eventually he does.

It is important to note here that his mum did not try to help him catch the star. Although it might have been very tempting for her – it is not always easy to see our babies struggling – she manages to resist the urge to step in. Patiently observing Igor as he gets frustrated by not catching the star, she can sense that this is a situation he can cope with. And thanks to her capacity to refrain from jumping in at the first hurdle, she is helping Igor to get a sense that catching the star is not the most important thing in the world – the trying is fun too . . . Allowing our babies to endure some reasonable and appropriate frustration – effectively placing the emphasis on the effort rather than on the outcome – helps our babies to feel more confident that they have the resources and the capacity to achieve what they want . . . even when all they want is to catch a star.

Play: our baby's secret language

Another aspect of playing that is often overlooked is how it offers a window into our babies' emotional life. When playing, our babies unconsciously explore their own feelings and emotions – and thereby communicate and share them with us, and anyone else close by.

As a child psychotherapist, play is at the centre of my work: it is by observing my little patients playing with the different toys in my consulting room that I get a sense of what is going on for them. The way they treat the family dolls, for instance: which ones they put in the house, which ones they leave outside, whether they handle them with care, or hesitation, or harshly and bullishly. All these details, as they try to make sense of the world through play, are little indications of how they feel about themselves and the world around them. They help me to get a picture of their emotional state, what internal conflict they may be struggling with.

Making sense of the world through play, and communicating some of that back to us, is also what our babies do, even when they have no words yet to attempt to explain what is going on for them. Play is their secret language and we, as parents, need to respect it, and try to understand it. That doesn't mean we need to translate every single action and noise as if it is an urgent message to us. We can just be open to receive some of their most obvious messages through calm and thoughtful observation. By playing with them, and watching them play by themselves, we can see what is troubling or exciting our babies, as they test what they like and dislike, what makes them feels safe and what scares them, what makes them happy and sad . . . Playing is their safe space, where they can experiment not just with their bodies but also with their feelings, letting us know what is going on for them without fear of retaliation or interference. They can push themselves to the edge of what feels safe, even beyond it a little, knowing that we are close by to help bring them back.

Elliot (six months) and Lydia

Lydia has just finished changing Elliot's nappy. Taking a big breath, she puts the palms of her hands on each of the soles of his feet, saying, 'All done.' As she does this, Elliot starts pushing on her hands, one foot after the other, as if he is slowly riding an upside-down bike. To start with, Lydia, looking slightly puzzled, follows the moves a few times. Then Elliot stops. Lydia moves her hands back a little but still leaves them in front of Elliot's feet, touching them very lightly. Elliot starts pushing on his legs again, looking at his mum with big, wide wondering eyes. Lydia now has a smile on her face, and says:' I know what you want to do.' Every time Elliot pushes on her hands she exaggerates a little more the impact it has on her. She makes a whooosh sound and, looking surprised, moves her whole body back slightly, as if being pushed away by the amazing force of little Elliot's tiny feet. When Lydia comes back to the initial position, Elliot's face is quite serious, but he also looks excited and pleased at the impact he is making on his mum. Recognising the power of the moment, she adds a little extra gesture: before putting her hands back onto his feet, she leans over and kisses them, almost as if acknowledging their amazing power. At this, he pushes his feet on her hands again, and as soon as she moves slightly back and makes the whoosh sounds, he starts laughing with all his heart. Lydia and Elliot play this game around six or seven times until Elliot's laughter has lost some of its pleasure quality and he is no longer pushing on her hands so hard. Lydia now places her hand on his tummy and, looking intently at him, says: 'Oh, I love you so much I could eat you . . .'

At first glance, Elliot and his mum's play looks like an ordinary fun game – mum bouncing off his feet and Elliot enjoying the sensation and the exaggerated feeling of his power. If we look a little closer, we can see that Elliot may also be exploring some deeper questions and feelings, and his mother's capacity to deal with them.

Remember that our babies love us when they feel we understand them immediately and respond to the needs they are expressing. But also how they can get annoyed with us when we get it wrong and frustrate them. We are far from perfect parents, and sometimes they might harbour some aggressive feelings towards us for the mistakes we have made (see Chapter 10 – When we feel low). With this in mind, it is possible to see Elliot's game of pushing his mother away with more and more vigour as a way of exploring his more negative feelings towards his mother and how she copes with them. If he pushes her away too much, will she stay away, or even walk away and leave him? Or will she come back to him, and make him feel better again and laugh with him?

Because Lydia is able to turn Elliot's aggression into a game rather than a retaliatory tit-for-tat, Elliot gets a sense that his mother can cope not just with his loving feelings but also with his aggressive ones. This is a huge relief for him, helping him to realise that in the presence of his mother he can be himself, that all his feelings and emotions are important and acceptable to his mother, and that, therefore, he doesn't need to hide a part of himself or mould himself into some ideal version of his mother's wishes and desires.

This game is also a way for Lydia to explore and express some of her own ambivalence towards her son. By telling him that she loves him so much that she could eat him, she is letting him know that, yes, she loves him, but also that there are times when she too feels more aggressive towards him and could eat him . . . With this expression, she is intuitively acknowledging her own ambivalence, her love (I love you, all the kisses) but also her very ordinary feelings of exasperation (I want to eat you) that comes with being a parent.

So you can see that, through this seemingly mundane game, Elliot is learning a profound life lesson – that when he pushes his mum away she will come back no matter what. He is learning about and experiencing his mother's unconditional love for him.

Move towards independence

As our babies become physically more independent, they start exploring the world a little bit further away from us. Thanks to all the playing we have done with them, they have started to learn that they are a separate being from us, with their own body and mind, their own feelings and emotions. And they have started to learn how to regulate some of those feelings, both in relation to us and, when we are not with them, to the world around them.

But crawling away from us, to explore on their own, takes both curiosity and courage. That is why, every now and then, our crawling babies come back to us, asking to be picked up or cuddled so they can recharge their emotional battery and be ready to go off again.

Lily (nine months) and Rose

Lily is sitting on the floor looking at a book. After a little while she crawls over to her mum, who is working at her computer. She grabs the leg of her trouser and pulls herself up. Rose picks her up and sits her on her knees, saying: 'Let me finish this email and I will play with you.' After pressing send, she gives Lily a kiss on her forehead and says: 'So, what do you want to do?' Rose carries Lily over to the area where all the toys are and sits her back on the floor. Lily grabs a ball and throws it. And when the ball rolls

---

behind the sofa, she crawls excitedly after it. As Lily disappears behind the sofa, Rose says, 'Where is Lily?' Lily stops in her tracks and comes back quickly, and then her mum says, 'Here is Lily!' Lily, who has been looking serious, bursts into laughter. Rose then takes the ball and gently makes it roll behind the sofa again. 'Where is the ball, Lily?' she says. Lily crawls after the ball, and as she disappears behind the sofa, Rose says: 'Where is Lily?' Lily crawls back as fast as she can, with a huge smile on her face, and Rosie says: 'HERE IS LILY!' At which Lily throws herself in her mother's arms, laughing. Seconds later, Lily takes the ball again and gently makes it roll behind the sofa. Again, Rosie wonders where the ball has gone, and, again, Lily crawls to find it, and when Lily is behind the sofa, Rose asks where has Lily gone and Lily crawls back as fast as she can, laughing delightedly at her mother's words. But, this time, she crawls right into her mothers' arms, and Rose lifts her up into a big hug, repeating 'Here is Lily, here is my baby!' and giving her lots of kisses. Lily laughs with even more delight and snuggles in her mother's arms.

Before she started playing with her mum, Lily had been spending some time happily playing on her own, looking at her picture books. On the face of it, this may seem like an easier, more relaxing task than throwing a ball and crawling to retrieve it. But actually both are quite emotionally demanding activities for such a little person. And Lily can only manage them for short periods of time and only if she feels safe and relaxed. At Lily's age, playing on her own is both physically and emotionally taxing. And as her play goes on, it is as if her emotional battery slowly goes down and her resilience gradually diminishes. She may, in the books she is looking at, have come across a picture that she found upsetting, or confusing. Hence her need to run back regularly to her mum to get that reassuring and recharging cuddle that will not only make her feel loved and safe again, but also boost her oxytocin levels, giving her the energy and courage to let her curiosity take her back out into the big world and have another go at playing. When her mum then takes her over to the play area, Lily is ready to do something even more adventurous. To begin with, throwing the ball may simply have been an expression of her frustration, or a distraction from some unwelcome thoughts, but it soon turns into an excellent game. Indeed, with this spontaneous game of hide-and-seek, Lily is beginning to understand that even when she cannot see the ball, or indeed her mother, neither actually cease to exist. She can rely on the fact that they will come back to her. Lily has been learning about this since the early peek-a-boo games she played with her parents. But it will take many more months and many more hide-and-seek games before it is well established in her mind.

Knowing and feeling that things and people exist even when she doesn't see them is a cornerstone in Lily's development and her understanding of the world. It will be really useful when she starts nursery. After her parents have dropped her off and disappeared, she will be able to enjoy her time with her friends in the knowledge that her parents, even though she cannot see them, have not gone away for ever. She can be confident they will reappear to pick her up at the end of the nursery day.

School is still some way off, of course. More immediately, Lily and her mum will be contending with another vital separation – bedtime – when it is especially important for our babies to know that we are not going away for ever as we leave them to go to sleep. And that's what we're going to do next.

Observe, follow and meet . . .

- observe your baby's face

- follow their gaze

- follow their lead, let them take you on their adventure

- meet them where they are (and not where you are . . .)

For those who are struggling . . .

- refrain from directing the play

- feel the difference between directing the play and simply adding your own twist (adding in your own twist is putting the cherry on the cake . . . directing the play is making the cake)

- try to enjoy the sense of potency and agency this gives your baby/child

16

Sleeping

An extraordinary emotional experience

S leep – our babies' sleep and ours (or lack of) – has become an obsession. Until our babies wreak havoc in our lives, very few of us really need to worry much about sleep. Apart from an unlucky few, a good night's sleep had mostly been taken for granted. But now that our babies are here, one of the things we long for most in our new baby world, is an uninterrupted night of sleep. We are so sleep-deprived that, at times, we can barely function. In desperation, we have read all the books and blogs, we have listened to all the advice, and still our babies wake up in the night – several times most likely – and we are totally shattered.

One thing we have discovered, though, is that there is no magic solution to help our babies sleep through the night. Anyone promising otherwise is peddling a fantasy. Sleep is a complex physiological and emotional experience that needs to be understood in terms of our *own* feelings and back story, before it can be 'managed' for and by our babies. So before we look at what falling asleep might feel like for our babies, we are going to explore what it really means emotionally for us to put them to sleep.

The ultimate moment of letting go of our babies

Putting our babies to sleep is a highly emotional experience, which is going to give rise in us to many different complex feelings.

Indeed, when our babies shut their eyes, when their breathing becomes deep, slow and regular, we have to face the fact that they are in their own world, with their own mind and their own dreams. In that moment more than in any other moment during the day, we are reminded that they are separate from us, that we and our babies are two different people. So we also have to persuade ourselves that they are going to be okay without us.

For nine months our babies, snuggled in our tummies, have been the closest anyone will ever be to us. And since they were born, we have had to witness their extreme vulnerability and take the measure of the immensity of our responsibility. So letting go of them, trusting that they are going to be okay without us, at least for a little while, can feel like a risky and frightening venture for us. And these anxious feelings can be at their most intense when we put our babies down to sleep: the dance we have been dancing together all day is now broken, and we have to let them drift off in a different world, a world where we are no longer needed and where they can, indeed must, look after themselves. So turning off the lights, kissing them good night, leaving them alone to sleep, becomes a pretty terrifying challenge as well as an extraordinary achievement.

We have spent all day close to our babies, feeding them, playing with them, changing them, locking eyes with them and bonding with them in all the ways we have explored together in this book. And now it is time to put them to sleep and say goodbye, hopefully (but also anxiously) for several hours. They are tired and we too are exhausted. We know we both need some rest and time apart. But managing that moment of letting go of our babies, of separating from them, is often much more complicated than it seems, as it is a moment packed with feelings that are not always easy to understand, let alone face. Indeed, as we get our babies ready, give them a bath, put them in their pyjamas, give them their last feed, walk to their bedroom (or ours) with them snuggled in our arms, lower them in their cot or tuck them up in our bed, we are, albeit often unconsciously, flooded by intense emotions and feelings. We are overwhelmed by the depth of our love for our babies; at the same time we may be undermined by worries about the quality of our parenting. And even more hidden, in the deepest, hardest to access recesses of our mind and memories, we are reminded about our own experience when, as a baby, we were put to bed and left alone by our parents.

So we need to look at all the feelings that are evoked in us when our babies shut their eyes and fall asleep (or not) because whatever we feel is inevitably going to affect how they are going to manage their own sleep and their own letting go of us. Indeed, our babies are masters at reading us, at feeling every hesitation in our hands when we lower them into their crib, every modulation in our voice as we tell them it is time to sleep, every slight alteration in our breathing as we leave the room. Our babies' incredible capacity to read us like open books means that they easily pick up on our emotional state. And this, of course, plays a part in determining whether they feel relaxed enough to fall asleep, or whether they are picking up cues from us that make them confused and anxious to be left alone, and worried to fall asleep. So being aware of our own complex feelings as we prepare to put our babies to bed, will help us bring a more realistic perspective to this daunting task. Ideally, we want to turn these inevitable and necessary separations into more ordinary events, so we can get the refreshment, rest and relief we all need.

Feeling good about putting our babies to sleep

Depending on our own experiences, we all attribute different meanings to the daily task of putting our babies to sleep, and the silence that ensues (if it goes well!). For a few lucky ones, it is quite a straightforward task that is accompanied by an unhurried feeling of satisfaction that we have done a good job today with our babies, and it is time for them to sleep and for us to get a well-deserved rest. We feel pleased, excited even, to have some space for ourselves and to be with our own thoughts for a while and attend to our own needs. Some of us may see our babies, quite early on in our parenting of them, as separate beings from us, with their own physiological and emotional lives. And when we imagine our babies asleep, alone in our bed or in their crib, we imagine them happy to be in their own space with their own dreams and their little body and brain growing. Of course we keep an ear out, but generally we are confident that they can look after themselves while asleep and don't feel the need to check on them every five minutes, or to be glued to the baby monitor, worrying if its batteries might have run out.

But, for a lot of us, putting our babies to sleep is not that simple. It can trigger much more complicated feelings, often tainted with guilt and worry. Before putting our babies to bed, if we pause for a few seconds, we might see that inside us there is something a bit like a boxing match going on: contradictory emotions, feelings and thoughts, fighting with each other for our unconscious attention. And the more aware of these feelings we can be, the easier it will be to process them ourselves so that we do not pass them on to our babies.

Feeling bad about putting our babies to sleep

Putting our babies to bed, letting go of them physically and emotionally, can trigger a mixture of confusing feelings. It turns the ordinary

304

task of putting our babies to sleep into an extra-ordinary one, which feels to us full of hazards and uncertainty.

For some of us, the difficulties around putting our babies to sleep has more to do with having to let go of our 'control' over them, along with the confusing sense that, after being at their beck and call for hours on end, we are suddenly no longer needed. It can be really hard, when we have been looking after them all day, taking care of their most minute needs, to switch off our 'full-on caring mode', and accept that there are things they can do on their own, like sleeping. When we have been in parenting mode all day, changing to 'own time' mode can feel difficult and uncomfortable. This is especially true for those of us for whom taking care of others has always felt easier than taking care of ourselves.

For many of us, being needed by our babies can feel very reassuring, as it offers a discreet but efficient way not to look too closely at our own needs and neediness. (Maybe now is a good time to pause and see if that is a pattern we also fall into with other people, for example siblings, friends, partner?) We are very good at putting our own needs second to our babies', as generally this has been a well-learned pattern since childhood, when our own parents struggled to put our baby needs before theirs. Having rarely had our own needs acknow-ledged as a child, it is much easier for us to deal with others' needs and expectations – for example, our parents – than to face and manage our own. Now, to have babies who find it hard to sleep without us beside them or can only manage to sleep in our arms or in their sling, allows us to continue to be busy with their care even in their sleep. So we may be unconsciously creating and perpetuating this dynamic, to serve our own purposes. This gives us an all-encompassing reason not to have to face our own needs, and even if that makes us totally exhausted, we carry on doing it . . . It doesn't, of course, suit our shattered bodies, yet we find it somehow emotionally convenient.

If we are not sure whether we belong to this category or not, one way of exploring what is happening is to ask ourselves: is having my baby asleep in my arms really helping them to feel better, or is it helping me to feel better? Of course, our babies love being in our arms, and it is important that they do spend plenty of time snuggled up against us, but it is also important, at times, to try to observe and notice what part we are playing in a situation. Am I keeping my baby asleep in my arms because I am really enjoying it or because, if I don't have my baby in my arms, I am not too sure what I am supposed to be doing, or I might feel lonely. If we recognise that, more often than not, we are keeping our babies asleep in our arms, because it helps distract us from other concerns or responsibilities, then that is the start of an awareness that may help us separate our feelings about our babies from our feelings about ourselves. And if we find that confusing or upsetting, it is perhaps a good idea to share our thoughts and feelings with someone who we trust can listen to our concerns without judging us, and thereby help us make sense of them. Once we become aware of our conflicting feelings, we can think of them in our mind, acknowledging and processing them, rather than passing them unconsciously on to our babies, making it easier for them to feel relaxed about falling asleep.

Our ambivalent feelings

Putting our babies to sleep is also a moment when we inevitably have to face our own very ordinary ambivalent feelings about our babies and about being a parent (see Chapter 10 – When we feel low). And for some of us, it can be hard to have to face that, yes, sometimes we'd love to have some time to ourselves, to have our own thoughts or even just to be able to go to the loo or have a shower when we want. We may feel guilty admitting to ourselves that there are moments when we miss our old life and we wish we were still free to do whatever we like, that caring for our babies is much harder than we thought it was going to be, and that sometimes we don't find it straightforward to love our babies. It's a good time to remind ourselves that such feelings are normal and needn't send our feelings of guilt soaring off the scale. In fact, in this context, a bit of regular, common or garden-variety guilt pretty much comes as standard.

But putting our babies to sleep can, for some of us, come to symbolise those moments of ambivalence, when we have to face some of our less than loving feelings for our babies . . . And as these feelings are at times hard to admit, this can lead us to be rather inconsistent with the way we handle our babies at bedtime, sometimes putting them to bed with confidence in our parenting but at other times feeling wobbly and guilty about the very act of putting them down to sleep. And, of course, our babies, who thrive on consistency, inevitably pick up on that. And as they struggle to feel safe enough to fall asleep on their own, they are likely to become clingy.

Let's listen to the words of the most sung lullaby in the English language:

> Rock-a-bye baby on the tree top,
> When the wind blows the cradle will rock,
> When the bough breaks the cradle will fall,
> And down will come baby, cradle and all.
> Down will come baby, cradle and all.

There are few lullabies that capture parents' ambivalent feelings so poignantly. It's really quite extraordinary, if you think about it, that we sing, in the gentlest and most soothing voices we can find, words that express our deepest and darkest fears, that our babies will crash out of their fragile sleep, as gentle rocking turns into a wild, terrifying fall . . . And yet gently hoping for the best, while calmly fearing the very worst, has clearly been deeply therapeutic for parents singing this song, and for babies gently drifting off to sleep, for centuries. It's worth considering here, that it's quite likely to be the calming of the singer, transforming their worst anxiety into something soft and harmless, that has the knock- on effect of soothing the baby they are singing to. So, as we sing 'Rock-a-bye baby', let's try to accept our ambivalent feelings as ordinary and healthy. And, also, let's not forget that, after all, if right now we want a bit of time on our own, it is because we have spent a lot of time with our babies today.

Too many difficult memories

Sometimes it is the silence and calmness that follow our babies falling asleep that can feel unsettling, as it leaves us alone with our own thoughts and memories, conscious or otherwise. And for those of us who have suffered a traumatic birth, for instance, or whose babies had to spend time in the Neonatal Intensive Care Unit, this can be a time when the memories feel overwhelming, sometimes even resulting in disturbing flashbacks. Revisiting the experience of giving birth (or witnessing our partner giving birth), or of our tiny babies surrounded by noisy machines, of things happening and decisions made that were outside our control, can flood us with scary feelings and make us feel very upset. Every bedtime can become a reminder of those very difficult moments of separation, and we might find ourselves very conflicted about letting go of our babies. Keeping our babies close to us can be a way to protect ourselves, a sort of armour from those intrusive images or thoughts. If that is the case, then talking to someone about this, perhaps a professional who can help with trauma, is important. This is especially crucial if the feelings are seriously preventing us from resting and sleeping, as the lack of sleep inevitably makes the traumatic memories more vivid and intrusive. This vicious circle can eventually lead to us feeling very low and possibly depressed (see Chapter 10 and the resources at the end of book).

Feeling like a neglectful parent

For some of us when we try to put our babies to bed, we can't help but feel we are blatantly depriving them of our support and love, withholding our deep and caring instincts for them, almost against our will. This makes it really easy to feel like a bad parent. Indeed, instead of imagining our babies content and safe as they sleep, we quickly imagine them lonely, sad, upset and may be even at risk. And it's all our fault!

Sometimes the feeling can be so strong that we cast ourselves as a neglectful parent and putting our babies to sleep becomes equivalent to some sort of abandonment, for which we deserve the harshest judgement. The separation that comes with falling asleep is experienced by us in such a negative way that, as we lower them in their cot, it is easy for our babies to pick up on those feelings and to quickly feel confused themselves. They may start to feel unsafe to be left alone. So instead of being relaxed and gradually falling asleep, they feel tense and worried, reflecting their anxiety back to us in a way that inevitably raises our own, in a negative spiral of worry.

Those powerful, spiralling feelings are very likely to come from our own childhood experience (our childhood 'sleep baggage', if you like) of being put to bed as a small child, or being left at school, or at granny's, or in any situation where we felt unhappy or anxious to be left by our parents. In those moments of separation, because of the way they were handled, it was easy for us to feel abandoned. We may even have worried that our parents were getting rid of us for ever . . .

And now, at our babies' bedtime, it is hard not to see our babies through the lens of our own experience, and imagine them feeling abandoned as we leave them to sleep. So negotiating a separation as ordinary and as necessary as sleep is fraught with frightening feelings, as we worry that we might be like our parents, and that our babies are going to feel as abandoned as we did. Sometimes that thought is so unbearable that we find it almost impossible to let go of our babies, or to handle the idea of our babies letting go of us, as with Eric, Anita and Joseph below.

Eric (seven months) and Anita and Joseph

Anita and Joseph came to see me because of sleep problems with their five-months-old baby, Eric. In the session, Joseph explained that Eric would only fall asleep at Anita's breast and holding very tightly on to Anita's long brown hair. During our work together, it became quickly apparent that Joseph found the situation difficult, as this meant he often felt excluded and on his own. Anita explained that she felt that by holding on to her hair so tightly, Eric was telling her that he did not want to let go of her and wanted her by his side all the time.

Trying to explore further, it became clear that, for Anita, the idea of leaving Eric on his own in his cot, filled her with huge anxiety. The possibility that he could wake up alone and possibly be upset without her in close proximity to instantly soothe and reassure him was so unbearable to her that she would insist on carrying him everywhere with her, even when he was fast asleep and could have been put down to sleep in his cot. Anita felt she was a good parent only as long as Eric was in her sight, or, even better, in her arms. The closer to Eric, the better she felt as a parent, and the bigger the distance between her and Eric, the worse she felt as a mother.

As we tried to understand why Anita was equating so strongly separation with bad parenting, in one session she burst into tears, recalling how, when she was around seven years old, she had been told off and made to feel silly by her mum for worrying about her much younger baby brother, who was often left crying upstairs for long periods of time, until he eventually fell asleep. Feeling so powerless at the time, Anita, albeit unconsciously, was determined that she was never going to feel like that again.

Anita and Eric's feelings had become very knotty and bound up together, and part of our work was to untangle the different feelings by finding out if it belonged to Eric or to Anita, then giving it back to its rightful owner. Picking up on his mum's anxiety and confusion, Eric hangs on to his Mum's hair very tightly, as she is unconsciously communicating to him that the only really safe place for him is in her arms. But, in fact, it is Anita who is struggling to feel safe when she is away from Eric: for her, being separate from her baby has become synonymous with being a bad mother, a feeling that, of course, she doesn't want to feel. The idea of Eric being left alone, even for a few seconds of soft crying, fills her with that terrible sense of powerlessness and guilt that she experienced when she was a child when she couldn't help her baby brother and, at the same time, was made to feel ashamed by her mother.

Listening to Anita's upsetting early experiences not only helped her to process some of the difficult feelings associated with them but also to see her baby in a different light. In the course of the six sessions we had together, Anita managed to slowly and thoughtfully let go of the image of Eric as a powerless baby, who if left alone would feel lonely and sad and fearful. Supported by Joseph, her partner, and encouraged to understand that what happened when she was a child was not her fault, she was able to come to see a strong and confident Eric, who sometimes needed his own space and place to rest, and who certainly had a powerful voice, which he knew very well how to use if he wanted to let her know when things were not okay . . .

Joseph, was also very instrumental in helping her change how she saw her son. For the first three weeks during our therapeutic work together, Joseph was in charge of bedtime. Although it was not easy to start with for Anita, this gradually helped her realise that Eric could manage falling asleep in his cot, that he did not have to be held for hours on end. As her sense of Eric's needs and abilities gradually changed, as well as her understanding of the experience of sleep, Anita could now convey to him gently and clearly, as she got him ready for bed, a feeling that sleep was a safe and nourishing experience and one he was now strong enough to manage in his own space. Feeling more relaxed and safe, Eric slowly could let go of his mum and start sleeping in his cot.

As we can see here, putting our babies to sleep for us parents often fills us with powerful and complex emotions. So, more than any other activities we do with our babies, putting them to bed is a moment when it is easy for our feelings and emotions to get tangled up with theirs.

So let's play the Untangling Game . . .

The Untangling Game

On little bits of paper, write the suggestions below: simple expressions of things that you or your baby might (or might not) be feeling.

I am feeling abandoned

I am feeling excluded

I am scared to be alone

I don't like the silence

I don't like the dark

I have had a good day and feel happy

I have had a stressful day and feel sad and fed up

I feel redundant

I feel calm

I feel tired/exhausted

I feel frustrated and wish I had done more today

I have done all I could today and feel content

Now fold up each piece of paper so you can't see what's written on them. Shuffle them around on the table. Then take different cups or glasses, one representing you and one representing your baby. Now, as you pick each piece of paper, try to think carefully, and in an unhurried way, whether the feeling written on the paper belongs to you, or to your baby – and put it in the designated cup or glass. If it belongs to neither, that's fine. Just put it to one side.

This simple exercise of self-questioning and self-acknowledgement can help us appreciate that a lot of the feelings that we attribute to our babies are actually ours. And this realisation can really help dis-empower those anxious feelings. This will make us feel much freer, less trapped by our negative thinking or our past, in the way we handle our babies as we put them down to sleep.

When we have sorted out or own feelings about this intense moment of putting our babies down to sleep, we can then look in a much clearer, unconfused way, at what falling asleep might really mean for our babies.

Falling asleep: our babies' experience

The first experience of sleeping for our babies, while we were preg-nant, was very much a co-sleeping experience, with them snugly curled up in our tummies. I mean that not necessarily in the sense that they slept inside our tummies when we slept (though sometimes that might be the case, or, on the contrary, that might have been when they decided to practise their somersaults), but that they slept in a way that was co-ordinated by our movements and habits. They were rocked to sleep by the movement of our bodies, and the sounds of our voices chatting with our partner and friends, the music in the room, the film on the TV, the radio in the car were their constant soothing lullabies. And through all of this they have the constant companionship of our heartbeat.

With their sudden and somewhat brutal departure from our tummies, our babies have lost that cosy snugness and all the softened, filtered background noise of their uterine lives . . . Now everything is different: they experience sometimes the harsh unfiltered sounds of our busy lives, and at others the brand-new silence of night. That's why our newborn babies love (and need) so much to spend time against our chest, hearing our heartbeat (a little fainter now than when they were inside us); or being rocked in our arms, with the gentle sounds of our humming and chatting voice, and the soft rustle of our clothing, giving them comfort. All of this makes the transition from uterine co-sleeping to 'real life' a little more bearable. It also helps them regulate their temperature as well as their own heartbeat.

But when the time comes for sleep away from our bodies, there comes with it the novelty of silence. There is no longer even our heartbeat, our blood flowing in our body, our gurgling digesting tummy to kept them company. Instead, the background noise of their uterine lives is now replaced by silence or at best a murmur of our grown-up lives nearby, and with it an inevitable sense of loneliness and a feeling of being excluded.

A place in our mind

Although our babies knew how to sleep in our tummies, they now have to learn from scratch how to sleep in this totally new world they have landed in. And it will take them months (perhaps just a few, perhaps many) for them to learn to trust that, when they fall asleep, they might fall (gently) out of our arms as we put them down, but they do not fall out of our mind. This sense that even though they are not in the same room as us, we have not forgotten them, they are still important to us, is essential for our babies to feel safe and relaxed enough to drift off. But to get that feeling that they exist in our minds, our babies need time with us, with lots and lots of cuddles and interactions.

Love-energy

In the same way we need to feed our babies with milk during the day so they have enough 'milk-energy' in their body to physically grow and last until the morning, we also need to feed them with our love so they have enough 'love-energy' to emotionally grow and last until the morning too. But when they are tiny, not only is their metabolism still too immature to last more than a couple of hours without needing more milk, but their mind, too, is still too immature to be away from us for very long without a top up of our reassuring love. And that is why our newborn babies generally prefer to fall asleep in our arms, and why they regularly wake up crying for us in the night. Their tiny minds have sparked into wakefulness, and their most urgent need, before even the nourishing milk they need, is a rapid refill of our love and reassurance that they are firmly lodged in our minds.

As their stomach grows, they can take more milk and don't need to be fed so often, and eventually they are able to last until the morning without a feed. And in just the same way, as their mind grows and with it their trust that we have not forgotten them, they also grow some storage space in their minds. Here they can store the good feelings and love we have lavished on them throughout the day, helping them not to need so much of our physical closeness in the night either. And with this metaphorical battery of loving feelings fully charged, they will start to find it easier to fall asleep on their own. And soon, if they wake up, they may even be able to fall back asleep without us, as they can still access that charge, and the feeling that they are safely in our mind.

Love-feeding

The great news is that love-feeding is, as we have seen throughout this book, what we do all the time: we feed it with our tender voice, our soft hands, comfy arms, delicious smell, loving eyes, warm smile, curious mind . . . We love-feed our babies when we milk-feed them (as we have seen in Chapter 14 – Feeding), but also when we change their nappies, give them a bath, dry them, put their clean clothes on, play all those fun games with them, smile at them, chat with them, sing them a song, cook them food, warm up their bottles, take them for a walk, show them the spring blossom, and the raindrops on the window, tidy up their toys, take them to play-groups or to see granny and grandpa, read them books, tell them stories . . .

With this rich input of our love throughout the day, by the time they are ready to go to bed, they are full of the feelings of being valued, of being important, of being interesting, of being worth knowing, of being well-loved. And it is with these incredibly delicious feelings that they are going to slowly fall asleep . . .

So, as we kiss them goodnight, as we slowly but confidently step out of the room, we are no longer leaving our babies on their own: we are leaving them with all those yummy, lovely feelings. Gently falling asleep, they can savour all the memories of the day, of the books read, of the warm bath water, of the tasty milk, of the funny songs, of the comforting cuddles, of the new noises, of our loving smiles and our shining eyes. And with our lingering sweet smell in the room, and the dreamy reverie of the memories of the day, they will slowly fall asleep . . .

And as time passes and our babies develop, sleep no longer means that feeling of loneliness and exclusion of the early weeks and months. Sleep becomes synonymous of that restorative state, when their bodies grow, their immune and nervous system get replenished and their brain and mind expand so they are ready for another day of dancing with us.

My view, as both a clinician and a mother of four babies, who all had very different sleep patterns, is that we are not going to solve the mysteries of sleep by clock-based routines of feeding and putting down, and waking up, and more feeding, etc. Of course, we all wish there was a magic trick that could make our babies sleep through the night from day one. But the reality is that it will take time for them to find their own rhythm. And one way we can support them is by playing the Untangling Game. Regularly sorting out which feelings belong to who will help us process our own anxiety around what it feels like for us to put them to bed at night. It will also give us a renewed enthusiasm to continue to nourish them throughout the day with our love and reassurance, and even a more carefree sense of fun while we play, so they can trust more and more that even when they are in their own sleepy world, they are still firmly anchored in our mind and our heart. We are always thinking of them.

17

Babies and the family

The home environment

So far, we have mainly focused on our individual relationship with our babies and the many different ways in which we can bond with them. But our babies are each born into a family – and home – with its own individual atmosphere. And that home, that family life, is also going to influence who they become.

When meeting families in my clinic, I try to get a sense of what life at home is like for them: is it a warm, caring place? Somewhere where everyone feels they are cherished, and can be themselves? Or is it perhaps rather chaotic and loud, and, if so, is this in a generally good-natured and forgiving way? How do the different members of the families interact with each other, and resolve the inevitable tensions that arise from sharing a living space?

The atmosphere at home forms the background of our baby's childhood and, at a neurological and hormonal level, it is going to have a strong impact on their brain development. As we have seen, when a baby experiences stress, their brain becomes flooded with cortisol – the hormone that puts them on high alert. If a baby grows up in a home full of disharmony, where difficulties lead to conflict and perhaps even violent arguments, and this happens regularly and repeatedly, rather than just occasionally, in the long term it is likely to have a detrimental effect on, among many other things, their ability to make close friendships at play and at school, and to stay focused in class. By contrast, a home where difficult things can generally be talked about and resolved is going to create a kinder hormonal cocktail, full of dopamine, serotonin, endorphins and oxytocin, allowing our babies to become more trusting of their relationships and the world.[1] So spending some time thinking about the environment our babies are going to grow up in is important.

The two main parents

Even if, for obvious biological reasons, a baby's earliest relationship is with their mother, they very soon start forming relationships with the other people around them too. Long gone is the time when it was thought that all the responsibility for our babies and children's well-being fell on their mother's shoulders. Depending on the family structure – and there are a great many of these – the other people in our baby's life can range from their second parent and step-parents, to their grandparents and siblings, nannies, nursery staff, close friends, even a friendly neighbour . . .

As we saw in Chapter 1, the second parent's relationship with their baby generally starts pre-birth, when their oxytocin levels match those of the pregnant mother, depending on how involved they become in the pregnancy. And this relationship is likely to have a vital influence on their baby's future. Many studies have shown that children who have had a good relationship with their second parent do better at school, have more friends and are more protected from mental health difficulties in their teens and later in life. So, for the moment, let's focus on the relationship between the two main parents (we will look at single parenthood in a moment, although a lot of what I say about co-parenting applies equally to single parenting) because, for our babies to have a strong relationship with both their parents, whatever their gender or type of relationship, those parents need to be getting on well, interacting respectfully and thoughtfully with each other.

How babies impact on couples

It is easy for first-time parents to think that they will get their baby to fit around their lives. But soon enough they come to the hard realisation that it is they who have to fit around their baby's life. As we have discussed, tiny babies have no routine: they eat when they are hungry, they sleep when they are tired, and when they want something they want it *now*. Whenever they are awake (and, actually, even when they are sleeping) what they like best is to be with us – all the time. As I said earlier, if anyone were to treat us in the way that a newborn baby treats their parents, we would be urged by our family and friends to leave that person immediately and move on.

So if you chose to have a baby because you felt that it would make your relationship with your partner happier and stronger, you might be in for a shock! Researchers studying the level of satisfaction in relationships have found that couples without children are generally more satisfied than couples with children, and that parents' dissatisfaction increases with each child that they have. One of the key findings was how much a baby tends to push parents back into stereotypical roles and gender expectations. And this may be partly why, in one particular study, 62 per cent of mothers of young babies said they were unhappy with their relationship with their partner.[2]

For many women, finding themselves suddenly stuck at home with a baby can be very oppressive. Only a few weeks ago they may have been out all day working, earning their own money, meeting up with their own friends and generally trying to maintain an equal relationship with their partner. After a baby is born, the domestic tasks feel more urgent and unavoidable: if recently they could happily have ignored a pile a dirty clothes, dirty dishes in the sink, or a smelly bin until their partner dealt with it, now that they are in the house all day they find it difficult to ignore these domestic responsibilities. Their partner going off to work each morning only exacerbates that sense of inequality.

Their baby's constant needs can also make mothers feel trapped. And, if they are breastfeeding, the feeling that they are potentially needed all the time can intensify this sense of their loss of freedom. It is interesting to note that the same study mentioned above highlights that higher socio-economic groups are more at risk of being dissatisfied in their relationship once they have a baby.[3] So it seems that the more educated and financially independent we are, the more difficult it is going to be to adapt to being a parent. And it is especially true for those who have been pushed from a young age to be high achievers at school. But one such study should not distract us from the fact that all mothers, of every kind, will sometimes feel trapped by motherhood. Staying at home with a baby who, even though they do not speak yet, is nevertheless a master at highlighting all the things that their parents are not (yet) very good at, is a challenge for everybody. Plus, unlike a job, which they were able to leave at the end of the day, parenting is a 24/7 activity, and it doesn't come with paid holidays!

So, yes, adding a third human being to a relationship can be hard to navigate for a couple, especially when that new addition is so helpless, vulnerable and demanding. And the relentlessness of parenting, especially in the first two years, can leave mothers feeling bewildered, resentful and increasingly disconnected from their partner. However, this does not mean our relationships are doomed and having babies is going to make us miserable. On the contrary, at a personal level, for the large majority of parents (70 per cent), having children makes their own lives, in the long term, more meaningful, bringing with it a deep sense of well-being.[4]

The tricky part tends to be the transition from being a couple without babies to a couple with babies. And many studies have shown that the more future parents take the time to think and talk about how their lives are going to change as a couple – imagining both the potential pitfalls of bringing a baby into the relationship and the joys – the smoother the transition and in the long term the happier they will be in their relationship.[5] The themes that parents have retrospectively found are the most useful to explore include how to share their home and the baby-related workload, how to make time for each other and how to share their feelings and show their appreciation of each other.

Preparing to be a parental couple

Staying connected requires good communication. So, taking the time to sit down together to think about what's coming down the line, and to talk about your relationship and how it is going to be affected, is a good habit to get into. Before you start, you might suggest that your partner reads this section (or indeed the whole book!) as a way of getting them into the same frame of mind as you. And when you've had some useful conversations and come to some conclusions, you could even sign up to some mutual agreements about how you are going to adjust and manage things.

Here are some suggestions about how you could start those conversations. And, by the way, it's definitely not advisable, or even feasible, to try to work your way through all these topics in a single session.

Perhaps you could take it in turns to choose the topics? And, of course, you should feel free to add other talking points that I may well have overlooked, if they feel important to you.

- How do each of you imagine your individual lives with a baby? What are your hopes and fears? Are they similar or different?

- How do you imagine your life as a couple with a baby? What are your hopes and fears? Are they similar or different? How can you help and support each other to manage them?

- How are you going to share the household chores? Who is going to do what? Rotating them and sharing them, rather than dividing them up between you, might well be more conducive to long-term harmony. On the other hand, one of you agreeing to always take care of something, so the other doesn't ever have to worry about it, could also be hugely appreciated, and therefore constructive. And if you feel the other is not doing their share, how are you going to talk about it? Creating a regular space in the week to review how things are going can help with resolving issues, making decisions, and avoiding resentment.

- How are you going to share the baby-related tasks? Who is going to get up in the night, change nappies? Which of you will take on the majority of the feeding? And don't forget the importance of play! Again, making a regular appointment to go over the arrangements can be useful.

- How are you going to support each other? List as much as you can of what you anticipate your specific needs will be.

- How are you going to ask for help if you need it? And how good are you going to be at accepting that help? It might be helpful to agree a time and a place for sharing worries and stresses, so they don't boil over in the moment they are most intensely felt.

- How do imagine your close family/friends are going to support you? How do you feel about parents and parents-in-law stepping in to help? Do you think paying someone to help alleviate the workload and stress might be right for you both?

- Talking about your feelings can seem exhausting when you are already tired from a long day of childcare. How are you going to tell your partner, for example, that you feel they are not listening to you or hearing you?

- Can you imagine yourself giving advice to each other on how to look after the baby? How are you going to handle each other's possible criticisms? Try to think of ways of turning potential criticism into constructive advice, so that you can be supportive of each other rather than undermining.

- Think about how you were both parented. Then imagine how you are going to parent your baby. Are you going to be like your own parents, or parent in a different way? What are the things you might do differently?

- How are you going to continue being a romantic couple – creating those special moments of connection when you do things together, making time for each other, eating together (no phone or TV), taking the time to watch a film or going out together, and also having time-out with friends?

- And what about sex? How do you think sex is going to be once the baby has arrived? Will you be able to talk about it and let your partner know how you feel about it?

What matters most, once your baby has arrived, is to keep talking to each other and to keep listening. It is the powerful feelings that come with being heard and understood by your partner that will sustain your relationship, especially in the early months when your world has been turned upside down by your baby. And if you manage to do that, if you manage to stay connected, then a quick catch-up every day on how things are going, and a regular (perhaps weekly) longer chat about what is going well and what is not going so well for each parent, and what changes would make a difference, will help to build and embed the habit of being mutually supportive and working together as a couple.

Parenting together: the magic triangle

Once your baby has made it into the heart of your family, the next matter that has the potential to bring you closer as a couple or to push you further apart is your ability (or inability) to be aligned in your parenting. This is not about how you are going to share chores and decide who does what and when. Rather, it is about your attitude towards parenting itself – how you as parents (in the widest sense possible – you certainly do not have to be in a romantic relationship to parent together) want to be with your baby and respond to their needs.

This ability and readiness of two people to parent together – i.e. to think more or less along the same lines – is another important aspect in the family dynamic that I keep an eye on (and ear out for) when parents come to see me in clinic. When listening to them and observing their interactions, I soon get a sense of whether talking to me about their baby's or child's difficulties brings them some relief and makes them feel closer. Or if, on the contrary, it is something that exposes the differences in their parenting and increases the tension between them.

It is usually at this point that I start drawing triangles on a piece of paper. At the top I write the name of the child; in the two bottom corners I write the name of each parent. Then, pairing the corners together with big circles, I point out that, since the arrival of their babies, the number of couples in the family has actually gone from one to three: two parent-baby couples and a parental couple. It is common at this point for parents to express some surprise: why am I circling their two names together? A lot of parents, who after the birth have put all their attention and effort into forming a bond with their babies, can easily forget that they were and still are a couple themselves, albeit also a couple of parents!

Let's look more closely at this parental couple for a moment, because it is such an important part of the parenting puzzle. Despite the myth put out all around us about perfect parenting, parenting together is not necessarily either easy or instinctive. For almost all of us it takes practice. And that's okay, because practising is good! It tends to bring us together. It is also likely to make parenting much more enjoyable – which, of course, in turn will greatly benefit our babies.

Creating a safe space

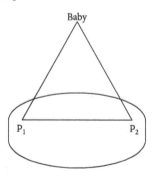

Spending nine months in utero, we might imagine, can give a baby a sense of being merged with their mother for ever. Their physical birth will, of course, go some way to shattering this illusion, but a baby also needs to experience a kind of 'psychological birth' to complete their separation, and become the autonomous person they need to be to have a life of their own. The good news is that, in a two-parent family, these psychological births, unlike the physical births, do not rest disproportionately on the mother's shoulders. On the contrary, the best way for parents to help their babies be born psychologically is by parenting together. And for this they need to create a safe space both physically (in their home) and psychologically (in their combined minds) to enable their baby to start the daunting adventure of developing their physical and mental independence, and eventually separating from them in a safe and healthy way.

When parents put their minds together, manage to think collaboratively and align their different perspectives to create a coherent and predictable atmosphere at home, their babies get that amazing feeling that is so important to their development: the feeling that they matter to their parents, that their well-being is important to them. It is as if, by bringing their minds together, parents co-create a cosy psychological womb, where their babies can feel safe and slowly build up the strength and capacity to start the challenging adventure of growing up.

Remember what we learned earlier about how much babies love interacting with us, looking at our face, which for them is like a mirror where they see their own emotions being reflected and can start learning about themselves and how they feel (see Chapter 8 – The power of being thought about)? Well, having two parents who can bring their minds together to think about them is like having an extra mirror where they are going to get a whole new reflection of themselves, but this time a more three-dimensional one. The experience of being looked at and thought about by two parents at the same time, as well as being exposed to the inevitable slight (but valuable) differences between our two perspectives, gives our baby a fuller and more complex sense of themselves.

Of course, there will be times when, firmly seated at the top of the triangle and witnessing their parents' co-operation, a baby will feel excluded and become a little envious and jealous. As they get older, they might even become suspicious of that close relationship: what if their parents were not just thinking about them? What if their parents were thinking about making another baby? Later on, it is not unusual to see toddlers and young children coming between their parents, to try to divide them in a bid to keep one of them to themselves – and perhaps even to prevent the possible appearance of a rival in the home. That is why it is a good idea for parents to keep that triangle in their mind and check every now and then how their parental couple is working.

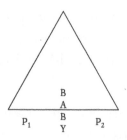

If, one day, in your triangle, you find a little child sitting in the middle, somewhere between the two of you, then it's time to gently move them back up to the top by bringing your minds together again. It is from there that your child will have the best view and most nourishing experience of the coherent narrative created by you, their parents.

And, more generally, when you find that the base of the triangle is getting wobbly, that your ideas about how to do things with your baby or child are no longer aligned with your co-parent's ideas, when parenting brings tension rather than pleasure, it is important to take the time to sit down and explore how best to work through your differences and start supporting each together again.

Bonding with each parent

For parents to be able to cooperate in their thinking about their baby, they each need to have their own individual relationship with them; and this requires that parents are able to 'share' their baby and generally give each other enough space to build their own distinct bond.

To begin with, it can be hard for parents to share their baby with each other. This is especially true for mothers, who, after carrying their babies for nine months in their tummies, and experiencing the intensity of giving birth, can find it emotionally complicated to let go of their babies, even momentarily. For these mothers, it can take a bit of time to be less permanently hands on, and ready to cede some of the care to their co-parent. Their co-parents might, therefore, need to be patient and ready, initially at least, to put up with a degree of scrutiny over how they do things (whether it be changing nappies, or giving them a bath), and take potentially un-wanted advice (that it is better to do it like this or like that).

One way to mitigate this is to try to spend as much time as possible together with your baby early on, literally sharing the tasks: taking time to bath your baby together, to get them dry, dress them, change their nappies . . . This allows you to create together your own parenting culture. This is reassuring not only for both of you – we now know that the other is going to do things roughly the same way you do them (or at least in a way you can cope with!) but also for your baby, who gets that consistency they so love and need. Simply watching your baby when they are asleep, wondering together what they might be dreaming about, or what that little twitching cheek might mean, or sharing how you each feel about your baby can be an extremely powerful way not only to bond and fall in love with your little one but also with each other – as parents and not just partners!

Push-me-pull-you

If some mothers find it hard at times to share their baby, equally some co-parents also find it hard to be interested in their newborn. It is still quite common, during sessions in my clinic, to hear fathers declare that babies are boring (I hope I have proved that they are not!) and that, until their babies are old enough to play football with them, they are not going to get too involved. I like to remind those fathers that, they'd better start building a good relationship with them now or they might find that that child is not very interested in kicking a ball around with them when the time comes. Indeed, to all co-parents, I say please don't wait for your baby to talk and walk before starting to get to know them: bonding and parenting start on day one and you need to keep it going every day.

That said, co-parents need to be given some time and space and encouragement to build a meaningful bond with their babies. And this may require the 'main' parent (usually the one who spends more time with the baby) to take a step back. As we have seen, having two parents makes our baby's emotional life richer. They find a different picture of themselves reflected in each of their parent's faces, and this variety, if you like, nourishes the development of different aspects of themselves that might not otherwise flourish in the same way. It also makes our own life richer: watching our co-parent interacting with our baby and slowly creating that deep bond with them (and later on kicking that football together) can be a source of tremendous joy and relief, reminding us in those moments that we are not alone, that not everything depends on us, and that if something were to happen to us they would be there to look after our babies and our babies would okay.

Our soft and firm parental minds

It has traditionally been argued that mothers and fathers parent differently because of their gender. Mothers have tended to be viewed as the primary source of empathy, while fathers have tended to be viewed as the enforcers of law and order. This perception is outdated not just socially, but scientifically, as it is now clear that *both* parents – and this should be reassuring for single parents and same sex parents – possess what have been called 'maternal capacities' and 'paternal capacities'. Whatever their gender, parents can both empathise with their babies and they can both set limits. Continuing to use gendered words to describe those aspects of parental care is therefore doing a disservice to parents and babies as, even if only subconsciously, it reinforces the outdated stereotype of mothers and fathers taking different roles, when actually more closeness and cooperation are what is needed. So instead of talking about maternal and paternal 'capacities' and characteristics, I prefer to refer to the different ways of being with our babies as *soft* and *firm*.

The soft facet of parenting is when, full of empathy, we jump into our baby's shoes and see the situation from their perspective. We become a fervent advocate of their emotions and feelings. By contrast, the firm facet is when we step out of our baby's shoes and, seeing the situation in a more objective way, are able to set some reasonable limits on their behaviour and demands.

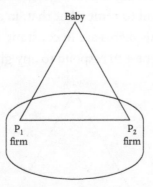

A more simplistic way of looking at the different parenting types would be to say that the soft parent says 'yes, yes, yes, I am with you', while the firm parent says 'no, no, that's not the way to go'. Our triangle now looks like this:

Viewed from a neuroscientific perspective, we can say that soft parenting comes predominantly from the right hemisphere of our brain, which as we saw in Chapter 7 – How do we know what our baby needs?, is associated with emotional processing and non-verbal communication and allows us to 'read' our babies intuitively and imagine what they might need from us. By contrast, firm parenting comes more from our left hemisphere, which is associated with logic, analytical and problem-solving skills, and is generally keen to get things in order. It is important to remember that, in a good working brain, the right and left hemispheres are in constant dialogue, each informing the other on how best to respond to any given situation.

In the first few weeks of our baby's life, in that period we call 'parental preoccupation' (see Chapter 3 – At last, we meet . . .), it is normal for us to parent mostly with our soft mind. Our baby's vulnerability is such that they need us to be in the 'yes, yes, yes, I am with you' mode pretty much all of the time. However, as they grow and develop and we get to know them and have a greater sense of what they can and cannot cope with, the art of parenting gradually demands us to use both our soft and our firm minds, to jump both in – and out of – our babies' shoes. As we will see shortly, growing up with parents who say yes, yes, yes all the time can be as detrimental as growing up with parents who only say no, no, no.

What we want is for our soft and firm qualities to be constantly talking to each other, weighing intuitively the pros and cons of either offering more empathy or imposing more limits. By holding our soft and firm minds close together, we enter into a powerful dialogue not only with ourselves but also with our co-parent, and this mitigates the risk of our parenting swinging dangerously from one end of the spectrum (being over indulgent) to the other (being over punitive). It also increases the chances of our parenting offering the consistency that our baby thrives on. With this gentle toing and froing, we should be able to find a middle ground we both feel comfortable with, and which our baby finds comfortable and supportive too.

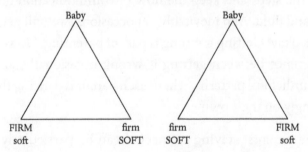

And, gradually, as we dance our parenting dance, with its synchronised and consistent patterns, our babies are able to internalise our soft and firm parenting qualities, and begin to develop their own varied sense of self. Their softer self will tend towards compassion and understanding, while their firmer self will try to curb the sorts of behaviour and habits that need reining in. To offer a crude example of how this might work, imagine for a moment your baby in years to come as a teenager, confronted with the constant temptation of playing on their phone – their soft side might say to themselves: of course you can go on your phone, you've had a long day at school and need a bit of rest and distraction. But the hope is that, after fifteen to twenty minutes, their firm side will show up and say: hang on, you've distracted yourself enough, and it is now time to finish your homework. Our soft and firm capacities are basic life skills, ones that we all need, and the earlier our babies are exposed to them in a gentle, reasonable way, the better they will be equipped to cope and make constructive choices later on.

When it is hard to parent together

Of course, parenting together, dancing those dances, is not always easy, especially when we are sleep-deprived and juggling with all the stresses of grown-up lives. It takes time to learn the steps, to stop and think together about our babies; it also requires determination to practise the steps and keep the flow of communication between us regular and fluid. And inevitably, on occasions, we will get it wrong. Which is okay! Getting it wrong is part of parenting. However, there is a difference between getting it wrong occasionally, and getting stuck in unhelpful patterns, where each parent is dancing their dance increasingly on their own.

For some parents, staying connected can be particularly difficult. Maybe they have inherited from their childhood an unhelpful model of parenting. Or maybe their relationship was already under strain before they had the baby and dancing the parental dance requires a degree of intimacy and cooperation that feels frightening or threatening. Or maybe they just find it hard to see things from someone else's point of view.

But it is a problem worth addressing, because having parents who feel emotionally stuck will inevitably impact on a child's own ability to be adaptable and flexible down the line – perhaps when they are ready to start nursery or primary school, or even later, on entry to secondary school. It tends to be at these moments of big transition that worried parents contact me, as their children struggle to cope with new social demands. Understandably desperate for strategies to manage their now 'misbehaving' toddler, or to help their 'under-achieving' child, these parents want a quick fix. They hope that by sending their child to a therapist, they will swiftly be made 'better', more co-operative, less anxious, easier to look after. But of course it is not as simple as that. And after drawing triangles with them to illustrate the conflicted dynamic in their family, I soon get them to understand that it is not so much with their child that I need to work, as with themselves: that they, as parents, have far more power than I do to 'fix' the problem. Generally, after a few sessions with the three of us putting our minds together to think about their child, they are ready to start the process of re-aligning and re-balancing their parenting and being supportive of each other. And before long their out-of-control toddler calms down, or their painfully shy child comes out of their shell, and starts to make friends and speak up in class.

When parents are not seeing and hearing the same baby

When parents struggle to put their minds together, it tends to be because either they share too similar an understanding of their baby's communication, or they perceive it too differently. When their baby cries in the middle of the night, for instance, they might both hear a vulnerable baby who needs them immediately or both hear a tyrant who wants to rule them and can certainly wait. Or does one hear only a vulnerable baby and the other only a tyrant? How we respond to our babies – whether we use our soft mind or our firm mind – of course depends on what we think our babies are trying to tell us and are asking us to do.

There are three main patterns of parental couple difficulties that I generally encounter in my clinic: 1) both parents are soft all the time; 2) both parents are firm all the time; 3) one parent is the soft one and the other is firm. Let's look at them in turn.

When both parents use only their soft mind

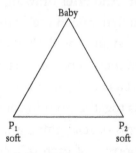

Some parents find it difficult to get out of that 'parental preoccupation' of the first few weeks and, even as their babies grow and become stronger and more able, they can only see them as vulnerable and helpless. Their parenting approach is therefore very soft and can soon turn into over-indulgence. And for their children, who from infancy have only known softness and 'yes, yes, yes, I am with you', the reality of life outside the home – when they start nursery or school – can come as a bit of a shock. Suddenly, they are confronted with a world of rules, and grown-ups who say 'no, that is enough'.

Pushing against the new limits, they can quickly get into trouble and are labelled 'difficult' or 'naughty'.

Let's imagine what it might be like to grow up with parents who are prone to over-empathise with their babies and can only bring their soft minds to their parenting. It would be a little bit like sleeping in a deliciously soft bed, but one with no bed frame. It might start as a nice feeling, but it would soon become pretty scary – perhaps like one of those dreams where you are falling and falling and don't know when, or even whether, you are going to land. No matter how soft we all want our mattresses to be, we also need something to hold them, a frame, a floor, something hard and strong. And it is the same for our babies: they want us to be soft, they want us to be able to imagine what it is like for them, to share and understand their feelings, but they also want us to hold them tight, to make them feel that, even though they have these strong feelings, they are not going to fall, that we are there to catch them, that there are limits. They need us to create a space informed by both our soft and our firm minds, where, feeling understood and contained, they can safely start their journey towards becoming themselves.

When both parents use only their firm mind

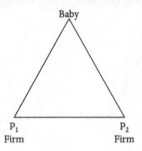

Baby

P₁
Firm

P₂
Firm

At the opposite end of the spectrum, if a baby has parents who can only respond to their cries in the middle of the night with their disciplinarian mind, who can only see their baby's behaviour as something to be managed and controlled and shaped, it will be like sleeping in a bed with a hard frame but no mattress. A fearsome place, cold and lonely. In some extreme situations, parents who cannot access their soft mind when they are with their babies can become abusive. Our babies want to feel firmly held and supported, but before that they want and need to feel understood, to feel that their parents can share their upset (and their joy). Of course, as our baby's autonomy increases, we will have to set more and more limits and rules to contain their explorations and their demands, using the firm side of our mind, but it is important to allow our soft mind to help impose those limits in a measured way, with kindness and respect.

When one parent is only yes, yes, yes and the other only no, no, no

Some parental couples can seem intractably divided. So when their baby cries in the middle of the night, the soft parent jumps out of bed, rushing at the first whimper, whereas the firm parent stays in bed, moaning that their baby is turning into a tyrant and needs reining in.

For these parents, I draw the following triangles:

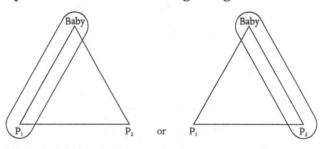

In this 'good cop, bad cop' scenario, there is a risk that, as the soft parent becomes increasingly over-protective of their baby, the firm parent will feel excluded, and become jealous and resentful of the soft parent-baby couple and their seemingly perfect relationship. Feeling pushed out by the other parent, maybe even undermined, the firm parent is likely to retaliate by being critical of their soft co-parent. So, instead of a supportive atmosphere at home, an atmosphere of rivalry and bitterness can develop, and hostility will creep into the couple relationship.

As for the baby, having a 'yes, yes, yes' parent and a 'no, no, no' parent can be deeply confusing. Being stuck between the two extremes of parenting, it becomes harder for them to develop a proper sense of themselves: they are either lost in the softness of their mattress unable to get a sense of where they as a person start and where they end; or they are being constrained so tightly by rules that they have no room to explore who they are. Often their only option is to adapt their behaviour and personality to please whichever parent they are with, which in turn prevents them from developing their own personality.

Another possibility is that they will lean towards the softer parent, and risk missing out on the possibility of a good relationship with the firmer one altogether. Excessive coupling with their soft parent can also make it harder for a child to deal with separation. Going to nursery or school, when they are required to say goodbye, might become a real struggle, and make it more difficult for them to take pleasure in learning and making friends.

The impact of our own childhoods

Why is it that two parents can each hear a different message from their babies? How is it that, for some parents, their baby's vulnerability tends to activate their right brain and soft mind, whereas for others it activates their left brain and firm mind?

How we perceive our babies can be profoundly influenced by the way our own parents, both individually and as a couple, perceived us and looked after us as young children, as we have seen throughout this book (and more specifically in Chapter 12 – The impact of how we were parented). Did they see in us the vulnerable baby or did they see the tyrant? Did they use both sides of their parenting brain and manage to create together a good balance of softness and firmness? Or did they have a tendency to lean too much toward being either indulgent or too strict? What was the atmosphere like in our childhood home? Was it supportive and fun-filled? Did we feel safe or was it impossible to really relax?

Exploring these questions as a parenting couple, and talking about how similarly or differently we were parented ourselves, can be hugely helpful in enabling us to begin to understand our respective perceptions of our baby. Are we generally on the same page when it comes to providing emotional support alongside imposing limits? If not, what was it in our own childhood that might be making us feel more readily inclined to use our soft mind or our firm mind? Were our own parents able to parent us in a mutually supportive way? Could they dance the dance together? Or did they struggle, so that we ended up clearly coupled with one of them, leaving our other parent often excluded?

Drawing our own triangle

At this point when working with parents in my clinic, I often ask them each to draw a triangle to represent their own childhood and explore what sort parenting model they feel they have inherited. And I think it is a good idea, if you feel like it, for you to do the same here.

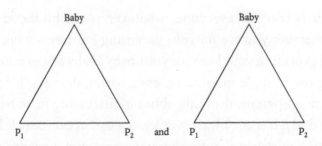

For new parents, thinking back to their own childhood and trying to talk with their co-parent about what aspects felt positive and what aspects felt more negative can be hugely cathartic – helping them to find their own way, and create their own parental culture and family atmosphere.

In theory, it is a good idea for parents to explore the impact of their own emotional heritage before a baby arrives. But sometimes it is only when we are in the thick of early parenting that we start becoming aware of it. It is only when confronted with the vulnerability of our own babies, for example, that we might start thinking about the time when we too were a vulnerable baby. Although that can feel alarming and may be upsetting (if we feel that our parents did not do a particularly good job), it is important to remember that we are no longer that baby/child. We are parents now, who can be different and who have a choice about whether or not to repeat the way our parents brought us up. We now have an opportunity to be the parents we want to be and draw our own triangle.

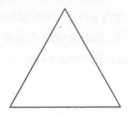

And this is true for everyone, whatever your childhood experience, wherever you are on your parenting journey – whether you are still expecting your baby, or your baby is already in your lives – keeping the triangle in mind or, even better, drawing it regularly with your co-parent, thinking about it, discussing it, re-balancing it if you find it has got a little wonky, is a useful exercise. It helps us to create a nurturing atmosphere at home and a secure psychological space in our minds, where our baby will feel both held and understood.

For our babies, knowing that we as parents agree on how to relate to them and how to keep them safe, while also letting them explore who they are and the world around them, gives them the impetus to grow and eventually to let go of us. Safely perched at the top of the triangle, our baby can enjoy watching us dancing the parental dances and gradually learn the steps themselves so that, one day, they too can dance the parental dance with their own partner in front of their own children . . .

Single parenting

Some single parents might feel a little deflated after reading so much about the importance of the parental couple. But please don't be, because the good news is that you do not need two parents to create that special triangle. As I mentioned earlier, every parent, no matter their gender, has within themselves both a soft and firm mind. And as a single parent you simply need to embrace both of the two bottom corners of the triangle. The dance you dance, therefore, is going to be more the internal one, like the one every parent dances individually within themselves.

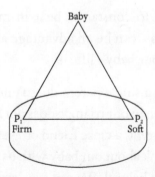

This means that, still firmly seated at the top of this triangle, your baby can witness you using both your soft and firm minds. And it is in this flexible space, created by the two sides of your mind working together, that you can build that special metaphorical bed with its soft mattress held by a strong frame. That will help you to nurture that special psychological atmosphere where your baby – experiencing both your capacity to empathise with their needs but also to set limits to some of their demands – will feel safe to start their journey of discovering who they are and becoming their own self.

Indeed, research has shown time and time again that what matters most for our babies to develop healthy bodies and minds is not whether they have one or two parents in the home, but having stability and consistency. And single parents are very well placed to achieve that and create their own consistent and coherent parental culture with its correct balance between indulgence and strictness.[6]

One of the possible drawbacks of single parenting is that it can be harder sometimes to spot when we are leaning too much towards our soft side or our firm side. Not having another parent to consult, or to counterbalance our natural inclination towards one side or the other, single parents might have to be a bit more on the lookout for any unbalance. That said, not having to align their parenting ideas with someone else – to constantly bear in mind another person's opinions and leanings – can be an advantage and bring more coherence and stability to our baby's life.

And, of course, being a single parent doesn't necessarily mean being alone. The third person in our triangle does not have to be a co-parent; they can be a grandparent, a close friend or even a therapist – anyone whom we trust to think about our baby with us and try to understand their behaviour can be helpful. We can even see them as a 'significant part-time' co-parent and have them join the triangle regularly but not constantly.

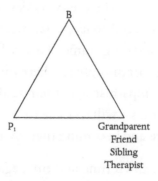

The rest of the family: grandparents and other people

Although our baby mostly draws their sense of self from their relationship with their parent(s), other key people in their life can also have a significant influence on their development. As we have seen throughout this book, babies are highly social: they love people, they love their faces, their voices . . . And, as they grow and their world gets a little bigger, having opportunities to form other key relationships can be very valuable for them. It can also be a source of pleasure for us – not least by providing an opportunity for some well-earned rest!

Family members, such as grandparents, aunts and uncles, as well as close friends, can be great at offering our babies that slightly different way of doing things, that slightly different way of looking at the world that will enrich their lives. But, of course, each of these people comes with their own ideas about how to rear a child (especially ours); and while some of you might be completely fine with that and be happy to hand over your baby and leave them to it, for others handing over your baby to someone else might be a source of great anxiety, especially if you feel that those people have ideas about parenting that do not concur with yours.

Imagine, for example, that your parents have offered to babysit to let you go out for the evening. You want to take up their offer, except that you are increasingly feeling conflicted about your childhood and have a lot of reservations about their parenting style and the way they brought you up. Your instinct might be to try and explain your way of doing things and make it clear that you expect them to follow *your* way to the letter. But this doesn't really make you feel much better, as you know your parents are firmly stuck in their own opinions and, of course, you can't be 100 per cent sure that they will not simply revert to their own way as soon as you have shut the door. On the other hand, if they follow your precise directives, your baby might find their care oddly mechanical and it might be harder for them (and their grandparents) to enjoy their time together.

So here is another option: why not use the parenting together/triangle model and invite one (or even both) of your child's grandparents (or an aunt, or friends, or an au pair . . .) to spend some time with you thinking about how to go about things, just as you have been doing with your co-parent: observing how your baby reacts to the world around them, wondering together what might be going on for them, chatting about what you have noticed that your baby likes and doesn't like, trying to imagine what your baby might be feeling when they cry or have to wait to get what they want.

Spending time with your baby's grandparents, for example, putting your heads together like this, will help everyone align their understanding of your baby's needs and personality. The grandparents will be able to listen to your views and see how you do things with your baby, but also you will be able to hear their views and maybe understand them better. Thanks to this collaborative thinking, your baby's grandparents will be much more likely to create that special space where your baby can feel safe to be themselves. Even better, it will make you feel less anxious about leaving your baby with them from time to time. While grandparents are figuring out the steps of their own dance with your babies, you can take a back seat for a bit, have a bath, see friends, spend time with your partner, go for a walk on your own, read a book, watch a film, do anything that feels nourishing.

Bringing our own parents into our babies' lives in this way is also a way of revisiting our own childhood, when they first became our parents. This can help us see them in a different light. By the time our parents become grandparents, they will have changed and become a slightly (or even very!) different people than the ones they used to be when we were a child. Now, witnessing our own mother or father being tender with our babies, being gentle and attentive in a way you feel they might not have been with you, can help heal some of the pain of what you think you might have missed in your own childhood. This, in turn, will help us and our own parents to get back in a more harmonious dance together.

Epilogue
Parenting is messy

Walking down the street the other day, my eyes and attention were caught by a display of photographs in a shop window, each one showing a family all smiles in their Sunday best. A mum and her three sons, who ranged from a teenager to a toddler; a mum, a dad and their identically dressed twin daughters; a pregnant mum proudly showing her big tummy; a baby in a basket with her parents beaming behind her; a baby on a floral blanket with pink petals floating around her . . . As I gazed at the pictures, at all these smiling people, I started to imagine what might have happened before and after the camera clicked. What sort of dances had they been dancing? I started to imagine the missteps, the trodden toes, the tensions between the mums and dads as they tried to get all the kids ready, the arguments between the teenagers as one accused another of stealing their favourite hoodie, the crying of the babies and their sudden regurgitation of the milk, the rivalry between the younger kids, fighting for who was going to be next to mum or dad in the picture . . .

As with our posts on social media and the articles we see in glossy magazines, these beautiful photographs show only one side of the story, the clean side, the side we are happy to reveal to others. But what happens on the other side, the not so polished one, the one behind closed doors? This is the side I have tried to describe in this book. And which I have tried to help you navigate with your baby, and to enjoy, even when it is messy and challenging. Why? Because the not so polished side, the one we tend to keep away from public scrutiny, is the true story of our lives, the one in which babies and parents grow and develop into real people.

Every time I hear of someone who is thinking of having a baby, I wish they could be sent an automatic message, saying: PARENT-ING IS MESSY. As we have seen, it is messy from the word go. We all dream of that perfect love with our babies, of those perfect pic-tures, of those perfect babies in their pristine clothes, lovingly smiling at us, entertaining us with their babbling but also leaving us enough time to carry on with our 'normal' lives . . . What is much harder to imagine is the tiredness, the bags under our eyes, the tears, the pain-ful birth, the sore nipples, the aching back, the dirty nappies (so many of them), the patches of dried milk on our shirts (or is it baby sick, or crushed bananas?); the tensions with our partner over who is going to get up in the middle of the night, or change the nappies, or fill the dishwasher or empty the bins; the boredom, the loneliness, the guilt . . .

I hope that, by throwing a light on the real story, I have managed to show that it is the messiness of parenting that makes it so exciting, that makes the whole crazy adventure worthwhile. If life only looked like those airbrushed photographs or social posts, boredom would soon get the better of all of us and we and our babies would in no time go quite mad. Parenting needs to be messy: it is because our babies make their nappies dirty that we know they are healthy. It is because our babies cry that we are able to enjoy their smiles. It is because sometimes they irritate us that we know the depth of our love for them. It is because, when we feel we've got it, when we have mastered whatever needed to be mastered – feeding, sleeping, play-ing . . . – and we wake up the next day to discover that our babies have moved on and whatever satisfied them yesterday is no longer to their liking, we know and are reassured that they are growing, changing and developing into their own selves.

There will be times when we are not the parent we want to be, that perfect parent we had imagined we were going to be at the begin-ning of the journey. And we will feel sad, disappointed, angry with ourselves and, most of all, guilty. But it is in those moments that we have a chance to get to know ourselves better, to accept our imper-fections and let go of self-judgement and self-blame, while also making some small adjustments to become a little closer to the parent we would like to be. It is also in those moments of imperfect parenting that we are revealing to our babies that we are not perfect, and that life is not perfect, and that indeed, they themselves never will be perfect! Nevertheless, if we can stay curious and connected, if we can continue to imagine what it is like for our babies, then the bond between us becomes ever stronger, and our parenting adven-ture more exciting, fulfilling and real.

Bringing up our babies – dancing those dances, making and nurtur-ing the bond that will stay with them for the rest of their lives – is one of the most human things we will ever do. Watching in wonder, as our babies become truly human themselves, will stretch us to our limits at times – and make us both feel very much alive.

Acknowlededgments

There are many people to thank. First, my little patients and their parents who have all taught me about the intricacy of human connections. Thank you for keeping me curious and making every session a new adventure.

I had been thinking of writing a book about the incredible stuff that happens between parents and babies for a long time, and it was Daisy Goodwin who, during walks on Golden Cap, persuaded me to get started. My agent Antony Topping, with his gentle but unfailing support, accompanied me all the way to the finish line. Aurea Carpenter helped it to crystallise with her generous and brilliant editing. And Gail Walker made incredibly helpful comments on the text. Thank you all.

My publisher Lindsey Evans gave me the chance to write the book I wanted to write, and her team at Headline who brought it all together beautifully. Thanks especially to copyeditor Anne Hervé and jacket designer Amy Cox, along with Kate Miles, Kathy Callesen and Inka Melson.

This book has been nourished by decades of conversations with all those who have accompanied me in my psychoanalytic journey:

Rachel Pardoe, Felicity Weir, Suzanne Sproston, Sabina Rosdarklin, Guy Baring, Nicky Loram and Kathy Garner; at the Tavistock Clinic where I trained: Catrin Bradley, Biddy Youell and Graham Music; my colleagues at the Bridge Foundation in Bristol: Georgina Taylor, Heather Mora, Annabelle Patel, Jessica Maliphant; at Exeter University: Richard Mizen, Taline Artinian, Marta Bolognani, Stephen Briggs, Jean Knox, Belinda West. Let's keep talking.

Thank you to the many friends who have supported and encouraged me, including (but not limited to) Angelle Wallis, Meetu Soni, Tessa Baring, Lizzy Ribeiro, Rosa Wallis, Stewart Dodd, Jane Cord, Jerry Skeet, Lucy Alexander, Emily Hill, Alexandra Chaldecott, Didier Kisala, Patricia Ikwo-Vandela, Ivan Samarine, Jess Upton, Rachel de Thample, Daisy Foster, Mary-Ann and Geoffrey Wilmot, Mary Hugill, Ali Herron, Tania Kovats, Natalia and Andryi Likhachova, Pako Koyalebo, Toby Clitherow, Dot Sim, Liz Robinson, Elvira Salva, Tom Faulkner, Sophy Fearnley-Whittingstall, Nick Harmer, Sophie Papin, Sue Wyatt, Kevin Labbé, Dave Olive and Tim Williams.

And even closer to home: thank you Jane and Rob Fearnley-Whittingstall for being such amazing grandparents – it has always been a pleasure to watch you interacting with the children; my mother (and wonderful Granny Denise) and brother Xavier Derôme who have kept a watchful eye on me from across the channel and provided a good supply of delicious cheese and wine. If my dad François Derôme was still alive, I know that he too would have kept my glass full.

Chloe, Oscar, Freddie and Louisa, my own – not so little now – children: watching you live your lives has been the most riveting and profoundly nourishing experience. Merci de tout mon coeur. Hugh, sharing the mad adventure with you has made it even more enjoyable. I love parenting our children with you and we love the delicious food you cook for us night after night. You have been the first reader of this book and your comments and suggestions gave me the courage to carry on, even when at times it all felt too much. Thank you.

Knotty, Kiki and Quiz, you have been the most loyal and patient companions on my writing journey, sitting by my desk for hours on end, without any critical comments whatsoever. Thank you for the Devon walks – as vital for me as for you.

Notes

1. The first nine months of life

1. Belluck, Pam, 'How Does Pregnancy Change the Brain? Clues Are Emerging', *The New York Times*, 16 September 2024.
2. Gholampour, F., Riem, M. M. E., & van den Heuvel, M. I., 'Maternal brain in the process of maternal-infant bonding: Review of the literature', *Social Neuroscience*, 15(4), 380–384, 2020, https://doi.org/10.1080/17470919.2020.1764093.
3. Carter, C. S. (2014). Oxytocin Pathways and the Evolution of Human Behavior. *Annual Review of Psychology*, 65(1), 17–39. https://doi.org/10.1146/annurev-psych-010213-115110
4. Machin, Dr Anna, *The Life of Dad: The Making of a Modern Father* (Simon & Schuster, 2018).
5. Feldman, Ruth, Ruth Feldman: Synchrony and the Neurobiology of Attachment @ the Simms/Mann Institute Think Tank, https://www.youtube.com/watch?v=ZaX02XQV09I

2. Giving birth

1. Morris N., Haddad F., 'The Effect of Anxiety on the Course of Labor', in McGuigan, F. J., Sime, W. E., Wallace, J. M. (eds),

Stress and Tension Control 3 (Springer US, 1989), pp. 235–40; Walter, M. H., Abele, H., Plappert, C. F., 'The Role of Oxytocin and the Effect of Stress During Childbirth: Neurobiological Basics and Implications for Mother and Child', Front Endocrinol (Lausanne), 27 October 2021, 12:742236. doi: 10.3389/fendo. 2021.742236. PMID: 34777247; PMCID: PMC8578887; Uvanäs Moberg, Kerstin, *Why Oxytocin Matters* (Pinter & Martin, 2019).

2. Hill, E., & Firth, A., 'Positive birth experiences: a systematic review of the lived experience from a birthing person's perspective', MIDIRS Midwifery Digest. 28(1):71–78, 2018.

3. At last, we meet . . .

1. Lee, G. Y., & Kisilevsky, B. S. (2014). Fetuses respond to father's voice but prefer mother's voice after birth. *Developmental Psychobiology, 56*(1), 1–11. https://doi.org/10.1002/dev.21084 DeCasper, A., & Fifer, W. (1980). Of human bonding: newborns prefer their mothers' voices. *Science, 208*(4448), 1174–1176. https://doi.org/10.1126/science.7375928

2. Longa, L. D., Dragovic, D., & Farroni, T. (2021). In touch with the heartbeat: Newborns' cardiac sensitivity to affective and non-affective touch. *International Journal of Environmental Research and Public Health, 18*(5), 1–18. https://doi.org/10.3390/ijerph18052212 Zhang, S., & He, C. (2023). Effect of the sound of the mother's heartbeat combined with white noise on heart rate, weight, and sleep in premature infants: a retrospective comparative cohort study. *Annals of Palliative Medicine, 12*(1), 111–120. https://doi.org/10.21037/apm-22-1269

3. Sai, F. Z. (2005). The role of the mother's voice in developing mother's face preference: Evidence for intermodal perception at birth. *Infant and Child Development, 14*(1), 29–50. https://doi.org/10.1002/icd.376

4. Wagner, J. B., Luyster, R. J., Yim, J. Y., Tager-Flusberg, H., & Nelson, C. A., 'The role of early visual attention in social development', *International Journal of Behavioral Development*, 37(2), 2013, pp. 118–124, https://doi-org.uoelibrary.idm.oclc.org/10.1177/0165025412468064.

5. Farroni, T., Csibra, G., Simion, F., Johnson, M. H., 'Eye contact detection in humans from birth', Proc Natl Acad Sci USA, 9 July 2002; 99(14):9602-5. doi: 10.1073/pnas.152159999. Epub 2002 Jun 24. PMID: 12082186; PMCID: PMC123187.

4. Born ready

1. de Lima, J., Lloyd-Thomas, A. R., Howard, R. F., Sumner, E., Quinn, T. M., 'Infant and neonatal pain: anaesthetists' perceptions and prescribing patterns', BMJ, 28 September 1996; 313(7060):787. doi: 10.1136/bmj.313.7060.787. PMID: 8842071; PMCID: PMC2352177; Bellieni, C. V., 'Pain assessment in human fetus and infants', AAPS J. 2012 Sep;14(3):456-61. doi: 10.1208/s12248-012-9354-5. Epub 2012 Apr 18. PMID: 22528505; PMCID: PMC3385812.

2. Nagy, E., Thompson, P., Mayor, L., & Doughty, H., 'Do foetuses communicate? Foetal responses to interactive versus non-interactive maternal voice and touch: An exploratory analysis', *Infant Behavior & Development*, 63, 2021, 101562-. https://doi.org/10.1016/j.infbeh.2021.101562.

3. Meltzoff, A. N., & Moore, M. K., 'Imitation of facial and manual gestures by human neonates', *Science*, 198(4312), 1977, pp. 75–78; Trevarthan, Colwyn, 'First things first: infants make good use of the sympathetic rhythm of imitation, without reason or language', *Edinburgh Journal of Child Psychotherapy*, vol. 31, no. 1 2005 91–113.

4. Nagy, E., Pal, A., & Orvos, H., 'Learning to imitate individual finger movements by the human neonate', *Developmental Science*, 17(6), 2014, pp. 841–857; Nagy, E., Pilling, K., Blake, V.,

and Orvos, H., 'Positive evidence for neonatal imitation: A general response, adaptive engagement', *Developmental Science*, 2020.

5. Trevarthen, C., & Aitken, K. J. (2001). Infant Intersubjectivity: Research, Theory, and Clinical Applications. *Journal of Child Psychology and Psychiatry*, 42(1), 3–48. https://doi.org/10.1017/S0021963001006552

6. Max-Planck-Gesellschaft, 'The power of imitation: Already in infancy, imitation promotes a general pro-social orientation toward others', 27 June 2013.

7. Trevarthen, Colwyn, 'What Is It Like to Be a Person Who Knows Nothing? Defining the Active Intersubjective Mind of a Newborn Human Being', *Infant Child Development*, 20: 119-135, 6 January 2011, https://doi.org/10.1002/icd.689.

8. Dondi, M., Messinger, D., Colle, M., Tabasso, A., Simion, F., Barba, B.D., & Fogel, A. A., 'New Perspective on Neonatal Smiling: Differences Between the Judgments of Expert Coders and Naive Observers', *Infancy*, 12: 235-255, 2007, https://doi.org/10.1111/j.1532-7078.2007.tb00242.x

9. Strathearn, Lane, Li, Jian, Fonagy, Peter , & Read Montague, P., 'What's in a Smile? Maternal Brain Responses to Infant Facial Cues', *Pediatrics*, July 2008; 122(1): 40–51. doi:10.1542/peds.2007-1566.

10. Als, Heidelise, 'The Newborn Communicates', *Journal of Communication*, Spring 1977, issue 2.

11. Delafield-Butt, J. T., Freer, Y., Perkins, J., Skulina, D., Schögler, B., & Lee, D. N. (2018). Prospective organization of neonatal arm movements: A motor foundation of embodied agency, disrupted in premature birth. *Developmental Science*, 21(6), e12693-n/a. https://doi.org/10.1111/desc.12693

12. Boiteau, Caroline, Kokkinaki, Thean, Sankey, Carol, Buil, Aude, Gratier, Maya, Devouche, Emmanuel, 'Father–newborn vocal interaction: A contribution to the theory of innate

intersubjectivity', {periodical title?}, 21 July 2021, https://doi.org/10.1002/icd.2259.

13. Winnicott, D. W., 'Primary maternal preoccupation' in Winnicott, D.W. (ed.), *Through Paediatrics to Psychoanalysis: Collected Papers* (Karnac, 1984 [1956]), 300–305; Winnicott, D. W., 'The Relationship of a Mother to her Baby at the Beginning', in *The Family and Individual Development* (Routledge, 1965, 1st edn), pp. 15–20, https://doi.org/10.4324/9781003209157-3.

5. Alone with our babies … Who am I?

1. Gerhardt, S. (2015). *Why Love Matters : How affection shapes a baby's brain* (Second edition.). Routledge.

7. How do we know what our babies need?

1. Rizzolatti, G., & Craighero, L. (2004). THE MIRROR-NEURON SYSTEM. *Annual Review of Neuroscience*, 27(1), 169–192. https://doi.org/10.1146/annurev.neuro.27.070203.144230; Fonagy, P., Gergely, G., & Target, M. (2007). The parent-infant dyad and the construction of the subjective self. *Journal of Child Psychology and Psychiatry*, 48(3–4), 288–328. https://doi.org/10.1111/j.1469-7610.2007.01727.x

8. The power of being thought about

1. Beebe, Beatrice, 'Mother-Infant Communication', https://www.youtube.com/watch?v=rEMge2FeREw

9. When loving our babies is hard

1. Chapman, E., & Gubi, P. M. (2022). An Exploration of the Ways in Which Feelings of "Maternal Ambivalence" Affect Some Women. *Illness, Crisis, and Loss, 30*(2), 92–106. https://doi.org/10.1177/1054137319870289
2. Parsons, C.E., Young, K.S., Bhandari, R., van Ijzendoorn, M.H., Bakermans-Kranenburg, M.J., Stein, A. and Kringelbach, M.L. (2014), The bonnie baby: experimentally manipulated temperament affects perceived cuteness and motivation to view infant faces. Dev Sci, 17: 257-269. https://doi.org/10.1111/desc.12112
3. Winnicott, D. W., 'Hate in the countertransference' in *Collected Papers: Through Pediatrics to Psycho-Analysis* (Routledg,1992), pp. 194–203.
4. Klein, Mélanie, 'Notes on some schizoid mechanisms', Envy and Gratitude and Other Works 1946–1963 (Hogarth Press and the Institute of Psycho-Analysis, 1975).

10. When we feel low

1. https://parentinfantfoundation.org.uk/powerful-mums-survey-results-launched-to-mark-start-of-infant-mental-health-awareness-week-2023/.
2. https://www.nhs.uk/mental-health/conditions/post-natal-depression/overview/.
3. Winnicott, D.W., 'Mirror-role of mother and family in child development' in *Playing and Reality* (Routledge, 1971), pp. 111–18.

12. The impact of how we were parented

1. Fonagy, P., Steele, M., Steele, H., Moran, G. S., & Higgitt, A. C. (1991). The capacity for understanding mental states: The reflective self in parent and child and its significance for

security of attachment. *Infant Mental Health Journal*, 12(3), 201–218. https://doi.org/10.1002/1097-0355(199123)12:3<201:: AID-IMHJ2280120307>3.0.CO;2-7

13. Healing from a traumatic birth

1. https://www.theo-clarke.org.uk/files/2024-05/Birth%20 Trauma%20Inquiry%20Report%20for%20Publication_ May13_2024_0.pdf.

2. https://www.theo-clarke.org.uk/files/2024-05/Birth%20 Trauma%20Inquiry%20Report%20for%20Publication_ May13_2024_0.pdf; Simpson, M., & Catling, C., 'Understanding psychological traumatic birth experiences: A literature review', *Women and Birth*, 29(3), 203–207, 2016, https://doi.org/10.1016/j. wombi.2015.10.009; AIMS Journal, 2019, vol. 30, no. 4, Gemma McKenzie reviews Reed, R., Sharman, R., and Inglis, C., 'Women's descriptions of childbirth trauma relating to care provider actions and interactions', *BMC Pregnancy and Childbirth*, 17:21, 2017.

3. Beck, C. T., & Watson, S. (2016). Posttraumatic Growth After Birth Trauma: "I Was Broken, Now I Am Unbreakable." *MCN, the American Journal of Maternal Child Nursing*, 41(5), 264–271. https:// doi.org/10.1097/NMC.0000000000000259; Sawyer, A., Ayers, S., Young, D., Bradley, R., & Smith, H. (2012). Posttraumatic growth after childbirth: A prospective study. *Psychology & Health*, 27(3), 362–377. https://doi.org/10.1080/08870446.2011.578745

4. https://www.theo-clarke.org.uk/files/2024-05/Birth%20Trauma%20 Inquiry%20Report%20for%20Publication_May13_2024_0.pdf.

5. Simkin, Penny, 'Just Another Day in a Woman's Life? Women's Long-Term Perceptions of Their First Birth Experience', Part I. Birth, 1991, 18. 203 - 210. 10.1111/j.1523-536X.1991.tb00103.x.

6. Ward, S. A. (1999). Birth Trauma in Infants and Children. *Journal of Prenatal & Perinatal Psychology & Health*, 13(3/4), 201-.

14. Feeding

1. Eleri Jones, Hope, Seaborne, Mike J., Mhereeg, Mohamed R., James, Michaela, Kennedy, Natasha L., Bandyopadhyay, Amrita, Brophy, Sinead, 'Breastfeeding initiation and duration through the COVID-19 pandemic, a linked population-level routine data study: the Born in Wales Cohort 2018–2021', BMJ Paediatrics Open, 2023;7:e001907.

2. Davis, A. M. B., & Sclafani, V., 'Birth Experiences, Breastfeeding, and the Mother-Child Relationship: Evidence from a Large Sample of Mothers', *Canadian Journal of Nursing Research*, 54(4), 518–529, 2022, https://doi.org/10.1177/08445621221089475.

3. Smith, L. J., 'Impact of Birthing Practices on the Breastfeeding Dyad', *Journal of Midwifery & Women's Health*, 52(6), 621–630, 2007, https://doi.org/10.1016/j.jmwh.2007.07.019.

15. Playing

1. Panksepp, J. (2004). *Affective Neuroscience: The Foundations of Human and Animal Emotions* (1st ed.). Oxford University Press. https://doi.org/10.1093/oso/9780195096736.001.0001

2. Creekpaum, S., Bellinson, J., & Charles, M. (2019). Child development through play. In *The Importance of Play in Early Childhood Education* (1st ed., pp. 11–18). Routledge. https://doi.org/10.4324/9781315180090-2; Cooke, B. M., & Shukla, D. (2011). Double Helix: Reciprocity between juvenile play and brain development. *Developmental Cognitive Neuroscience*, 1(4), 459–470. https://doi.org/10.1016/j.dcn.2011.07.001

3. Siviy, S. M. (2016). A brain motivated to play: insights into the neurobiology of playfulness. *Behaviour*, 153(6–7), 819–844. https://doi.org/10.1163/1568539X-00003349

17. Babies and the family

1. Bachler, E., Frühmann, A., Bachler, H., Aas, B., Nickel, M., & Schiepek, G. K. (2018). The effect of childhood adversities and protective factors on the development of child-psychiatric disorders and their treatment. *Frontiers in Psychology*, 9, 2226–2226. https://doi.org/10.3389/fpsyg.2018.02226

2. Twenge, Jean M., Campbell, W. Keith, and Foster, Craig A., 'Parenthood and Marital Satisfaction: A Meta-Analytic Review', *Journal of Marriage and Family*, 65, no. 3, 2003, pp. 574–83, http://www.jstor.org/stable/3600024.

3. Nelson, S. K., Kushlev, K., English, T., Dunn, E. W., and Lyubomirsky, S., 'In Defense of Parenthood: Children Are Associated With More Joy Than Misery', *Psychological Science*, 24(1), 3-10, 2013, https://doi.org/10.1177/0956797612447798.

4. Cowan, Carolyn Pape, & Cowan, Philip A., 'Interventions to Ease the Transition to Parenthood: Why They Are Needed and What They Can Do', *Family Relations*, 44, no. 4, 1995: 412–23, https://doi.org/10.2307/584997; Cowan, C. P., & Cowan, P. A. (1992). When partners become parents: The big life change for couples. Basic Books.

5. Landry, S. H., Smith, K. E., Swank, P. R., Assel, M. A., & Vellet, S. (2001). Does Early Responsive Parenting Have a Special Importance for Children's Development or Is Consistency Across Early Childhood Necessary? *Developmental Psychology*, 37(3), 387–403. https://doi.org/10.1037/0012-1649.37.3.387

6. Lippold, M. A., Davis, K. D., Lawson, K. M., & McHale, S. M. (2016). Day-to-day Consistency in Positive Parent–Child Interactions and Youth Well-Being. *Journal of Child and Family Studies*, 25(12), 3584–3592. https://doi.org/10.1007/s10826-016-0502-x

Further Reading

Baradon, T., ed., *Working With Fathers in Psychoanalytic Parent–Infant Psycho-therapy* (Routledge, 2019, 1st edn.), https://doi.org/10.4324/9781315106830.

Beebe, B., & Steele, M., 'How Does Microanalysis of Mother-Infant Communication Inform Maternal Sensitivity and Infant Attachment?', *Attachment & Human Development*, 15(5–6), 583–602, 2013, https://doi.org/10.1080/14616734.2013.841050.

Beebe, Beatrice, 'Mother-Infant Communication', https://www.youtube.com/watch?v=rEMge2FeREw

Briggs, A., ed., *Surviving Space: Papers on the Infant Observation: Essays on the Centenary of Esther Bick* (Karnac, 2002, 1st edn).

Bion, W. R., *Elements of Psycho-analysis* (Heinemann, 1963).

Bion, W. R., *Learning From Experience*, vol. 22 (Routledge, 2020), https://doi.org/10.4324/9780429476631.

Bowlby, J., *The Making and Breaking of Affectional Bonds* (Routledge, 2005).

Bradley, E., Emanuel, L., *What Can the Matter Be?: Therapeutic Interventions with Parents, Infants and Young Children* (Routledge, 2008, 1st edn.), https://doi.org/10.4324/9780429484797.

Brown, A., & Tulleken, C. van, *Breastfeeding Uncovered: Who Really Decides How We Feed Our Babies?* (Pinter & Martin, 2021, 2nd edn.).

Davis-Floyd, R., & Sargent, C. F., eds, *Childbirth and Authoritative Knowledge: Cross-Cultural Perspectives* (University of California Press, 1997, 1st edn.), https://doi.org/10.1525/9780520918733.

Daws, D., & de Rementeria, A., *Finding Your Way with Your Baby: The Emotional Life of Parents and Babies* (Routledge, 2021, 2nd edn).

Daws, D., & Sutton, S., *Parent-Infant Psychotherapy for Sleep Problems: Through the Night* (Routledge, 2020, 1st ed.), https://doi-org.uoelibrary.idm.oclc.org/10.4324/9780429198212.

Dockrill, L., *What Have I Done?: An Honest Memoir About Surviving Post-Natal Mental Illness* (Vintage Digital, 2020).

Edwards, J., 'The Elusive Pursuit of Good Enough Fatherhood, and the Single Parent Family as a Modern Phenomenon', *Journal of Child Psychotherapy*, 48(3), 362–377, 2022

Feldman, R., 'Parent-infant Synchrony and the Construction of Shared Timing; Physiological Precursors, Developmental Outcomes, and Risk Conditions', *Journal of Child Psychology and Psychiatry*, 48(3–4), 329–354, 2007, https://doi.org/10.1111/j.1469-7610.2006.01701.x.

Feldman, R., 'The Adaptive Human Parental Brain: Implications for Children's Social Development', *Trends in Neurosciences*, 38(6), 387–399, 2015, https://doi.org/10.1016/j.tins.2015.04.004.

Feldman, R., 'The Neurobiology of Mammalian Parenting and the Biosocial Context of Human Caregiving', *Hormones and Behavior*, 77, 3–17, 2016, https://doi.org/10.1016/j.yhbeh.2015.10.001.

Feldman, Ruth, 'How Parent-Infant Synchrony Supports Children's Regulatory Capacities', https://www.youtube.com/watch?v=mUgd6s-DPe4&list=PLGaKMsexhTsWgWQYQQyBvrrBcCydcH59d&index=18&t=481s

Feldman, Ruth, 'Synchrony and the Neurobiology of Attachment @ the Simms/Mann Institute Think Tank', https://www.youtube.com/watch?v=ZaX02XQV09I&t=2s

Fonagy, P., Gergely, G., and Target, M., 'The Parent–Infant Dyad and the Construction of the Subjective Self', *Journal of Child Psychology and Psychiatry*, 48: 288–328, 2007.

Gerhardt, S., *Why Love Matters: How Affection Shapes a Baby's Brain* (Routledge/Taylor & Francis Group, 2014).

Glaser, E. (2021). *Motherhood: a manifesto*. 4th Estate.

Hazard, L., *Hard Pushed: A Midwife's Story* (Arrow Books, 2020), https://developingchild.harvard.edu.

Hazard, L., *Womb: The Inside Story of Where We All Began* (Virago, 2024).

Joeli Brearley. (2021). *The Motherhood Penalty: The Truth About the Motherhood Penalty and How to Fix It*. Simon & Schuster.

Jones, L., *Matrescence* (Pantheon, 2024).

Klein, Melanie, 'Notes on some schizoid mechanisms', *Envy and Gratitude and Other Works 1946–1963* (Hogarth Press and the Institute of Psycho-Analysis, 1975).

Knox, J., *Self-agency in Psychotherapy: Attachment, Autonomy, and Intimacy* (W.W. Norton & Company, 2011).

Lowy, M., *The Maternal Experience: Encounters with Ambivalence and Love* (Routledge, 2020, 1st edn.), https://doi.org/10.4324/9781003124344.

Machin, Dr Anna, *The Life of Dad: The Making of a Modern Father* (Simon & Schuster, 2018).

Meltzoff, Dr Andrew, 'Bodies, Brains & Emotions in Infant Development', https://www.youtube.com/watch?v=7HmRA6sxoeU

Murray, L., *The Psychology of Babies : How Relationships Support Development from Birth to Two* (Constable & Robinson Ltd, 2014).

Music, G., *Nurturing Natures: Attachment and Children's Emotional, Sociocultural and Brain Development* (Routledge, 2024, 3rd edn).

Music, G., *Womb Life: Wonders and Challenges of Pregnancy, the Foetus' Journey and Birth* (Mind-Nurturing Books, 2024).

Odent, M., 'The First Hour Following Birth: Don't Wake the Mother!', *Midwifery Today*, no. 61, pp. 9–12, 2002.

Oster, E., *Expecting better: Why the Conventional Pregnancy Wisdom is Wrong – and What You Really Need To Know* (Penguin Books, 2024).

Palmer, G., *Why the Politics of Breastfeeding Matter*, vol. 6 (Pinter & Martin, 2016).

Parker, R., *Torn in Two: The Experience of Maternal Ambivalence* (Virago, 2005, revised edition).

Campbell, P., & Thomson-Salo, F., *The Baby as Subject* (Routledge, 2018, 1st edn.), https://doi.org/10.4324/9780429481178.

Perry, P., *The Book You Wish Your Parents Had Read: And Your Children Will Be Glad That You Did* (Penguin Books, 2020, 1st edn.).

Raphael-Leff, J., *Parent-Infant Psychodynamics: Wild Things, Mirrors and Ghosts* (Routledge, 2018, 1st edn).

Schore, A. N., 'The Human Unconscious: The Development of the Right Brain and its Role in Early Emotional Life', *Emotional Development in Psychoanalysis, Attachment Theory and Neuroscience: Creating Connections*, pp. 23–52, 2004.

Schore, A.N., 'Back to Basics: Attachment, Affect Regulation, and the Developing Right Brain: Linking Developmental Neuroscience to Pediatrics', *Pediatrics in Review*, 26, 204 217, 2005.

Scotland, M. S. L., *Birth Shock: How to Recover from Birth Trauma – Why 'At Least You've Got a Healthy Baby' Isn't Enough* (Pinter & Martin, 2020).

Scotland, M. S. L., *Why Postnatal Depression Matters* (Pinter & Martin, 2015).

Siegel, D. J., *The Developing Mind: Toward a Neurobiology of Interpersonal Experience* (The Guilford Press, 1999).

Stern, D. N., *Diary of a Baby* (HarperCollins, 1991).

Stern, D. N., *The First Relationship: Infant and Mother* (Harvard University Press, 2002, new edition), https://doi.org/10.4159/9780674044029.

Stern, D. N., *The Interpersonal World of the Infant: A View from Psychoanalysis and Developmental Psychology* (Routledge, 1985, 1st edn.), https://doi.org/10.4324/9780429482137.

Stern, D., Bruschweiler-Stern, N., & Freeland, A., *The Birth of a Mother: How The Motherhood Experience Changes You Forever* (Bloomsbury, 1998).

Sternberg, J., & Urwin, C., *Infant Observation and Research: Emotional Processes in Everyday Lives* (Routledge, 2012, 1st ed.), https://doi.org/10.4324/9780203133941.

Sunderland, M., *What Every Parent Needs to Know: A Psychologist's Guide to Raising Happy, Nurtured Children* (Dorling Kindersley Publishing, 2023, new edition).

Sutton, S., *Psychoanalysis, Neuroscience and the Stories of Our Lives: The Relational Roots of Mental Health* (Routledge, 2019, 1st edn).

Svanberg, E., *Why Birth Trauma Matters*, vol. 15 (Pinter & Martin, 2019).

Thomson-Salo, F., *Infant Observation: Creating Transformative Relationships* (Routledge, 2018, 1st edn.).

Trowell, J., & Etchegoyen, A., *The Importance of Fathers: A Psychoanalytic Re-evaluation*, vol. 42 (Routledge, 2002, 1st edn).

Uvnäs-Moberg, K., *Why Oxytocin Matters*, vol. 17 (Pinter & Martin, 2019).

Waddell, M., *Inside Lives: Psychoanalysis and the Growth of the Personality* (Routledge, 2002, 1st edn).

Walker, R., *Baby Love: Choosing Motherhood After a Lifetime of Ambivalence* (Penguin Books, 2007).

Webber, L., *Breastfeeding and the Fourth Trimester: A Supportive, Expert Guide to the First Three Months* (Headline, 2023).

Winnicott, D. W., 'Hate in the countertransference', *Collected Papers: Through Pediatrics to Psycho-Analysis* (Routledge,1992), pp. 194–203.

Winnicott, D. W., 'Mirror-role of Mother and Family in Child Development', *Playing and Reality* (Routledge, 1971), pp. 111–18.

Winnicott, D. W., 'Primary Maternal Preoccupation', *The Collected Works of D. W. Winnicott* (Oxford University Press, 2016), pp. 183–188, https://doi.org/10.1093/med:psych/9780190271374.003.0039.

Winnicott, D. W., *The Child, the Family, and the Outside World* (Penguin Books, 1964).

Witkowska, A., *Understanding Babies: How Engaging with Your Baby's Movement Development Helps Build a Loving Relationship* (Pinter and Martin, 2021).

Associations Offering Information and Support

The Association for Infant Mental Health: https://aimh.uk

The 'Getting to Know Your Baby' videos have been designed to help parents, caregivers, and health professionals to know how to support the development of a baby's emotional wellbeing.

National Child Trust: https://www.nct.org.uk

Tommy's: https://www.tommys.org

Post-natal Illness

PaNDAS, Post-Natal Depression Awareness and Support: https://pandasfoun dation.org.uk. A charity that offers hope, empathy and support for every parent or network affected by perinatal mental illness (call 0808 196 1776).

APNI, Association for Postnatal Illness: https://apni.org. Their helpline is open 10am–2pm (call 0207 386 0868), or email info@apni.org for advice on the management and treatment of post-natal illness. They can also put women in touch with other mothers who have suffered PND.

Mind: https://www.mind.org.uk

Birth and Traumatic Birth

AIMS (Association for Improvements in the Maternity Services): https://www.aims.org.uk

Birthrights, Protecting human rights in childbirth: https://birthrights.org.uk

Five X More is a grassroots organisation committed to changing and highlighting Black maternal health outcomes in the UK: https://fivexmore.org

Maternal Mental Health Alliance: https://maternalmentalhealthalliance.org

Following Traumatic Birth Experiences

The Birth Trauma Association:
http://www.birthtraumaassociation.org.uk offers an online search tool for a therapist specialised in birth trauma in your area.

Make Birth Better: https://www.makebirthbetter.org/

Breastfeeding

The Breastfeeding Network:
https://www.breastfeedingnetwork.org.uk. Breastfeeding information and support, available 24 hours a day, every day of the year (call 0300 1000 212).

Psychotherapeitic Support

ACP, The Association Of Child Psychotherapists:
https://childpsychotherapy.org.uk Offers online search for a child psychotherapist in your area who could help with post-natal depression or any aspect of the bonding relationship between parents and their babies.

British Association for Counselling and Psychotherapy:
https://www.bacp.co.uk

British Psychotherapy Foundation:
https://www.britishpsychotherapyfoundation.org.uk

British Psychoanalytic Council: https://www.bpc.org.uk

Dads

Dope Black Dads is a digital safe space for fathers who wish to discuss their experiences of being Black, a parent, and masculinity in the modern world: https://dopeblack.org//join/#dads

Dad Matters provides support for dads worried about suffering from anxiety, depression and post-traumatic stress (PTSD): https://dadmatters.org.uk/national

LGBT+

https://www.fflag.org.uk

A national voluntary organisation and charity dedicated to supporting families and their LGBT+ loved ones.

Maternity/Paternity rights

https://workingfamilies.org.uk

https://pregnantthenscrewed.com

https://maternityaction.org.uk

Index